The Faraway

The Gutter

New Pen

The Whins

Penside

Beck Bank

Penside Gorse

Rushy Pasture

The Gully

THAT
STRANGE
ALCHEMY

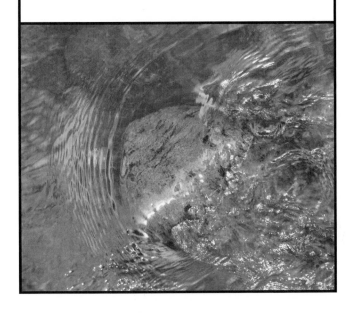

Also by published by Merlin Unwin Books

Private Thoughts from a Small Shoot Laurence Catlow

Once a Flyfisher Laurence Catlow

Confessions of a Shooting Fishing Man Laurence Catlow

The Shootingman's Bedside Book Compiled by BB

Geese! Memoirs of a Wildfowler Edward Miller

Rough Shooting in Ireland Douglas Butler

Vintage Guns for the Modern Shot Diggory Hadoke

The Fisherman's Bedside Book Compiled by BB

A History of Flyfishing Conrad Voss Bark

Tying Flies with CDC Leon Links

www.merlinunwin.co.uk

THAT
STRANGE
ALCHEMY

Pheasants, Trout
and a Middle-aged Man

LAURENCE CATLOW

Merlin Unwin Books

First published in Great Britain by Merlin Unwin Books, 2008
Text © Laurence Catlow, 2008
Photographs © Rod Calbrade, 2008
(those on pages 49, 69, 88, 243, 256, 259 © Merlin Unwin)

MERLIN UNWIN BOOKS LTD
Palmers House
7 Corve Street, Ludlow
Shropshire SY8 1DB, U.K.
Tel 01584 877456
Fax 01584 877457
email: books@merlinunwin.co.uk
website: www.merlinunwin.co.uk

British Library Cataloguing in Publication Data:
A catalogue record for this book is available from the British Library

ISBN 978-1-906122-03-4

Designed and typeset in Bembo by Merlin Unwin Books, Ludlow.
Printed in Great Britain by TJ International, Padstow.

CHAPTER ONE

First Day of the Season

I had been in Italy. I had wandered round Pompeii and Herculaneum and thought how interesting they were; I had gazed into the crater of Vesuvius and thought that it was perfectly hideous. The beauty of Capri, on a cold, bright spring morning, had caught me unawares and moved me beyond expectation. The lunches had been delightful, with tiny clams and mixed fries of small fish, with spaghetti tossed in wonderfully simple sauces of oil and garlic and then scattered with parsley and chives; the wine had been unexceptional, but it had been good to drink it in the sunshine; it had gone well with the food and I had even discovered a taste for the small glasses of limoncello that came free with the coffee and the bill. The lunches had been delightful and they had left me feeling less drowsy and self-indulgent than midday wine usually does but even so I still ended most afternoons dozing on my bed for an hour or so, oppressed by the aftermath of the wine and the strange conviction that always comes over me on my rare excursions abroad: a conviction that I have temporarily separated myself from real living and turned into a spectator of scenes to which I do not belong, a detached and interested and unprurient sort of voyeur.

Once or twice, as an alternative to lying on my bed, I went to evening mass, feeling for forty minutes or so that I was no longer just watching life but suddenly living it seriously and living it to the full. Just for those forty minutes I had stopped wandering as an observer through the life of a foreign country: now I was at the core of it, as much a part of it as anyone else. And the church, standing on its white cliff above the sea, was very cool and very beautiful and it was good, after the end of mass, to gaze out over the blue water and say a few Hail Marys before thoughts of dinner chased them from my mind: *Santa Maria, madre del Dio, prega per noi peccatori, adesso ed in ora della nostra morte, amen.*

I enjoyed my Italian holiday. The point of mentioning it is that it happened in March and that both the Wharfe and the Eden opened for trouting while I was hundreds of miles away from both of them, admiring antiquities or peering into the crater of a dormant volcano or sitting at a table drinking wine. I had not thought much of fishing in Italy, though I had acknowledged that it had started again; and I had looked over one or two foreign bridges and told myself that the water flowing beneath them was unlikely to be full of trout.

But when I woke up on the morning after my return, realising that my holiday was over and that it was time for something more important, I immediately decided to go fishing. I had, in fact, more or less decided this the night before, only reserving final confirmation for the next morning in case I felt too tired for a challenge as serious as the season's first fishing day. I could have pottered round in the morning and then tied a few flies, with perhaps a couple of hours rabbiting in the afternoon. I could have prepared myself for going fishing, putting away my holiday frame of mind and replacing it with something more suitable for a fisherman, something steadier and more determined. It might have been better to wait a day before going fishing, but I woke up feeling rested and feeling well, feeling strong enough to cope with a fishing day; and so the decision was made; it was made (provisionally) while lying in bed and ratified while shaving.

After letting the dogs out I ate two scrambled eggs and drank two cups of coffee, made a sandwich and filled my flask with tea, put two of my rods and my waders and my fishing waistcoat, together with my long-handled net and my creel, into the Land Rover; and then, after checking repeatedly that I was not about to leave something indispensable behind, I lit my pipe and drove off for the Eden.

Going fishing is a serious business. We fishers all know this and the rest of the world fails to understand. The rest of the world thinks we are in search of entertainment or relaxation or escape; the rest of the world does not realise that we fishers go fishing because we have to, that we go to rivers because we cannot keep away from them. We could easily lead contented lives without ever going to Italy; but we would find life insupportable without ever going fishing. We do not really think of fishing days as days of sport and pleasure, though they often bring both; we do not think of them as restful interludes on either side of more central things. We think of them, believe it or not, as fishing days, which are altogether different from holidays. They are days that belong in the heart of our lives; there can never be enough of them and the first fishing day of another season is a very special day indeed.

If your first fishing day of the season follows your return from a week in Italy, it would probably be best to recognise a contrast between your holiday and your fishing weather. After the bright Mediterranean light, after those southern skies that were unequivocally blue, after the glare and the shine and the dazzle, it would be good to go fishing in something grey and soft and damp and English.

On this particular first day of the season the air was warm and the sun was bright and the sky was just about as blue as those I had seen over the bay of Naples. There were, I suppose, subtle differences; perhaps the light was less intense; there may have been a white undertone to the blue above me; there were certainly no vines, no blossoming almonds or fruiting lemons on the edges of the road, and Kirkby Stephen, come to think of it, looked nothing like Sorrento. There were, now that I am really thinking about it, very obvious differences, but at the time I was scarcely aware of them. I was too eager to get to the river and, once I had got there and was standing on Musgrave Bridge, I was too busy looking at the river Eden, which after almost three weeks without rain was running very low, flowing with that intense and startling clarity that belongs to low water in spring.

In summer a thin river is clear in its own way, but it is a very imperfect imitation of the same conditions at the start of the season; in summer low water, the riverbed is clouded with strands of moss and weed and slime, and the surface is clotted with dust and foam and with a thousand bits of things that come from the summer riot of growth and decay.

There are no conditions more difficult for a fisher than low water in the spring of the year, when the river bed is still bare and the water is untainted by the year's profusion; it is beautiful and frightening in its purity. Look at the reflection of tree trunks in the pools; think how lovely they are and think too that you may have to be content with these waving images as some sort of reward for your day's efforts, since you are likely to struggle in your search for that still better beauty of a spotted trout on the pale grass of the riverbank.

The early fishing last year was very demanding. April passed almost without rain. There were days on the Eden when the spring olives came in wild abundance, and not only in brief bursts but for hours on end from noon until late in the afternoon; and there was not, as sometimes happens right at the start of the season, a half-hearted response from the trout. There were big fish guzzling in every pool and run, and I was lucky if I went home with a single one of them in my bag. I tried them with traditional patterns, with Waterhens and Greenwells and Orange Partridges, with Rough Olives and Imperials; I tried them with progressive flies, with Klinkhamers and sparkle duns and funnelduns and anything else that I could think of; and none of it worked, except on those odd occasions when a particularly greedy or a fatally inquisitive or a plain stupid trout suddenly swallowed one of my traditional or progressive offerings. I hate to admit it, but I think my few successful patterns were all of the progressive type.

There were one or two days when I never caught a fish; there were three or four days when it happened only once. On the first day of the season, when the water had fallen nothing like as low as it fell within a week or two, it happened twice, and it happened with the first rising fish that I came across. He swallowed my parachute Imperial at the third or fourth offer and he weighed a pound and a half. I think I put a fish down a few minutes later, but then the Imperial captured a trout of one pound five ounces, and soon afterwards the hatch, which had never been on the grand scale, petered out altogether, leaving me with a brace in my bag and the feeling that I had started the season in the best possible way.

You do not want to catch scores of fish on your first day of the season. You should wait until May for your first big bag, for half a dozen fat trout with as many or more returned. The early weeks of the season are just a beginning, there is a sense of prelude to them and a brace or a leash of trout is more than enough reward for a day's fishing, which will not be a full day, anyway, since at the start of the season there is no point in starting before eleven in the morning and little point in fishing on much after four in the afternoon.

The rich days, days when trout feed for hours on end and can be caught from early morning right into the last light and beyond, the rich days come later with the leaf and the blossom and the swarming life of late spring and summer. It is best to build up to them, catching a fish now and then and telling yourself that in a few weeks you will be catching them in scores on the same day. A brace is undoubtedly the ideal bag for the first day of all.

Arthur Ransome writes delightfully on the start of the season. He thinks you should miss the first trout that rises at your fly. The second he allows you to hook in the hope that it will prove undersized. Only the third rising fish, according to Ransome, should end up in a fisher's creel, his theory being that there should be preliminary stages to the taking of our first trout; the miracle is too marvellous to happen at the first opportunity. I know what he means, but I would rather catch and kill the season's first trout and then miss or return the second one. Perhaps I am short of confidence. At any rate I need to reassure myself as soon as possible that I can still do it: can still fool a trout into eating my fly, still keep the hook in his mouth until he is ready for the net, can then lift him from the river and find with enormous relief that I am still primitive enough to knock him on the head without the slightest compunction. Once all this has been accomplished I can cope with failure much more successfully, for I have learned that the age of miracles has survived another winter. Failure with the first trout of the season always strikes me as a bad omen for the months ahead.

This season I had to wait until the afternoon for my first rise. There was some fly before noon, but it was never much more than a trickle and there were no rings spreading across any of the pools. I searched the river with a Klinkhamer – the water was too low for speculative casts with a couple of wet flies – and I felt very happy to be fishing again.

I realised that my left wading boot was still leaking, but in a seeping rather than a soaking sort of way, which is, of course, perfectly acceptable. Most experienced fishers let in water through at least one of their waders; perhaps it deepens our sense of communion with the river and the fish; perhaps we also abuse our waders, leaving them (when they are not on our feet and legs) to lie crumpled in heaps in the backs of Land Rovers from the middle of March to the end of September. And those holes, those tiny punctures that seem, when we first get into the river, to admit no more than a hint of moisture (a hint that soon develops into unambiguous wetness), those holes and punctures are almost impossible to find and patch. Anyway I was untroubled to discover that a small portion of the river Eden was trickling down my left leg. I tried my hand at long casts and roll casts and casts with little wiggles put in them in order to delay drag.

They were not all successful demonstrations of the fly-fisher's art (I find the wiggles particularly difficult), but some of them pleased me and I delighted in the power and delicacy of my eight and a half foot Loomis GLX, wondering why it had taken me so many years to throw off my stubborn allegiance to split-cane.

It was all very delightful and the sun was warm and the river was beautiful; there were redshank along the edges of the river, redshank and wagtails and piping oyster-catchers; there were lapwings and curlews over the pastures and purple heads of butterbur were already beginning to push themselves out of the earth. There were celandines and coltsfoot all over the place and there were clumps of primroses too. It was all, I now realise, very different from Italy; it was all very delightful but, after two hours with no sign of a trout, I confess that I was beginning to feel bored. I realised that it was time to rest for a while and then to persevere; the search for the season's first trout should never be abandoned before the middle of the afternoon.

I had lunch above Musgrave bridge, sitting on the bank and looking at the old red church across the water and at the daffodils in the graveyard. I looked for sand martins too, for they are usually back by the end of March, brown-backed and busy round the high banks pitted with their nest-holes, but there were none to be seen. I had been tempted to put half a bottle of wine in my creel, so that I should be able to drink a lunchtime toast to the first day of the season and perhaps to its first trout. The thought had come to me while shaving, and had repeated itself during the scrambled eggs; but then I told myself that I already drank quite enough without solitary binges on the riverbank and besides, there would be wine in the evening, which was where – except in Italy – wine should belong. In honour of the start of the season, moreover, I had made sure that my evening wine was of the better sort, and I should enjoy it all the more as the first red wine of the day; and even if it had been preceded by a generous glass of Manzanilla, it would speak to me, as I drank it, of my moderation and self-control.

In this way the temptation of the half-bottle had been successfully put behind me. Lunch was eaten without wine, which explains why I was feeling quietly virtuous as I sat there drinking tea and chewing a ham sandwich. It was half way through the sandwich that I saw the rise in the middle of Church Run. He came up two or three times more as I chewed on; there were further well-spaced rises while I took a few last temperate swills and a few pulls on my pipe. I did not want to rush into action and bungle the season's first real chance of a trout. I took the risk that he would go down before I got to him.

He weighed one pound ten ounces; he fought hard and was in superb condition. He took a size twelve Klinkhamer, far bigger than any spring olive that ever floated down the currents of a river, and he made me very eager for the brace. There was another fish rising at the top of the run, but, in spite of a change of fly as soon as the big Klinkhamer was refused and in defiance of several rather skilful casts with deftly imparted wiggles, I could not bring him up and he had soon stopped rising. I did not find another feeding fish and very soon the thin trickle of olives had failed.

It was a first day of only one trout, but he was a fine trout and at the end of it all I was happy with him. A day of one trout, unless he is an altogether exceptional fish, scarcely makes a red-letter day, but the first day of the season is an altogether exceptional sort of day: a day when small rewards can bring almost complete contentment. And, as Arthur Ransome observes, 'perhaps the greatest satisfaction of the first day of the season is the knowledge in the evening that the whole of the rest of the season is to come.'

Chapter Two

Iron Blues of Spring

We fishers like rivers with lots of water in them. We like them full of water because it helps us to catch fish, although, if you think about it for a few minutes, you will realise that this is only half the reason; in fact half the reason we are fishers at all is that we like rivers. Some of us go beyond mere liking, developing a strange and powerful affinity with the rivers that we know best. There are bits of them that move us very deeply, usually the bits that seem most strongly to express their individuality or the bits that have treated us most generously; long separation hurts and reunion is often wonderful.

We feel happier by our rivers than we feel in most other places (even in pubs), which could, I suppose, be because we are emotionally deprived – some of us at least – desperate for something to love; it could be that we are human failures, lonely and sad and incomplete; but, whatever the truth of all this, it is beyond argument that we find rivers with water in them – not a brown torrent of it, not an angry surge, but a full, bright and lively flow of the marvellous stuff between the banks – it is beyond dispute that we find rivers generously supplied with water much more beautiful than parched rivers with creeping trickles of moisture and mocking remnants of pools.

Rivers look much healthier when they are flowing as they should; they are very obviously more full of life; and, although they are thousands of years old, they look young again whenever the water is up and running; and we fishers, loving our rivers, love this youthful vitality of theirs; it is a contagious sort of vitality, which makes us feel vigorous ourselves as we walk along the banks. The world seems a

cleaner and younger, a better and much brighter place from the edge of
a full and clear-flowing river, which is how we always see our rivers as
we sit at home and wonder when we shall next be able to spend some
part of a day along the edges of the Wharfe or the Eden or whichever
the rivers are that have wound themselves into our hearts.

Although fishers prefer rivers with plenty of water in them, we
expect each summer to bring whole weeks, perhaps even months on
end, when our rivers are not as we should choose; water-starved rivers
are part of the summer scheme of things. We cope with this as well
as we can; and there are undoubted satisfactions to be drawn from
extracting a few trout from an August river that has become more rock
than water, doing it with small flies, except when bigger ones do the
trick, but usually with small or even tiny flies and with many failures
and with lots of pride in a brace of trout at the end of the day.

There are arguments in favour of low water in July and August;
not the least of them is the evenings that follow hot summer days, those
evenings when the spinners and the sedges promise sackfuls of trout and
very occasionally deliver a second brace to add to the brace that cost us

The Wharfe at Yockenthwaite

so much sweat in the glare and swelter of the day. Whatever the results of these summer evenings they are full of hope and they are cool and they are beautiful; it is a blessing to be out in them and a blessing to take long swallows of bitter beer at their end.

I expect low water at some stage of the summer. I do not expect it in March and April; in fact I resent it very bitterly in the spring of the year. I do not want to find my rivers already stale and tired when I return to them at the beginning of another season; they should be full from the winter rains, full and clear and flowing with all the promise of the reviving year, so that I can look at them, feel refreshed just by the sight of them and think that, if only the olives come, I may go home with a brace of trout.

That first day after my return from Italy was perfectly acceptable. The river was certainly low but it was clean and beautiful and there was rain forecast before the weekend. The next day I went fishing on the Wharfe; again I caught a single trout – a lovely fish of one pound six ounces – and again I went home happy: happy there was a fish in my creel and even happier that, according to the weathermen, the rain was on its way. I felt sure that, when next I waved my marvellous Loomis GLX (or one of the Sages) over the Eden or the Wharfe, whichever river it might be would be better supplied with water and might even manage to put a brace in my creel rather than just a singleton.

All this creel-talk reminds me, by the way, that I now write neither imprecisely nor metaphorically in talking about a creel. When I mention my creel I no longer mean a plastic bag stuffed into the inside pocket of an old Barbour (there was a time when this was exactly what I did mean); nor do I mean the back pocket of my fishing waistcoat (which is where my creel migrated when at last I acknowledged that a fishing waistcoat was a good idea). And I no longer mean one of my old game bags, where dead trout once lay in a litter of pheasant feathers and rabbit fur and were not always improved for the table by the stale nest that kept them warm for half a day.

When I mention my creel now I mean what I say: a basket of brown wickerwork, rather a big one, bow-fronted in the traditional fashion with a traditional hole in the lid and lots of air inside, a basket that keeps dead trout fresh even on the hottest of days. I suppose it looks like an affectation; doubtless it also looks rather incongruous, hanging on one side of my fishing waistcoat with the Loomis or one of the Sages waving above it. It should rub against an ancient sports jacket and the trout that fill it should be put there by split-cane. It only cost me thirty pounds, which is the reason I bought it, unless perhaps it was because, finding that I had suddenly and surprisingly turned into an almost modern sort of fisher, I bought it to preserve at least some sort of connection with the old ways.

My creel was most certainly a bargain and, now that I have got it, I rather think that every fisher should have one, except, of course, for those mistaken fishers who never kill a fish. My creel certainly keeps trout much better than pockets or plastic bags or old game bags ever did. It is very light and very spacious; there is room for my thermos flask and my lunch and for a light waterproof in case of rain. It is also a welcome presence in my study, sitting there in one corner of the room and smelling discreetly of trout. I often glance at it when I am working at my desk, hoping that one day soon it will be hanging from my shoulder with a brace of trout inside. I can see my creel as I write these words and I am rather hoping that, come the weekend, it will spend some time hanging almost heavily from my shoulder.

There was a succession of days in the first half of April which, at the end of each one of them, saw me returning my creel rather bitterly to the back of the Land Rover. There were, in fact, three such days;

they were all blank days and, while gazing despondently at my creel, with all that air inside it but not a single trout to keep fresh, I kept telling myself that the lightness of my creel was not my fault; it was the fault of the weather, which had produced water of springtime clarity but at a level that usually comes with long summer drought.

It was hopeless for fishing and I decided that I would not hang my creel from my shoulder again until the weather had remembered how to rain. I had gone to London believing that Northern downpours were a certainty. There had been no downpours, there had not been a single drop of rain and there would be no more fishing for me until things improved.

It began, about a fortnight later, just before the end of the month, with gardeners' rain: useless stuff for fishers, no more than a few showers and a morning or two of misting drizzle: enough to seep an inch or two into the dry soil and set the seeds growing: enough to make gardeners smile but nowhere near enough to bring relief to thirsty rivers or fresh hope to fishermen. I knew it was no use because, in spite of the drizzle and the showers, my Land Rover was still bouncing over the hard earth of my little farm on the edge of the hills. I began to think it would be like 1984, when the drought began early in spring and, with the exception of two or three thunderstorms, stretched right through the summer almost to the end of August. It was the summer when I first resorted to the upstream worm.

I was never much good at the upstream worm and I gave it up years ago, but I began to wonder if I might soon be starting again and trying to get better at it; I began to suspect that within a few weeks I should be digging worms after a lapse of at least ten summers. But then there came a Thursday when the drizzle lasted all day. The worms were given at least a temporary reprieve.

There was more drizzle on Friday and some of it was of the soaking sort. The rivers round Sedbergh did not respond in any way that I could see. Saturday afternoon was wet, not very wet, but wet enough to make me wonder whether it was heavy drizzle or more like proper rain. I went to evening mass in Kendal so that, if the Eden rose overnight, I should have the whole of Sunday for fishing. On the way home there was unambiguous rain; there was no pelting against the windscreen, there were no torrents falling from the sky, but the wipers were kept busy and, in every hollow of the road, my tyres were splashing very happily through shallow pools of standing water.

I ate a rabbit and drank claret with two friends, looking out of the window from time to time to see if it was still raining (it seemed lighter but it was still coming down); it was trying harder again when I took the dogs out just before midnight and I wondered whether, over the hills in Mallerstang and down through Kirkby Stephen, the Eden was perhaps already stirring in the darkness, lifting its voice a little and just beginning to spread itself an inch or two over those banks of shingle that had so long been dry.

I was on the Eden by eleven o'clock (there is no point in being earlier until May comes along) and I found that it really had stirred. Whether it had risen one inch or six I cannot say; I can never remember what was covered and uncovered when my rivers were on their bones, and so I am never able to make remotely dependable comparisons, but I was not bothered with inches as I stood by the river and got ready to fish. I was concerned with the look of things and I was delighted by

'I was on the Eden by eleven o'clock...'

what I saw; for I could see that the Eden was most certainly refreshed and beyond doubt much livelier, still flowing clear but now flowing invitingly. I guess that the level had risen about three inches. The rain must only have started to seep into the river once the earth had soaked up those two days of drizzle, but this seepage had accomplished a transformation, and perhaps the greatest change was in me, knowing that this gentle lift of water had been much better than a sudden rush, knowing that this creeping overnight rise had turned the Eden back into a fisher's river, knowing that, if only the fly came, I should be a lousy fisherman if I did not manage to catch a few trout.

And the fly did come – enough of it to bring fish onto the feed – and I did catch trout – more than a few of them – and the fishing in itself was in some ways almost unmemorable, although it was certainly very enjoyable. I am now going to tell you about the fishing, but it was the rainless weeks that preceded it that made the day special. The fishing itself was undemanding and fairly ordinary. Being a fairly ordinary sort of fisherman I enjoyed it enormously.

There was not a huge hatch, but there were three sorts of dun on the water together and the presence of two of them brought particular pleasure. For perhaps half an hour there was a scattering of iron blues, very dark under the cloud, very welcome to see because they have become scarcer and scarcer over the years and it is good to know that the Eden still manages to breed a few of them. There was a scattering of iron blues and there was a very occasional March brown, big and mottled and eventually confirmed as the real thing.

The true March brown is not as big as a brook dun, which is the most mottled of its impostors; and most of the rest come later in the season; their wings are heavily veined rather than mottled, and, in the wings of a true March brown, there is something like a clear patch in the middle of all the mottling, which makes you hope that you are looking at the genuine article; and since it is an article that you thought had almost vanished from the Eden, you start rummaging in the pockets of your waistcoat until at last you find the covered lens that has survived from the scientific stage of your interest in fisherman's flies, a stage which even led you to a microscope and, with its help, to viewings of the male genitalia of various spinners that you hoped to identify with absolute certainty. You gave up the microscope long ago, but somehow the lens has stayed with you and moved into your waistcoat; you have found it now and, knowing where it is, you go on fishing – perhaps catching a trout or two – but what you are really doing is waiting for the next big fly with mottled wings; and when at long last it appears – as long as it is somewhere within hope of capture – you waste five minutes chasing it round an eddy with one of your fingers until it floats away down the river or flutters off into the sky.

Ten minutes later a second chance occurs and this time, after another pursuit with the index finger of your right hand, you make a capture, lifting from the water a large fly with heavily mottled wings. With mounting excitement you seem to see the distinctive clear patch in the middle of each wing; you apply your now uncovered lens to one of your captive's median or posterior legs and, seeing very clearly the diagnostic femoral blotch which sets this fly apart from all its imitators, you heave a sigh of satisfaction and say under your breath, unless you say it aloud, 'this is the true March brown'.

Flyfishers get very fond of flies – if they don't they should do – especially of those that come from the rivers they fish rather than those that fall on the water because carelessness or the wind has put them there. I cannot think tender thoughts about hawthorn flies and black gnats, even though they often produce wonderful sport and though for days on end they bring fishers their only chance of trout. Hawthorn flies, after all, are downright ugly and black gnats are scarcely beautiful. Much the loveliest, anyway, of our river-bred flies are the duns and the spinners they turn into, and when two of the threatened species decide to hatch on the same day, even though they come in such small numbers that they never influence your choice of artificial fly, then you go home feeling delighted that you have seen them and ever so slightly reassured about the future of your fishing and the future of your planet. There is, at least, still room for hope.

The flies that mattered to me as a catcher of fish were large dark olives, bigger than the iron blues, much smaller than the march browns. I always think of them as spring olives, because it is in March and April that I see them on my rivers, and I suppose this is one reason why the spring olive is my favourite fly: the fly of spring, the fly that hatches when fishing starts again, the fly that, almost every season, I thank with almost passionate sincerity for the first trout of another year.

I am, of course, deeply attached to blue-wings; when they come thickly and the two-pounders start eating them – and if I start catching the two-pounders – then I declare myself head over heels in love with them. I also have a soft spot for pale wateries; and I am always delighted when I come across a turkey brown or a purple dun, although I do not suppose they have ever helped to put a single fish in my creel. There was a time when I got excited about large spurwings and started trying to devise imitations. Small spurwings and medium olives are often lumped together with pale wateries; you have to get your hands, very delicately, on a male and study the eyes to know what you are talking about. Small dark olives – Skues called them July duns – are a further complication.

When they hatch in profusion on the Eden you should undoubt-edly fill your creel, unless you have made a mistake and are filling it because the trout are eating pale wateries or small spurwings or even medium olives. They are all roughly the same size (small); they are all beautiful in the same understated fashion; they are very difficult to tell apart and this is perhaps why, although they are all important fisher-man's flies, I can never quite surrender my heart to them, for I am never quite certain whether I have just fallen for *baetis bioculatus* or *baetis vernus* (unless it is, in fact, neither of these, but either *baetis scambus* or just possibly *centroptilum luteolum*).

With spring olives – *baetis rhodanus,* in case you are interested – there is no problem of this sort, for in March and April, there is unlikely to be any other species of dun floating on the water in their company, unless it is the iron blue or the march brown, neither of which can possibly be mistaken for my favourite fly. I like flies more when I know what I am looking at; this is one reason I am so fond of blue-wings, which very considerately grow three tails and, in doing so, set themselves apart from all the duns with which they might otherwise be confused. I have said nothing of olive uprights; they are less common on the Eden than they used to be; there used to be huge hatches and very greedy rises. Anyway they are easy to identify, noticeably bigger than the various olives and pale wateries but considerably smaller than all the March brown tribe, although they are, as it happens, close relatives of the true March brown and share with him the glory of a femoral blotch. They are handsome flies, especially the males, which have big black eyes; and both male and female have lovely blue-grey wings. I should love to see a big hatch of them again, with big fish busy stuffing themselves all over the river.

I seem to have lost my thread. There were no olive uprights the other Sunday; there were a few iron blues, one or two March browns and a fairly good hatch of spring olives. It was the olives that brought the trout onto the feed, although it was a typically patchy spring rise. There were pools with duns floating down the current in threes and fours together but with no trout rising to suck them in. I had come to a place I call New Pool – it was formed four or five years ago – before I saw a rise.

I sat down at once and lit my pipe in order to take stock of the situation. I often pause in this fashion when I have seen a feeding fish. It is only partly an analytical pause during which, with Skues-like penetration, I observe whether the trout are slaughtering duns or spinners or hatching nymphs and, with this settled, tie on a fly that my observation suggests is appropriate, at the same time deciding whether to dispatch it over the rising trout with a conventional cast or a roll cast or a side cast, whether to put an artful wiggle in the line and whether to place my fly two inches or perhaps two feet in front of the fish I hope to kill.

There is, in fact, very little of this going on in my mind when, having just spotted a trout, I promptly sit down on the bank and light my pipe. What I am really doing is enjoying the luxury of hope, delaying the disappointment that is likely to replace it once I stand up and get in position and then throw my fly somewhere in the vicinity of those hopeful and enticing signs on the surface of the river.

On this occasion, when I sat down and put a match to my pipe, there was a fly of the Klinkhamer style attached to my cast; it was a sort of Greenwell version of the Klinkhamer, with a body of primrose wool and a furnace cock hackle; it was tied on a size fourteen hook and it was still there when I had smoked my pipe for a few minutes and prolonged the pause by pouring myself half a cupful of tea. During all this I noticed that as many as half a dozen of New Pool's trout were busy eating insect flesh; it was to the nearest of them that, with the smoking and drinking finally done, I cast my fly, finding within a minute or two that he weighed one pound five ounces.

The next fish was a little smaller and a lot thinner and he went back; the two that followed were both just over the pound, they were both fat and they went into the creel. One of them took the Orange Partridge that I forgot to mention was dangling some feet above my modish Greenwell variant, put there in the hope that perhaps a few Eden trout would remain faithful to tradition by swallowing a spider pattern to seal their doom. There was only this one traditionalist; all the others, the three others that I killed and the two that I returned, preferred the modern thing on the end of my cast.

The all-purpose Klinkhamer

There are times when the irresistible attractions of flies built along Klinkhamer lines make me feel despondent. I begin to wonder whether I shall ever again think it a good idea to tie a Waterhen Bloa to the end of my cast. I love the old upstream wet and the simple, beautiful patterns that belong to it; but I fish them much less than I used to and in its various forms the Klinkhamer is the main culprit; for, dressed in different colours and sizes, it will draw hidden trout from the bottom of the river; it will deceive fish eating sitting or crippled or hatching duns; it will disappear into the mouths of trout gulping down sedges or black gnats or hawthorn flies. Perhaps we should stop talking of fishing wet or fishing dry; perhaps the time is coming when fly-fishing – apart from fishing a fall of spinners or immoral practices like fishing with goldheads and fishing the Czech nymph – will simply mean fishing Klinkhamer. It is, of course, a wonderful tribute to Hans van Klinken, but there are still times when his influence on the recent course of flyfishing begins to depress me.

The other Sunday was not one of these times, for the Orange Partridge managed a contribution and, anyway, I was very happy to be catching trout at all after the weeks with no rain. And they were spring trout, with a cold breeze blowing over the river and with a grey sky giving the river a soft shine and a silver slide. I gave three of my trout to friends who like eating them; I ate one of them myself and found the flavour of its pink flesh a complete and satisfactory explanation for its death earlier in the day.

There was no wine with my trout, for there was work to be done when I had finished eating it; but, once work was over, I drank a glass or two of whisky and read Skues. He was, of course, busy catching dozens of trout, but there was no jealousy in my response to his tales of slaughter, because, whenever I chose, I could look at the creel in the corner of my study and think to myself that, for the first time this season, it had come home with me at least half full of trout.

Chapter Three

Something Missing in Eden

I was sitting in the Land Rover almost at the top of the Eden. I had eaten a Cornish pasty and drunk half a cup of tea. I was planning to smoke for a while, finishing the tea and looking out of the window while deciding what sort of Klinkhamer to put on the end of my cast when at last I got out and then got ready to go fishing. I was almost at the top of the Eden, a mile or two above Kirkby Stephen and no more than a few miles from the source.

I was there because I was ready for a change. In the first three weeks of May, with the river constantly refreshed by rain, I had spent four successful and rather easy afternoons further downstream. I had also spent an afternoon of many trout way up the Wharfe beyond Yockenthwaite and Deepdale. After the April drought it was turning into a fisherman's spring and it was time for something difficult, time for some delicate and demanding fishing with the chance of an exceptional trout as a reward for it all.

The Eden is, in one respect at least, a peculiar river, in that the further upstream you go along its banks, the bigger grow the trout that swim between them. This statement is undoubtedly based on inadequate research; in spite of this it is probably true. I have never been on the river down towards Carlisle; I am thinking of the better portion of the Eden, on which I have fished as low as Little Salkeld and Lazonby, catching lovely fish of twelve ounces and a pound; further upstream, at Warcop and Musgrave, I have almost reached two pounds. But all my genuine two-pounders – and there has been a scattering of them over the years – all these two-pounders have come from the stretch above the inflow of Scandal beck, or from the beck itself where I once caught a trout only a few ounces short of three pounds.

I have never brought a two-pounder home from the river above Kirkby Stephen, from the Wharton Hall water or from Mallerstang, but several times I have left a hook in the jaws of a trout that I thought made two pounds seem small. The highest miles of the Eden flow over limestone; they also flow, for much of their course, beneath a thick cover of trees. You need recent rain to fish the high Eden, for it drops thin and clear very quickly; most of it you cannot fish at the weekends, when the main owner very sensibly keeps his trout and his river for himself.

This difficult and limited access means that it is not much fished. I should be surprised if more than thirty or forty trout are removed from the top of the river in the course of a normal season, which means that many of the trout of Mallerstang have the opportunity to grow big; and, since the stock, in terms of numbers, is fairly small – it is not one of those stretches of water where you see dozens of trout rising at the same time in the same small pool – since the head of trout is much smaller than is often the case on the headwaters of a moorland stream, and since the water is rich limestone water, the trout that swim there – some of them at least – grow long and fat and a few of them are very big indeed.

When, from time to time, I am visited by the urge to catch a trout to put inside a glass case, then I usually head off for the top of the Eden. Three and a half pounds, by the way, will be big enough; three and a half pounds of wild river trout will be more than big enough for the honour of a glass case. If ever I come home with such a trout, the odds are that I shall be coming home from Mallerstang or from somewhere near Wharton Hall.

It was not really the thought of three-and-a-half-pounders fit for glass cases that sent me to Mallerstang the other day. It was more that I wanted a change and knew that I had not fished there a single time last season: proof, if you want it, that stuffed trout in glass cases are not very high on my list of fishing priorities. It will happen if it happens; if the three-and-a-half-pounder is ever drawn over my net, as long as it is wild and beautiful as well as three and a half pounds, then it will end up in a bow-fronted case. If this never happens then I shall not, for want of it, die an embittered old man.

I had parked the Land Rover on Mallerstang Common because I felt like a change and because I also felt that I did not fish the secluded and beautiful water near the top of the Eden anything like often enough. There was also the thought that I should do something about this sooner rather than later, since I suspected that, in another ten years, I might have grown too decrepit to spend an afternoon squirming between alders and stumbling down high banks and wading a river full of treacherous limestone slabs where every second step threatens a slip or a fall. The Eden above Wharton Hall is something of an obstacle course; at any rate you spend as much time negotiating the obstacles as you do fishing for trout.

I had eaten my Cornish pasty and drunk a cup of tea. Before facing all those obstacles I needed a few moments with my pipe, which unexpectedly proved impossible because I now found that I had forgotten to bring it with me; and there was not, as there usually is – at least there did not appear to be – an old and forgotten pipe lurking somewhere in the confusion that spreads itself all over the two passenger-seats in the front of the Land Rover: a confusion of match-boxes and used matches, of fives balls and shotgun cartridges, of bills and mittens and handkerchiefs and tobacco ash and mud and dust and Lord knows what else. The front seats of my Land Rover are probably a health hazard. Two or three times a year the squalor becomes so repulsive that I do something about it, rearranging parts of it, getting rid of most of it and making what remains look almost neat.

Nothing looked neat when I began my search; the front-seats of the Land Rover had been going through one of their periods of random accumulation and were very squalid indeed, which actually filled me with hope. I had soon unearthed one with no stem, which had found its way into an empty cartridge-box, and, although its uselessness provoked me to bad language, I refused to despair, transferring my hope to the tray beneath the dashboard, where I suddenly felt convinced that I should uncover a complete meerschaum. I could remember coming across it once or twice when I had been looking for something else; I thought that I could remember meeting it last week; but, although the tray yielded up, among other things, a Swiss Army Knife – presumed lost on the riverbank – a shrivelled tangerine, a dog whistle and a few used pipe-cleaners, there was most definitely no meerschaum pipe.

It happens once every second or third season; usually it is the tobacco that is forgotten rather than the pipe. Once it was the matches and always there is the same desperate rummage which, when it has failed to turn up what I am looking for, always inspires the same anguished debate: whether I should grin and bear it or refuse to do either, spending perhaps an hour of what should be sacred fishing time driving to the nearest shops and buying an ounce of any sort of tobacco (or a cheap pipe or even a packet of cigars). Occasionally I have done this but more usually, once I have acknowledged that four or five smokeless hours lie ahead of me, I persuade myself that it is no bad thing, that I rarely smoke for more than a few minutes together when fishing, that I can sit down and rest without putting a pipe in my mouth, that I shall probably be just as happy fishing without tobacco and that I might as well seize the opportunity to give up the filthy habit altogether. It generally starts with me thinking along these commendably positive lines.

So it was that, after tackling up and tying a Greenwell Klinkhamer to my line, I set off down the Eden in the direction of Wharton Hall, thinking without much conviction that I was on the threshold of a new and healthier life. The river was very beautiful: clear but still glowing from the recent rain, with the yellow limestone shining through the water, with the pools half hidden beneath the young leaves all along the banks and with here and there the signs of a rising trout. There was the sound of the river; there was the sound of the birds; there were swarms of black fly in the air, suggesting that a different and smaller sort of Klinkhamer might soon replace the Greenwell variant; it was warm and still beneath the cloud and it seemed, in all but one respect, almost a perfect afternoon to be out with a fishing rod.

It took me about twenty minutes to reach my starting point. The main barrier had been a particularly high and rickety fence, the sort in which most of the posts are rotten and the whole structure seems almost certain to collapse when you are swaying on top of it; there had been this fence and one or two walls rather less close to disintegration. Most of the obstacles still lay ahead of me, once I began to struggle along the river back towards Mallerstang Common and the Land Rover. I sat down to rest for a few moments in order to prepare myself for fishing. In telling myself that I was quite happy sitting there without inhaling smoke I was telling myself a lie, and a pointless lie because I was not taken in by it for a moment. I should have loved to be sitting there breathing smoke in and then breathing it out again, while calmly deciding whether to change to a black and smaller Klinkhamer before I started fishing, or to try the Greenwell version over a fish or two and change it if it failed. Instead of this I sat there breathing only air and the truth of it is that it was just about endurable.

It was better when I started fishing, at least it was better until I caught a most beautiful trout of one pound twelve ounces. He was everything a trout should be: deep-bellied and yellow-bellied, deep-bellied but nothing like gross, yellow-bellied and shining black-backed with silver between the black, with long, dark amber fins and with a broad tail, delicately translucent all down the vertical edge. He shone in all sorts of ways and I could tell immediately from the look of him that his red flesh would taste wonderful; but it was impossible for me to celebrate his capture with a box of matches and a pipe of tobacco, lying back in the grass and the buttercups for a minute or two, blowing out smoke, listening to the river and to the birds and acknowledging that the second half of May is incomparable: unquestionably the best time of the year to be sprawling by a river with a pipe in your mouth and a trout approaching two pounds already in you creel. I did not sprawl; I did not bother with a repetition of the great lie. After killing my trout I admired it for a few seconds and then I went on.

I had soon caught and returned a second trout just under the pound. Soon afterwards I went over the top of my waders. The river was much more thickly overgrown than I remembered it and there were many places, usually the places where a fish was rising steadily, where any sort of cast was a plain impossibility. After something like half an hour of tribulation, slipping and stumbling through the river, almost falling at every third or fourth step, fighting my way forward

round great bankside trunks and beneath low branches, prodding my
way over the seamed and shelved bed of the river, after about half an
hour during which only a fraction of my time was spent doing what I
had come to do, I abandoned any idea of further progress through the
water, struggling up a steep and very tangled and slippery bank before
taking the overland route to the next possible point of entry.

By this time the strain of it all was beginning to tell and I had
abandoned any thoughts of giving up tobacco. I was determined to
continue fishing, for it was only three o'clock and there was no reason,
tobacco excepted, why I should return to Sedbergh before six; but I had
already decided what I was going to do when at last I got back there: I
was going to pour myself a huge whisky (very rarely allowed so early
in the evening); next I was going to fill my biggest pipe brimful with
Player's Medium Navy Cut; then I was going to sit down, sniff the
wonderful smells that rise from an inch or two of Glenmorangie in the
bottom of a deep glass, take an appreciative swallow, put a solemn match
to my pipe ; and, with all this done, then, for the next half hour, I was
going to revel in the intoxicating pleasures of my double addiction.

Returning to the river and pushing the prospect of Glenmorangie
and Player's Medium Navy Cut firmly to the back of my mind, I began
to think fishing thoughts again. I came to an old pack-horse bridge and,
beyond it, to a slow and shadowed winding of the river beneath alders:
smooth, slow water for the most part, but with seams and ripples of
faster flow, shaped by the bedrock or by jumbles of roots or by juttings
of the bank. There were fish rising at tiny black things; some of them I
could cover with improvised flicks and rolls that sometimes went where
they were meant to go. I was fishing a damp little wisp of hackle and
herl that has often caught big fish for me, but now the trout would have
none of it. When I left it in a tree I resorted to a biggish and brownish
Klinkhamer, hoping to find a trout greedy enough to forget polite
sipping for just a moment and gulp down a genuine mouthful.

It was one of those casts with no name, nearer a roll than an
overhead performance, more like a jerk than a roll. I shall call it a jerk
cast and I shall make no attempt to analyse its several stages, because I
cannot remember them and could almost certainly never repeat them.

The jerk cast was called forth by the place that demanded it and, surprisingly, it worked, putting the brownish Klinkhamer to a spot under the bank where what I guessed to be a good trout was rising from time to time. The trout absorbed the Klinkhamer – with more of a sip than a gulp – and immediately I knew that I was attached to a monster, for as soon as he felt the hook he leapt half out of the water and then, swimming down into the pool below me, he sulked invisibly.

Already I was thinking of the glass case, for he was certainly very big and my brief glimpse of him had suggested that he was probably beautiful as well. I was determined to employ infinite patience in order to bring him over the net and I was encouraged by his apparent lack of enterprise. Mostly he hung on the end of a tight line; sometimes he swam a few yards to one side or the other; now and then he swam towards me or moved off a little further downstream. Once or twice he approached the surface and almost revealed his tail. He was undoubtedly huge.

There was, I suppose, a minute or two of this; it was more like an endurance test than a fight and my arm was soon aching from the strain of holding the little Sage high while three – or perhaps even four – pounds of trout were pulling on it from the other end. The biggest trout I ever caught weighed two pounds twelve ounces and, from what I could remember of the struggle, the fish with which I was now engaged felt a whole lot heavier. The one-and-three-quarter-pounder in my creel was certainly a midget in comparison; perhaps this sulking brute really did weigh four pounds, in which case, even if he lacked something in beauty, he would still qualify for the bow-fronted case with, behind him, an artistic impression of running water and, rubbing against him, a few green strands of weed.

I am sure the inactive phase of the struggle lasted at least three minutes; for there was time for me to think back to a big fish from last season, an Eden trout of two and a half pounds that had behaved in a similarly dour fashion, hanging on the line and shaking his head and swimming very slowly this way and that. I seemed to remember that it had taken me five minutes to land him; and that had been with the more powerful Loomis; with my soft-actioned little Sage, and with perhaps a pound and a half more of trout, things might still be unresolved in a quarter of an hour.

The fight now took a livelier turn; several inches of tail appeared above the surface and swished round menacingly. There was a vague glimpse of a huge form attached to this small portion of tail; then there was a wide and bad-tempered circuit of the pool, with sudden pulls on the line and petulant head-shaking. It seemed that he was about to come to the surface; perhaps he would splash and wallow there; perhaps there would be an opportunity for the net, for sometimes big trout tire very quickly. This one didn't. Instead of coming to the surface he decided to dive, with an irresistible demonstration of strength and purpose that left me standing in the water and unwilling to believe what a loose line and an unbent rod were telling me very plainly. I pulled on the line, I lifted the rod, feeling for the trout that was no longer there. We all do it, I think, but we cannot do it for more than a second or two. This time I may have done it for a few seconds longer, until I could bring myself to acknowledge that I had just lost contact with an enormous trout and was as yet uncertain precisely how I felt about it.

I knew of course that I should have preferred to catch him and find out how much he weighed. I knew that he was big and guessed that he was at least three and a half pounds. I knew that I would rather not have hooked him than to have had him on and then to have lost him, hook and all. I also knew that if it had happened twenty years ago it would have hurt abominably and haunted me for days on end. Aged fifty three I did not know precisely what I felt about my loss (for it is a loss, whatever old Isaac Walton says); there was disappointment; there was unsatisfied curiosity; there was some sense of failure but there was no burden of incompetence because I could not tell myself that I had done anything obviously wrong. As we get older we generally get better at catching big fish; undoubtedly we get much better at losing them. This was almost certainly the biggest trout I had ever lost and I never fought back a tear. I did not even swear.

I was unsure quite how I felt about hooking and losing a very large trout. I knew that the proper reaction to this situation was to get out my pipe. Since this was impossible I also knew that I did not want to go on fishing, but to get back home as quickly as possible and pour myself that whisky, before sitting down and filling my pipe and then filling my lungs and thinking the whole thing through.

There were no startling insights inspired by a very large Glenmorangie and half an hour's heavy smoking, except that the afternoon had been special in its own way and that the top of the Eden would be seeing me much more often than in the past. I did not brood obsessively on the loss of a great fish; I did not vow to search him out as soon as possible and reclaim my brownish Klinkhamer from his enormous jaws; but the thought of him was with me throughout the evening. I ate my supper and drank my half bottle of wine, thinking how the eating and drinking would have been filled with a spirit of quiet celebration if only that huge trout had come home with me. When I took the dogs out just before midnight, I put two old pipes in the Land Rover, together with two boxes of matches and a packet of dry and repulsively aromatic tobacco. Knowing that these emergency supplies were in place I had a second Glenmorangie; then I got into bed and slept very soundly. I wonder if he was really a four-pounder?

CHAPTER FOUR

A Week on the Wharfe

The end of May usually brings me a whole week's fishing on the Wharfe. It is probably the only time in the season when I fish on each of seven consecutive days, and one of their best pleasures is driving to the river on the morning of the first day, driving over the hills to Wharfedale and looking at the rivers and streams that I drive along or drive over, in order to guess the condition of the Wharfe and at the same time telling myself, as I drive to Sawes and then head up the steep road to Cam Houses, that for the next week, my life will concern itself almost exclusively with trout; and not just with thinking about them and wondering when next I shall be able to try to catch a brace or two of them, not just with books about them and with tying flies designed to deceive at least a few of them.

For a week I will be concerned with real trout in a real river, with seeing them rise and wondering what they are taking, with wading the water and casting over its currents, with lost flies and changes of fly and flies refused and sometimes swallowed, with trout missed at the strike or pricked, or hooked and running and slow to surrender, with little trout and big trout and trout on the bank with me wielding the priest and then gazing at a dead trout in thankful acknowledgment of its marvellous beauty.

It is good for a fisherman to be able to tell himself that for a whole week his life will, in one way or another, be full of trout; and full of them, if he chooses, from ten o'clock in the morning until after ten o'clock at night. If he is a sensible fisherman, he will have brought only fishing books to read in those rare times of the week when he will not be out somewhere with his rod, or not be eating food or drinking wine (unless he is drinking bottled Guinness instead) and talking about fishing with his friends. This probably leaves only half an hour before sleep for his books which, as long as they are fishing books, will round off the day rather nicely, encouraging his dreams, should any come, to concern themselves solely with trout.

This year, as I drove over to the Wharfe with a couple of John Gierach's wonderful books stuffed in my bag, I was feeling more than usually contented, for I knew that the river would be full and I also knew that the forecast for the week was good, which offered the prospect of fishing a falling river, of following it down the valley from day to day, fishing in different places and finding a different sort of fishing all the way. On my first morning I was heading for the beginnings of the Wharfe; I was heading for the river above Deepdale and I was planning to fish the beginnings of the Wharfe right up to its first pool, up to the place where Oughtershaw Beck and Greenfield Beck fall into each other and make my favourite river.

There is something unusually satisfying about catching trout in the first pool of a river, from a little hollow in the bedrock, a little gravelly hollow with a huge boulder at its neck, a little hollow no more than two or three yards long and a yard or two wide. A two-pounder would be out of place here; you want bright little half-pounders to give back to the river's first pool, with the hope of a three-quarter-pounder to take away in your creel; and you want to know that the trout you return, and the odd trout you kill, have all of them lived in the river where you have just caught them, from the time when they were eggs, waiting down there in the gravel for the end of winter to turn them into miniature trout.

Up beyond Deepdale the fish are wild – at least most of them are – and it is one of the delights of fishing there. They are small by the modern fisher's standards and they are very beautiful; and there is beauty of a complementary sort in thinking, as you cast among them, that they are where they and their ancestors have been for thousands of years, living in the little river that follows its rocky course through those steep fields between the fells. Fishing for wild trout appeals to the imagination in a way that fishing stocked water never can.

On Sunday, anyway, I started fishing for the wild trout of Deepdale just before noon. There was an awkward downstream wind – which meant the powerful eight-and-a-half-foot Sage with a number six line – and there was an almost perfect water, much smaller than when I had been there a fortnight earlier, smaller and falling, but still full and shining and not so full that it engulfed the small scale of things, overwhelming all those little features that between them make up half the joy of fishing near the tops of rivers. It was a full and shining water, still glowing from the peat down the deeper runs, but it was no longer an impatient push of water hurrying on its way to spread itself between wider banks. There were slow glides and steady runs between the boisterous bits. There were eddies full of foam; there were little holes where the water rested; there were shelves of yellow rock where the spilling water was churned white, but along all the shallow edges the water was already clear. It was the sort of water that helps a little river to express itself most fluently; it was also the sort of water that suggests to a fisher that he has a good chance of catching fish; and it looked wonderful between the sloping fields, with the moorland rising steeply above them to the broken, impatient sky.

A particular delight to me was that it seemed a water in which to fish wet flies upstream. Klinkhamers of one sort or another might come later but, with no fish showing, upstream wet was undoubtedly a rational as well as a traditional first tactic. I should have liked to tie on a Waterhen Bloa and an Orange Partridge, but these great flies are for rising trout. If you are looking at a water that suggests you ought to catch fish, but a water that shows no signs of them feeding, then start with something a bit bulkier and brighter on a fourteen hook; start with a hackled Coachman and a Simple Simon; if this doesn't work try them in bigger sizes and then try your traditional spiders; when they fail as well it is, of course, time for the Klinkhamer, and time for a big one too.

If you are a fisherman who pines for loneliness, who wants himself and no one else for company, then the top of the Wharfe is not your place. You are very unlikely to meet another fisher, unless one of your

Solitude at Deepdale

friends wanders up from a lower beat half way through the afternoon; but a road runs along one side of the river and a path takes walkers up and down the other side, while you follow the banks and cast your flies somewhere in the middle of it all. Down below Yockenthwaite you get away from the road, but the path is still there and even busier than between Deepdale and Beckermonds.

I suppose I should prefer no path and no road running along the beginnings of the Wharfe. Fishing is a sort of withdrawal, a sort of retreat; cars and parties of ramblers are likely to get in the way of a fisher's lonely communion with himself and the water and the landscape, and there is undoubtedly something compelling about unpeopled places. Unfortunately the top of the river Wharfe is not such a place. It is very beautiful, the fishing is very good and, especially at the weekend, there is lots of traffic on the road and there is always at least a steady trickle of men and women in walking boots, heading upstream for Beckermonds or downriver towards Hubberholme. I try not to hook them with my back cast; I smile at them whether or not they smile at me (which they usually do); if they ask me about my fishing I give them an honest reply. Not one of them has ever suggested to me that, as a catcher and killer of trout, I am a heartless, a cruel or a wicked man. Perhaps I should

love the top of the Wharfe even more without the walkers; but I love
it as it is; I am happy to share it with them and, just in case you were
wondering, yes! I do enjoy catching trout with a group of spectators
standing on the bank and marvelling at my skill. Once or twice I have
been photographed in the act and I enjoyed that too.

Simple Simon and the Coachman worked very well on Sunday.
In almost every pool the line twitched or jerked a time or two; most
of the trout were small, seven or eight inches long, but they were all
lovely fish, with big black spots and smaller red ones and perfect fins.
I was broken by a larger trout in the twisting run a few yards below
a little fall. Further up towards the beginning of the Wharfe a three-
quarter-pounder went in the creel; he was joined by another fish of the
same size from the first pool of all, which, as I have already insisted, is
always a special satisfaction. But even with the powerful Sage the wind
was bothering me and I decided to move. Doubtless my technique was
to blame rather than the rod; probably my loop is not tight enough, or
something of that sort.

Anyway thinking of the sheltered water below Yockenthwaite, I
drove downstream a mile or so to the old pack-horse bridge that crosses
the river below the farm-house built on the slope above. It is a surprisingly elegant farmhouse; up there at the bare head of the valley you
would expect sturdiness and defiance in the form of rough stone and
small windows; you would not expect regular proportions or dressed
yellow limestone between town-house windows and a door with a
moulded architrave; least of all would you expect a summer house of
the same dressed stone, built on to one end of the main house and
standing in a walled garden. It is a surprise, a tasteful surprise and, after
a century or two, it has mellowed into a weathered surprise so that, if
it ever looked out-of-place in its surroundings, it now most certainly
belongs.

I did find shelter from the wind down below Yockenthwaite;
and the air smelt of May blossom, and the meadows, between the tight
pattern of their limestone walls, were full of buttercups and orchids.
There were trout rising here and there and I caught perhaps half a
dozen of them with a little brown Klinkhamer. I kept one just over and

another just under the pound and finished at six o'clock. When I got to Arncliffe and *The Falcon* I found that I knew everyone who was there and that they were all fishers (or fishers' wives). There was wine with dinner – a spicy *Cotes du Rhone* – and then I had a bath and wrote up my diary and drank a few bottles of Guinness before going to bed.

There was time for half an hour's Gierach before I put the light out, time for me to feel bitterly ashamed that, in a previous book, I wrote dismissively of *Trout Bum*. It was a grave critical error. I have read it at least three times since then; I have read half a dozen of Gierach's other books as well and they are very fine indeed. He is a passionate fisherman but his writing about fishing always seems relaxed. The tone is all his own and on first encounter I badly misjudged it. He cares deeply about rivers and fish but writes lightly about them. Very clearly he holds strong views about things, particularly about how not to treat rivers, but there is never any unpleasant stridency to his expression of them. He has almost rejected American materialism, but he is aware of the 'almost'; he is aware of his own inconsistencies and he never rants or preaches; he is telling us how he lives and what he values rather than telling us what we should do and think ourselves. He has devoted his life to fly-fishing and to writing about it because it is beautiful and fascinating and fulfilling.

There is a sense of relief in this but no sense of moral superiority, no sense of contempt for others who have chosen differently. His books are about more than fishing; some sort of philosophy of life emerges from them, but it emerges as a personal preference rather than as the one true way. His writing communicates a strong and very attractive sense of personality and is often very funny. Gierach is a consummately skilful writer; one of the best things about his writing is that it is never heavy-handed; it never shouts at you. His books on fishing are amongst the best there are and they are perfect reading for half an hour before sleep at the end of a long fishing day. It had been a good fishing day, but certainly the most special thing about it had been that there were six more of them to come.

On Monday I went to Kettlewell and rejoiced in the lightness of the wind and the refined strength of my Loomis. Gierach, of course, if he had been with me, would have been waving bamboo. I used my American Loomis, fishing a Greenwell-style Klinkhamer, and caught two most beautiful trout. They were both just over the pound and both as silver as sea-trout, the silver telling me that their flesh would be pink; but in general the river was quiet and in the afternoon I went back to Yockenthwaite, where I found a very soft, grey afternoon with a mixed trickle of olives and a few rising trout; it was one of those afternoons when casting a fly was almost enough in itself. There were places for side casts and roll casts and a few places for ordinary overhead casts; and I seemed to be on form and the quiet sound of the line was a delight and the May blossom was sweet and the buttercups and the orchids were very shining softly in the grey light.

The river was yellow and brown and silver and grey, and the trout that I caught from time to time – all on the Greenwell Klinkhamer – these five or six trout were more than was needed. I kept three of about a pound and when, sometime after six, I was stowing my tackle in the Land Rover and looking down over the rock pools through which the river flows below the old bridge, looking down at the slip and the slide

Bridge over the Wharfe at Yockenthwaite

and the ripple of the brown water and seeing a trout rise hard against the bank in the lowest and longest of those four lovely pools, I felt a sudden longing to forget about *The Falcon,* about dinner and wine and fishing-talk, to forget about all this and take hold of my rod and go back to the river for just as long as I wanted.

It is a feeling that visits me once or twice a season, almost always at Yockenthwaite as I stand there looking at the river and the bridge and at the old farmhouse across the water. This feeling is most powerful on still evenings in September, when the bracken on the fells is just beginning to turn, when the sheep graze more slowly and more quietly, when the farmhouse chimneys are sending up straight columns of white smoke. It is a feeling I associate with late September, when the walkers have gone and when a cloudy afternoon is beginning to fade into the brief autumn evening but, at Yockenthwaite, it can come over me at any time of the season; there is a wonderful quality of quietness about the place which, on a calm grey evening, often seems a compelling reason to stay there and keep fishing, searching the little pools with a fly and drawing from the water the complementary excitements of the river's trout. Once or twice I have surrendered; I have finished fishing and started all over again and kept going deep into the twilight.

On this occasion I resisted the urge to stay. But I did fish again after dinner, not at Yockenthwaite but on the beck that runs down the valley behind the hotel. I did not want any more trout in the creel; five was more than enough for me with five more days still ahead. A two-pounder in good condition would, I suppose, have come back with me through the darkness, but I was relieved no two-pounder came my way. I did not want more dead fish; I wanted to cast wet flies through the dimming light and to watch my white line for the twitch of a taking trout.

I suppose I did not fish for much more than an hour; it was an hour and a bit with something of magic about it, and I mean magic, which is a tired, misunderstood and ill-used old word; it appears in sentences and to describe circumstances where it does not belong; it has lost most of its power and been reduced to an almost ordinary word. But it most certainly belongs, in all its true mystery, to that hour on the beck, which was a transforming hour, one that somehow managed to make the world seem a place of nothing but wonder and beauty and peace.

The air was absolutely still and the sky was grey. There were some sort of sedge flies fluttering silently up the beck. There were the shapes of the surrounding hills. There were the shapes of rabbits scampering through the grass, with the dark shapes of mallard flighting up the valley and the sound of their beating wings. There was the softer sound and movement of the water and the dim shine of my line sliding over it; and now and then it twitched and often the trout were too quick for me or were only plucking at the flies; but three times a fish was drawn over the net, indistinct and gleaming in the last light, and then slipped back into the current.

It was almost dark when an inextricable tangle put an end to my fishing. Without the tangle I should not have finished; I should have gone on to the next pool and then to the pool beyond, drawn on by the enticement in the water and in the air and in the sudden twitches on my line.

Tuesday was an ordinary sort of fishing day, spent below Kettlewell. There were few fish feeding, but I got a nice trout of a pound and a quarter from a long glide beneath a tall, leaning sycamore. The fly was August Black. There were also one or two small trout from places where I expect big ones, and then it was time for lunch. The afternoon was quiet as well, but from the same glide, this time with a little Black and Peacock Spider, I killed a trout of one and three quarter pounds. It was an ordinary sort of fishing day but the brace was a considerable satisfaction, especially since both fish came to wet flies.

Most of Wednesday was frustrating and dispiriting. I spent it above Kettlewell and hoped to do great things. At three o'clock I had not caught a trout, not even a troutling to unhook and return to the water. I had cast over rising fish, with Klinkhamers of various sizes, with little black floaters and with little black flies that sank or were meant to sink. There had been a pull or two but I had failed to set the hook and they had probably been toying pulls anyway. By three o'clock I was despondent; my casting had gone to pieces and I could not see how I was going to kill a trout. The air was warm and the sun was on the water. There were fish rising and I had tried flies that should have caught some of them. I did not know what to do next and I even thought of calling it a day. I only thought of it, but even the thought of it shows how deeply the gloom had come down.

The Wharfe above Kettlewell is one of my favourite stretches of the river. It has given me some fine bags and some fine fish. This made things worse on Wednesday, because, in most of the places where I put fish down rather than catching them, I could remember big trout from earlier days, and I did not think I could remember a single day above Kettlewell Bridge that had sent me away with an empty creel. And the water was a good fly water. Within a day or two it would begin to drop low but, on Wednesday, it was still a generous water with the last remains of colour from the recent rains.

The sun was bright, but that should not cause problems in a good water in May. Bright sunshine only hurts fishing when rivers are on their bones, and even then I am not sure that it is the enemy it is said to be. There was fly on Wednesday; there was lots of tiny and not so tiny black stuff. There were plenty of rising fish and, in my experience, fish eating black fly in May are not usually very difficult to deceive. Everything was in my favour and there I was at three o'clock in the afternoon without a single trout in my creel.

I had come to a lovely stretch of water where, between two sharp corners, the river flows down a long and very lively run, with trailing willows at the top, with on one side a high bank and with dappled light on the water from the sycamores and ashes that line this bank. But I was not in the mood to appreciate surrounding beauties. A couple of two-pounders in the creel would doubtless have opened my eyes to the infinitely varied delights of shade and sunshine and flowing water, but there were no two-pounders in my creel; there was nothing there at all except for a thermos flask and, when I saw what was clearly a good trout rising in the slacker water at the bottom of the run, I did not feel pleased. I acknowledged that I should have to go through the motions of trying to catch him, which would inevitably mean putting him down and then moving on in search of further humiliation.

I was fed up with variations on the theme of small and black. I could no longer cast cleverly enough to know where they came to water (which makes hooking fish very difficult). I was disillusioned with Klinkhamers and so, for no particular reason, I tied on a little parachute pale watery with a tail of gold. This tail, consisting of seven or eight strands of Krystal Flash, is meant to represent a nymphal shuck and it is not my invention. Whether or not fish take it as intended is open to question, but there are certainly times when they find flies with flashing tails very attractive.

I tied on my parachute pale watery because I had to tie on something. I expected it to fail, for I was by now convinced that I should leave the river, when eventually I had had enough of not catching trout, with what Skues calls a toom creel. Within five minutes a fish of one pound six ounces, a beautiful yellow-bellied fish with a small head and a big tail, meant that my creel was toom no longer. I now saw that, right at the top of the run, just below the willows, a big snout was sticking itself out of the water from time to time. My casting really had gone to pieces; I could not put my fly within a foot of where I wanted to; there was some trouble with timing and there was a sort of forward drift to my forearm of which I was aware but which I could do nothing to control. The truth is that, on top of everything else, I was suddenly very nervous, which was, I suppose, ridiculous and shameful in a fisher of fifty three, but trout matter to me and, after five hours of frustration, the prospect of turning a blank into a brace – a brace of big fish – had fairly set my arm shaking.

I managed not to cast heavily. I inched the fly forward and it fell behind and to each side of its target until at last it fell where it was meant to fall. The snout was in a co-operative mood and protruded itself once again; and suddenly there was an angry fish running hard, charging down almost to the bottom of the run and then racing back and heading straight for the willows and their roots. I thought he must be at least two pounds, perhaps even two and a half. I was terrified of losing him and he was very slow to tire. He did not weigh two pounds; he weighed one pound fourteen ounces and I did not care a fig. I had made the brace, a brace of wild and beautiful fish. They had come within less than ten minutes; failure had turned into glory and, as I knelt in the dappled grass and gazed at them, at their spots, at their fins, at their tails, at their shining flanks and their dark backs, as I knelt there gazing at my brace and drinking in its magnificence, I was as happy as a fisher can be, loving the bright sun and the bright water and the half-shadowed run that had just put in my creel two trout that between them weighed four ounces more than three pounds.

It is absurd that, in a world full of important sorrow, two trout can bring such happiness; it is absurd and wonderful and it is what makes me a fisherman. Not all the trout we catch make us look at the world with different eyes; many of them are just ordinary trout; but if I ever find that none of them can still work this strange alchemy upon me, then at least half the reason for being a fisher will have disappeared.

There were no more trout; they returned to their finicky ways and my casting remained erratic. I wondered what had made those two fish different from all the other trout in the river. Why had they so readily swallowed my little parachute pale watery with its tail of gold when no other fish would even nose it? There were a few pale olives on the water, but it was a few. Anyway I thought that both halves of my brace had probably been treating themselves to occasional olives

'It is absurd that, in a world full of important sorrow,
two trout can bring such happiness...'

rather than fattening up on an exclusive diet of black fly. I did not care very much; I was so happy they were in my creel. And I did not fish in the evening, partly because the beck was already falling low but more because that marvellous ten minutes seemed somehow enough for the whole day. I was also tired and half a bottle of wine made an armchair seem a place in which to stay, until at last I got to my feet, told my friends that Guinness time had come and shuffled off to the bar.

By the Thursday of a full week's fishing I sometimes begin to wonder if I might have had enough. This may be because I am finding trout very difficult to come by, although usually this makes me determined to keep trying; more often it is because things have gone well and I am beginning to feel that a few days without trout might whet my fisher's appetite and send me back to the river with a renewed hunger for more of them.

This year there was never any feeling of satiety. Sunday and Monday had brought plenty of trout to net. Tuesday and Wednesday had brought little beyond the brace killed on each day. The trout-hunger was still on me and, during my last three days on the Wharfe, my attempts to satisfy it centred on the glide below the leaning sycamore that had yielded Tuesday's trout. It was not just a whim or an infatuation. It was because the beats below the Stepping Stones were seething with stock-fish that had been in the river less than a month and were very ugly and very easy to catch. I wanted nothing to do with them and they did not seem to have spread above the stones – at least I came across none – but I also came across far fewer rising trout than I expected to find there in a good water at the end of May.

I caught some beautiful little seven and eight inchers. I put down or missed what were probably bigger fish; but there were at least half a dozen places where experience told me that trout would be rising and where, each day when I came to them, no rising trout were to be seen. There were a few tiddlers splashing about in the romantically called Sewage-Pipe run, but I associate it with big trout and there were none in evidence. From the short run above it, little more than a deep groove in the yellow bedrock beneath a tall ash tree, from this little run I have caught trout over two pounds and I never come to it without expectation; more often than not there has been a trout there eating something and he has very rarely been small. This week there was no sign of a fish under the branches of the ash; further downstream there is a long straight glide over the rock where something is almost always showing near the straggling willows in the slightly rougher water right towards the head. This week there was nothing showing above or below the willows and there were never any fish to be seen in the little pools and runs beneath the high, walled bank that carries the path from Kettlewell down to the Stepping Stones.

It puzzled and disappointed me, this seeming absence of good trout rising where they are meant to rise, but it did not worry me too much, especially since the weather turned hotter and more humid as the week passed. It will take more visits with few signs of trout before I begin to think that there is something wrong with the Wharfe between the Stepping Stones and Kettlewell. Trout are peculiar creatures; they behave just as you expect them to behave almost all of the time; then, for a day or a week, they confound your expectations and behave quite differently. Always there will be a reason for it, but it will often be a compound reason composed of such subtle and elusive elements that it is beyond a fisher's powers of analysis. Anyway the fact that, on three or four days, fish are untypically hard to find on a given stretch of water, does not inevitably mean that poachers have struck by night and taken them all away. You need not fear something of this sort, or something even worse, until three or four days have turned into at least a month.

The strange thing about my days on the Stepping-Stones-beat this week was that, although over most of it there was a marked absence of rising trout, there were always fish feeding away for all the world to see in the long glide beneath the leaning sycamore. It had given me a brace on Tuesday. On Thursday it produced a trout of one pound two ounces (to a dry Black Gnat); on Friday a tiny Black and Peacock Spider brought a fish of one pound twelve ounces to net; on Saturday a Griffiths Gnat came up trumps with a trout that honesty compels me to admit was just one ounce short of two pounds.

All three days were days of just one trout with perhaps half a dozen smaller fish returned. I spent half of those three days sitting by the edge of the Sycamore Glide and wondering what fly to try next; then I would try it and catch or more usually fail to catch one of the half dozen trout busy feeding there, which indicated that it was time to wander off for a time in search of trout rising elsewhere, before returning to my smooth rock at the bottom of the glide, sitting down on it and wondering all over again which fly I should attach to the end of my line.

I suppose it is a pool really rather than a glide, a shelving bowl of limestone with the sycamore across the river – on your right as you sit there looking upstream – with this sycamore leaning its branches over the river where the water flows into the pool over two or three transverse shelves of rock. I think of it as a glide because, in a normal or low water, the current, flowing under the sycamore and then moving just a little nearer the middle of the river, is a gentle movement rather than a rush and soon almost loses itself in the slack water of the pool. The trout rise all along the edges of this leisurely flow, and they are difficult. I have caught them in the past, but not many of them, and I confess that I have not always tried very hard, because there has been lots of easier water both upstream and down.

This week my choice of rising trout was limited and I tried my best with the trout of Sycamore Glide. There were usually at least half a dozen of them feeding there, very clearly busy with little black things. There were little sipping rises that I knew were almost certainly the work of big trout. And the trout beat me much more often than I beat them. Most typically they ignored my fly. Sometimes they nudged it and refused to take; once or twice they did take and I bungled the strike. They were all wild, at least all the trout I caught were wild or fully naturalised fish. Four of them I killed and the biggest came last; and, just five minutes after acknowledging that I had not quite caught a two-pounder, another big fish sailed up to my fly – I could see him in the clear water – and, striking too soon, I only pricked him.

He was a big disappointment, that pricked fish; a brace would have made my last day and I have a feeling that he might just have weighed two pounds. But it had been a varied and interesting week. I had not fished my way steadily downstream as I had intended. Twice

I had gone up rather than going down and the stock fish had kept me from exploring below the Stepping Stones. In spite of this it had been a good week, with the fishing becoming steadily more difficult, with a magical evening on a little beck, with a wonderful half hour above Kettlewell, with some fine trout to show for my efforts and with that progressive concentration on the challenge of a single pool. It was a week that sent me home wondering when I should be able to go fishing again and thinking that, if all went well, I might be able to spend Tuesday evening somewhere on the Eden.

CHAPTER FIVE

The Secret Rea

When, six or seven years ago, I looked for the first time at Shropshire's river Rea – it was not much of a look because most of the water was lurking somewhere beneath an impenetrable mesh of branches and a wild riot of bankside growth – immediately I felt depressed. It did not seem to my eyes that this dark and shrouded river was a river for trout or trout-fishers. I did not look at the Rea and feel impatient to get my waders on; from what I could see of it, I felt that fishing the Rea was almost certain to be a waste of time.

The reason for this, I think, was that we north-country fishers carry in our minds a very clear picture of what a troutstream looks like. It is, to begin with, full of clear water, unless it is fining down from flood and glowing with the dark radiance of peat; it flows over bright gravel and over smooth rock and in many places it is boulder-strewn; here and there the water lingers in long pools and flats, briefly losing its sense of urgency; but in general our typical trout stream gets a move on; it is a river of rapid currents, foaming over slabs and steps of rock and rushing down narrow channels and pushing its way through restless pools. There may be dramatic moments where it passes beneath high cliffs or forces its way through a deep gorge or plunges down steep falls; in such places it may be hidden from the surrounding landscape, but by and large it is an open river, an obvious and welcome presence in the fields through which it flows.

Judging from my first and severely impeded view of it, the river Rea, or the Rea Brook as it is perhaps more properly called, corresponded to none of these generalities. The water, for a start, was very far from clear; it was creeping on its way in a red-brown haze. It appeared to be a sluggish sort of river or brook; the bit of it I could see, at any rate, seemed barely to be flowing at all. There was no sign of a rock or boulder. The banks were of reddish clay although this was largely obscured by the jungle that covered them, and it looked as though the bed would be an oozing mass of mud and silt.

Worst of all was the fact that the Rea flowed whole yards below the level of the surrounding fields; the banks were high and steep; there were trees – alders, willows and poplars – all along them. I should scarcely have suspected the presence of the Rea if I had not been promised that it was there, taken right up to it and told where to look. It seemed almost a subterranean watercourse, hidden away from the land to which it belonged. There was sunshine over the fields; there was very little of it on the Rea.

There was something dispiriting about it, about the murky water sliding down its dark channel between those high and tangled banks and beneath the midsummer gloom of all those trees. There was an air of neglect to it all; there was something forbidding about the sunken little brook and the dismal chaos of its banks. I thought there might be a chub or two somewhere in the Rea, a few chub and a few roach and perhaps a few half-starved pikelets; I could not believe there were any trout. My first impression of the Rea, in fact, was of a ditch rather than a trout stream; my first impression of the Rea was as misleading as any such impression can be.

Once I had tackled up, wondering why I was bothering, and largely out of politeness to my host, once I had got ready to go fishing and then struggled down the bank and finally got into the Rea, I realised almost at once that things were rather better than they had seemed from above.

To begin with, the water did move; there were short runs under the banks and on the corners; knotted masses of roots grew out into the stream and made little glides and deflections of flow through the shadows. There was much more splash and gurgle than I had been expecting; the little river slipped over brittle shelves of slatey rock; it rippled over pebbled shallows; under constriction it rushed into one or

The Rea: 'almost a subterranean watercourse'

two of the pools and was altogether much livelier than my first sight of it had suggested. The water flowed with the colour of the clay and the rock, but it was bright and clean; there was haze only in the deeper, siltier pools. It was a river of shadows but it was also a river of sunlight; there were patches of it, patches and dappled patterns and sometimes great pools of flowing light where the canopy opened up.

Throughout the day there was a constant trickle of duns and, whatever my first impressions had told me, the Rea was unquestionably a trout stream, for I caught some of them: not the three-quarter-pounders that I had been told to hope for – though my friend Merlin got a brace of these – but little seven and eight inchers, wild fish with red fins and red spots and with a bright red rim along the transverse edges of the tail.

Since that first day I have grown very fond of the Rea. I fish it two or three times a season and almost always it is kind to me, sending me back to my friends in Ludlow with a brace or a leash of lovely wild trout. The Rea is quite different from my own rivers and this difference has become a chief part of my pleasure in fishing it. There is a special feeling of withdrawal waiting to take possession of fishers who go to the Rea. First they must beat a path down the tangled banks, accepting stings and scratches as part of the price of their day's sport; but then, with this barrier now established between themselves and the rest of the world, then they can follow the course of the hidden stream, hoping for just a few of its red-finned trout as a reward for all those scratches and stings, and finding, after an hour or two, that they have fished their way into a deep seclusion of green leaves and shadows, of sliding water and dappled sunshine and welcoming loneliness.

There are things about fishing the Rea – even apart from the discomfort of getting in and out of it – that sometimes make the seclusion seem less than ideal. You must expect to lose flies, catching them in low branches when you are trying to cover what looks like a good trout; you must expect to find fish rising in places where even the thought of a cast is an absurdity; you will be lucky if only one of your wading boots gets full of water; you may well fall in and get wet all over. But it is worth it. The delights of fishing the hidden stream are very great indeed.

My most recent encounter with the Rea Brook came one Monday early in July. On Sunday I had fished the Onny, on a very sleepy afternoon when only troutlings splashed at my flies; on Saturday it had been the Rea, and I had returned to Ludlow in the evening with a trout of a pound and with two trout of ten ounces; perhaps a dozen fish up to half a pound had been released and I had felt pleased both with myself and with the Rea. Monday was my last day in Shropshire and, of course, I went back to the Rea.

It was a hot, bright morning with big white clouds floating very slowly between the blue and with a warm breeze, just drifting upstream. For some reason I was in a mood to explore and walked much further down the river than I had ever been before, finding the water slightly less over-arched with trees and the banks not quite so thickly overgrown with nettles and thistles, with willow herb and twining masses of goosegrass.

There was a Klinkhamer on the end of my line, a little brown one. It was the fly that had deceived all Saturday's trout – by some miracle I had managed not to lose it – and it still looked only a little more dishevelled than it had looked when it had just been tied. I have caught Rea trout on the wet fly – there was a morning a few years ago when a hackle Coachman brought me two fish of a pound in less than ten minutes – but, in July at least, I think the Rea will give better sport to the dry-fly.

Typically the trout feed on the day-long trickle of duns and on the miscellaneous insects that drop from the branches – or flutter from the banks – onto the surface of the stream. I believe that some seasons there is an enormous hatch of Mayfly, but I have never been there in Mayfly time. I have never been there in the evening and so can say nothing about the evening rise, although I know from my own rivers that daytime trickles of duns often produce enormous falls of spinner as the light fails.

In writing about the Rea I am thinking of high-summer days between ten and six o'clock when it is, in my experience, a water for the dry fly. And, in my experience, the trout, as long as you can get into position and then drop your fly in the right spot without frightening them, are generally easy to please. It is as well that they are, for everything else about fishing the Rea is of the demanding sort; casting a fly is a very delicate business on the Rea; getting in and out of the water is often a very indelicate and decidedly arduous business. You are bound to get hung up; you will probably begin to suspect that those tall nettles and thistles and those leaning branches are seizing your flies on purpose, in retaliation for your invasion of their territory.

And though the trout may be, in most respects, accommodating, there are limits to their tolerance and you are certain to frighten them with improvised casts that sometimes work but more often put your fly in a thistle or a branch or in the middle of a tangled heap of nylon on the surface of the river. You cannot expect to settle down to a fish on the Rea, trying him with seven sorts of dun and four sorts of nymph and one or two sorts somewhere in between. If you cover him once you have done well; expect some sort of disaster on the second attempt.

It is a good job the Rea trout are broad-minded in their approach to food. There are problems enough without ticklish problems of fly-selection. On Monday the 7th of July, anyway, I had faith in my little brown Klinkhamer as I walked down the river in the sunshine, peering into shadowed pools and seeing here and there the marks of rising trout. Perhaps I had walked half a mile, perhaps a little more, when I came to a place where the river turned against a steep wooded bank, which seemed to be telling me that I had come far enough and that it was almost time to start fishing; it was, in other words, time to sit and smoke for a few minutes, gathering my strength to deal with all the tribulations to come.

After a few minutes I tried to make a start and found that I could not get into the river where I wanted to, which was at the bottom of a pool where two or three trout were rising. The banks were too steep and too thickly overgrown for me to fight my way down to the river. It was pretty obvious, anyway, that the water was too deep and it was equally clear that, even if I managed to get into position without getting most of the river Rea on the wrong side of my waders, I should be very unlikely to find any sort of cast possible. I gave up on those trout, slid into the water at the top of the pool, saw a rise in the little run ahead of me and had almost immediately caught a trout of at least seven inches.

The fishing had begun and now wound its course along the margins of the Rea for the next six hours or so, in deep or sun-dappled shadow, occasionally beneath untrammelled brightness, and with a sense of growing remoteness from anything but this light and these shadows, and the moving water on which they lay and the wild banks above the water where the alders and poplars and willows that spread their branches so quietly above the sliding stream and over the trout that swam there and over the flies that buzzed and fluttered in their shade.

The little Sage, with its soft and easy action, was a delight on the little river. My rolls and flicks and switches worked just as often as they failed, and this new stretch of the Rea, although it was by absolute standards densely overgrown, was fairly open in comparison with the

higher reaches where I had always been before. There were one or two
small trout returned to the water. I left my little brown Klinkhamer
somewhere in a tree, tied on another and then, on a sharp corner where
the flow deepened under the far bank, I covered a rise, hooked a big fish
and guessed him at least a pound. He was exactly a pound and a half; he
was the biggest fish the Rea had ever given me and it was time for me
to sit in the reeds and smoke, feeling very happy to be a fisher and very
happy to be fishing the Rea Brook.

I began to wonder, as I sat there, how my life would have been if
it had not been full of fishing. I began to wonder what might have taken
its place. It might have been full of golf (which was a brief adolescent
addiction). More likely it would have been full of walking or perhaps
even bird-watching. It would certainly have been much fuller of Latin
and Greek. Without fishing I thought that I might have made a real
scholar of myself, I might have turned into a distinguished classicist
rather than a competent schoolmaster.

It did not take me long to decide that I was perfectly content with
the schoolmaster-fisherman; for I decided that I did not have either the
intellect or the dogged perseverance for true scholarship and, anyway,
the thought of a life without fishing was a dreadful thought; and there
was also the thought that writing about fishing has given me as much
pleasure as the fishing itself. Could I have written books about walking
or bird watching? Would scholarly monographs have given me as much
satisfaction as rummaging round in the events and experiences of my
life as an angler?

It was, of course, not the first time I have thought along these
lines and asked myself similar questions. Sometimes my response to
them has been less unequivocal; never have they found me as compla-
cent and serene as in the July sunshine of a Monday morning on the
banks of the Rea.

It was soon time, anyway, to look for trout again, down the glides
and runs of the stream, on all the corners and in all those currents
against the roots. When fishing I can never really relax, not even by the
side of the little river Rea, until there is a brace in my creel; I would
rather go home with two three-quarter-pounders than a single trout

of a pound and a half, which is doubtless an incorrect preference but it is never going to change. There is comfort in a brace; a single trout, however large, is one trout too few for me; and so, in spite of my happiness, I was very keen for my Rea monster to have some company in so big a creel. He was lonely for rather longer than I was expecting.

There were two trout – and they looked good ones – rising in a long straight run only partially overhung by trees. This is as near as you get to open water on the Rea; if I see fish rising in such a place I count them already half caught. But the first of these two trout thought nothing of my little brown Klinkhamer. I changed to a much smaller black thing and this put him down. I tried the fish above him with a sinking black thing and he stopped rising immediately. Their faddishness both surprised and annoyed me: it was not what I looked for from the trout of the Rea Brook. I felt that it was my duty to cover them with a fly and that it was their duty, as long as mine had been adequately performed, to swallow whatever fly I had chosen on their behalf.

Moving on, and tying on one of my gold-tailed pale wateries, I returned a few trout and began to fear that the rest of the day would be full of six and seven inchers. It is, of course, good to catch small trout, for they are very beautiful and, in a wild river like the Rea, they mean healthy spawning beds. Small trout are a delight, as long as at least two bigger ones are mixed in with them. I had to wait for the second half of my brace for at least an hour, until I came to a pool that was large by the standards of the Rea. There was a lively run into it, pushing its influence right through to the tail, where I saw a rise and had soon caught a trout of twelve ounces. And then, half way up the pool, my brace turned into a leash with a genuine pounder.

It was time for lunch now – at three o'clock in the afternoon – time for a mug of tea and a sandwich and then tobacco, while I sat among forget-me-nots on a half-grassed bank of gravel at the bottom of the pool, sitting in a patchwork of shadow and sunshine with my rod resting on my creel and with those three trout stowed inside it. There was the squeak and flash of a kingfisher (believe me that I am not making him up because he ought to have been there); there was this kingfisher and the sound of him, there were olives fluttering off the water – I think they were blue-wings – and soon I should be ready to go fishing again. But for ten minutes it was good to sit there and think easy thoughts on the edge of the Rea Brook.

Before long I caught another trout, of about twelve ounces, and put him back. Then I wandered down the river almost to where I had started. It was hot in the open fields beneath the sun. The fat Shropshire sheep had all retreated into the shade. It would soon be time to finish, for I was happy with three trout and I never much enjoy fishing once my creel is as full as I want it to be. I thought that I would take a fourth fish if a good one came my way, but I was not much bothered and this meant that another hour's fishing would certainly be enough.

I followed the sheeps' example and withdrew from the sun, sitting on a fallen trunk beneath the trees and anointing with spittle the stings and scratches all over my arms. I decided that, however hot the weather, a long-sleeved shirt was essential on the Rea and, although I had only once gone over the top of my waders, I wondered whether I should make an exception to the rule that I go fishing in thigh waders, allowing myself the chest sort on the Rea.

I did not reach a conclusion. I was beginning to look forward to the evening, to wine and smoked trout, to dry feet and the company of friends. There was a sense of comfortable remoteness in the fields all round me; but soon it would be time to leave them in search of food and drink and talk. And, since I had rashly promised to provide trout fresh from the river for smoking, it suddenly seemed that a fourth trout would be a good idea after all.

I looked for him in the long run of fastidious trout, but they were no longer rising and so it was impossible to find out whether they were still behaving like jaded epicures. I found a few small fish here and there, but it was not until I reached the kingfisher's pool that the fourth trout went into the creel. He weighed twelve ounces, and he meant that it really was time to finish and drive off to Ludlow, although I cleaned my trout first, throwing their guts and gills into the river as food for whatever creatures of the river might fancy them. If there are crayfish in the Rea, then some of them will have had a feast.

The trout were smoked in an old army field oven, a rusting hulk of an oven which looks ridiculous but produces wonderful smoked fish. We drank red wine with them and it worked very well. And it somehow rounds off a fishing day when you cook your catch the same evening and then sit in a garden as the night gathers round you, eating and drinking and just occasionally thinking of the little river from which your trout came. It will be almost a year before I fish the Rea brook again.

A black poplar by Shropshire's Rea brook: 'a growing sense of remoteness'

Chapter Six

Low Water Thoughts

I rarely fish much in August, not at least before the end of the month; sometimes there is an hour or two in the evening; sometimes there is part of an afternoon; very occasionally, if the Eden is irresistible, there is almost a full day. But most of August is for my pheasant poults at High Park, for feeding and watering them, for trying to coax them back into their pens, for setting traps to catch mink and stoats and feral cats, for baiting these traps with delicious slices of sardines (in oil) and mackerel (in tomato sauce). August is for pheasants and for getting my shoot in order for late-autumn and winter sport; there is not too much time to spare for pheasants once September has sent me back to school, and so August – apart from its last week – is mainly for my poults, with just a few bits of fishing here and there.

This year there were not even any bits. Throughout the month the Eden was so low that I did not want to be standing in what was left of it with a rod in my hand; and, anyway, the days were so hot and so stifling that I returned from High Park far too tired and much too sweaty to think of a quick supper before setting out again to fish the evening rise. There were times out on the farm, generally about two o'clock in the afternoon, when I thought that I was beginning to melt; once home I usually took my body to bed for an hour or so; lying in a darkened room was a very deep delight and usually it sent me to sleep. After my sleep I had to face the heat again, heading off for the vegetable garden to pick courgettes and beans for my supper, digging a few potatoes and perhaps cutting a few sweet peas for the table. Then it would be time for a bath before the ordeal of the kitchen, which generally made the bath seem a waste of time by renewing the feeling that my flesh, like the butter in the pan, was starting to liquefy.

At last the bliss of sherry-time would come, bringing a large glass of manzanilla as a first reward for a day's labour under the sun; with food there was always half a bottle of wine and always, somewhere near the end of drinking it, I would light my pipe and sniff my glass and pray that, with my poults now settled, there would be rain to make rivers flow again before my trip to the Wharfe at the end of the month. Then it would be time for a whisky and after the whisky it was time to lie sweating in my bed, where in spite of the sticky air – and perhaps partly because of the wine and the whisky, not to mention the day's work – sleep usually came easily and usually lasted until around eight o' clock the next morning.

But the rain did not come as I had been hoping. One Sunday there was a thundery downpour that lasted about two hours; it cleared the air and it settled the dust, but it did nothing to bring relief to weary trout streams. There were one or two mornings of misting drizzle and there was nothing else but humid air and hot sunshine. It was ideal weather for pheasant poults but it offered little prospect of good trouting on the Wharfe in what had soon shrunk to less than a week. I never thought of cancelling my late-August fishing. I had not fished for almost a month, since two delightful days at Driffield and Foston, so I was determined to go to the Wharfe even if it had forgotten how to flow; which is the reason why, on the evening before my fishing trip, I went down to the vegetable garden, this time with no thoughts of gathering beans or courgettes (they had already been brought in). I went right down to the bottom of the garden with a fork in my hand, down to the compost heap, and you may have guessed already that I went there to dig worms.

Gathering worms is almost a sport in itself, especially during the middle of a drought. There was a time about fifteen years ago when I did a fair amount of it, until my brief enthusiasm for the upstream worm faded away, partly because of a succession of wet summers, more importantly because I realised that I much preferred catching trout on the fly. I had been drawn to the upstream or clear-water worm by reading Stewart, Pritt and Nelson and by their praise of it as a skilful

and deadly way of catching trout; it seemed to have an honourable place
in the tradition of Northern fishing; at the beginning of my short affair
with the worm, it seemed to me almost as much a part of this tradition
as the Partridge and Orange and the Waterhen Bloa.

My first attempts with the worm were a comedy; I could never
manage to cast it more than two or three feet. Very slowly two or
three feet was extended to six or seven, although this progress was not
rewarded with any trout. Then I learned that the modern wormer did
not, like Stewart and the other old masters, use a long rod and a fly line
with a six or seven foot leader and then cast or flick or urge his worm
ahead of him; the modern wormer, living in the age of monofilament,
fished with a centre-pin reel loaded with nylon, which made throwing
a worm a much easier affair. I will not claim that I became a practised
hand at the modern style of worming; but I caught fish with it in very
low rivers before deciding that it was too easy and therefore immoral.
Then I turned back to tradition in the form of a fly line, learning at
last how to urge my worm forward a respectable distance and learning
as well how to catch a few trout by the method of Stewart and Nelson
and Pritt.

For three or four summers in the mid-Eighties, I fished the worm
when rivers were on their bones, and then I gave it up, finding that I
preferred the fly even in times of drought. Sometimes I thought of the
upstream worm at the end of a blank day, sometimes I thought that, if
there was no rain, I might try it out next week; but I never did, either
because the rain came or because I forgot about worms and did what I
could with the fly.

It was a long time, anyway, since I had searched the compost heap
with a fork in preparation for a day's sport with the worm. I had forgotten
that the centre of the heap, the rotting heart of it, provides a home only
for tiny red worms; there may be seething masses of them but they are
no use for the upstream wormer, who wants thicker worms an inch and
a half to two inches long, worms that live out their dark lives in the rich
and damp soil on the margins of the heap. Once I had remembered this,
I had soon gathered about fifty admirable worms, drawing them into
the unwelcome light before storing them in the moist gloom of a tin

box stuffed with damp newspaper. I was not determined to use them on the Wharfe; but, if it was as low as the Eden and its tributary streams, and if sport with the fly proved completely unrewarding, I wanted my worms as an available stratagem. It was a long time since I had urged a worm ahead of me into the trickling currents of a drought river; I was rather looking forward to giving it another go.

When I reached the Wharfe on the Wednesday, with my tin of worms in the back of the Land Rover, I found that the water was low (the keeper had told me as much over the phone) but it was not as low as I had been expecting. It was a low summer water, but unquestionably the Wharfe was much less weary and diminished than the Eden. The keeper had mentioned thundery rain the week before, insisting that its influence had been short-lived; but I think he was mistaken – it must have been a real downpour over the dry fells – because, standing on Conistone Bridge at half past eleven, although I was looking at a low and clear summer river, I was also looking at a river in which a fisherman might hope to catch trout on the fly. And so the worms stayed in the back of the Land Rover. I thought I might return for them in an hour or two but, to begin with at least, I went to the river armed only with artificial bait.

The day was still and cloudy and soft; there was a brief and thick hatch of blue-wings that brought me a trout of one pound five ounces to a Greenwell Klinkhamer. I failed with two or three fish and realised too late that they were feeding just under the surface on the nymph; the hatch had already finished when it suddenly occurred to me that a Partridge and Orange would probably have done the trick and that I had missed my chance to catch fish on the greatest of the spiders. Anyway, after the blue-wings had gone the trout turned to smut and I turned to little black things; but an inspired intuition also tied a hackle Coachman to a single high dropper and, although my little black things caught a few fish of seven or eight ounces, the Coachman provoked two savage takes in the remains of fast runs. The first trout weighed one pound seven ounces; the second was just two ounces lighter. Three trout weighing almost four pounds is as much as you can ask for from a thin river in need of rain; they were trout with the bold colouring of autumn fish, but they were still firm-fleshed and none of them was far gone in eggs or spawn.

For the trout fisher, autumn begins in late August, with cold mornings and slow starts on the river, with afternoon hatches of duns and early falls of spinner, with flocking swallows and full-grown ducks and with robins already singing their end-of-summer song. It was on the second of my four fishing days – the day that is the point of this chapter – that I realised how the autumn mood had come to me as well as to the robins. Perhaps they helped to make it; perhaps the still air and the gathering swallows helped as well. But it was not only in the afternoon that I began to feel properly autumnal; during most of the morning I felt fed-up too, fed-up and frustrated by my failure to catch any trout.

I was on the river up towards Kettlewell and there was very little doing. The worms were still in the Land Rover and once or twice I wondered about going to get them, but the fly had worked the day before and it seemed to me that I should spend a whole day without trout, a day involving a fruitless display of twenty or thirty patterns, before resorting to the upstream worm. I was not altogether sure that I still approved of it.

I did not use even a dozen patterns in the morning; the fish were smutting – the few that were feeding – and none of my four or five smallest patterns on a black theme interested a single one of them. I tried two or three big, bushy floaters to see if they might shock a trout into taking; they shocked a trout or two but not in the direction of my fly. Worm-thoughts recurred while I ate my sandwich; again they were rejected and I decided to walk right down to Watersmeet and fish my way back to the stepping stones; I would stick to the fly and, if it let me down, I should turn into a wormer the next morning.

There was a huge congregation of swallows hunting midges in the long pasture on either side of Black Keld. They were swooping low,

the air was full of their talk, and the sight and the sound of them was a pleasure even to a troutless fisherman, a fisher who sank into back-end thoughts as he walked down through the swallows and the tufted grass and the seeding thistles, as he climbed the stile above Spout Dub and then made his way slowly to Watersmeet, with parties of ten and twenty duck rising from the river and deepening the mood – this time in a predatory way – by turning his mind to the prospect of September flighting and the first mallard of another autumn.

I have this habit of drifting into the third person when writing about myself. I suppose it makes me feel important and somehow representative. Mentioning this habit is a good way of slipping back into the right pronoun, though it is not a trick that should be used more than a few times. I reached Watersmeet, anyway, and, fishing the lovely glides and runs under the trees up from the junction pool, I began to catch a few trout, and began to think what a beautiful thing fly-fishing is, especially when the day is calm and soft.

They were beautiful fish too, fish of the river's breeding, silvery and delicate-finned fish between half a pound and three quarters. In late May, when they were between six and ten ounces, there were lots of them on all the beats above Watersmeet. There were still lots of them and they had grown, but in the thin water they were now much more difficult to catch. Before too long I had managed three of them and killed the three-quarter-pounder, wondering if I was perhaps a greedy fisherman, but captivated by the beauty of his wildness and convinced that he would taste wonderful on a plate (he did).

Knocking this fish on the head inspired a nag or two of doubt; it should not have done and, to be honest, the nags were not a serious discomfort. There are many big fish in the Wharfe; many of them should not be there and one of their worst effects is to corrupt the judgement of fishers by teaching them that a wild trout of three quarters of a pound is too small to put into a creel. I knew better than this; my nags were really no more than nods in the direction of modern error, showing that I too have been influenced by the cult of the stock-fish, a cult which persuades us to think a trout of two pounds – obese, pallid, deformed and often very easy to catch – somehow a worthier trout than a shining, long-finned, full-and-slender-tailed silver trout of three quarters of a pound.

I sat and smoked for a few minutes. It was quiet and cloudy and very peaceful; the nags drifted away on my pipesmoke and I welcomed the evidence that the Wharfe, with no help from any stock pond, has bred a plentiful generation of very beautiful trout. I decided to postpone the worm for at least another day, for one of its problems is that trout often take the hooks deep down in the throat, forcing a merciful fisher to kill trout of eight and ten ounces along with those memorable trout of three quarters of a pound.

It was very comforting to think that the Wharfe was producing its own trout in abundance. Moving on I came to a long and gentle run where a trout or two was rising. When my little Black Gnat had not only failed to catch them but put them down as well, I looked more closely at the river and realised that there were blue-wings coming off the water. It was not a thick hatch but there were two or three duns floating together in most of the eddies. Leaving the trees and coming to the next run, I no longer found a trickle of fly; suddenly I found that the whole river was crowded with the dark and jostling silhouettes of their wings. By now it was undoubtedly a thick hatch, much thicker than it had been the day before, meaning that successive days had produced more blue-wings on the Wharfe than I had seen for something like twenty years.

It may seem surprising but it was this thought, rather than the sudden hope of trout, that filled me with such delight as I watched the blue-wings sailing down the slack currents of the river. I could remember huge hatches from my first years on the Wharfe and I could not remember anything comparable with the present one for a very long time indeed. I was sitting by a river that was breeding flies as well as fish, a river that seemed until very recently almost to have lost the knack of doing either. Perhaps, next spring, the dark olives would come in wild abundance; perhaps, next May beneath the cloud, the iron blues would be littering the water like black confetti scattered there by the wind.

Now the day when you realise that your favourite river, which winds its way almost forty years back into your life, the day when you realise that the river Wharfe is much healthier than you have long thought it, is beyond any doubt a special day. The time when this happens – about four o'clock in the afternoon – is a time to sit on the bank and hope that someone will appear from nowhere with a bottle of champagne. If no one shows up with a bottle and a couple of glasses, you will have to make do with your thermos-flask; you will pour yourself a mugful of tepid tea and then light your pipe and sit there on the edge of the water, smoking and drinking and feeling very happy for your favourite river and happy above all to be sitting beside it in the cloudy stillness of a late-August afternoon.

Look round, watch the swallows, listen to the robins and remember the great hatches of your youth, those days when the blue-wings began at noon and were still going strong when you left the river at seven; remember those hatches and remind yourself just how long ago they were. It is, after all, the beginning of your autumn fishing and it is entirely appropriate that, as a middle-aged fisher, you should sit there on the bank and feel the gentle pressure of passing time. Look at the wealth of fly on the water and, seeing all those wings, pray that when you are dead, in five or thirty years, some other fisher may sit where you are sitting and, seeing the same sight, think something like the same thoughts.

I should have liked to sit there longer, surrendering more completely to the mood and telling myself that I had sat and smoked in the same place almost forty years ago; which is, of course, precisely what I did tell myself. But I was sitting there with blue-wings thick on the water and with many trout rising to them, and with only one trout in my creel, which is why I did not feel that I should stay sitting there for the next half an hour. I might be fifty-three, but I was also a practising fisherman, conscious that it would be a neglect of duty to lose myself in conventional and mildly self-indulgent middle-aged thoughts while the trout were busy feasting on the biggest hatch of blue-wings that I had seen for years and years. It was time to get on my feet and try to catch a fish or two.

It was a long hatch as well as a thick hatch; it was not an affair of twenty minutes like the hatch of the day before. Well under way by four o'clock it was beginning to slacken only when I left the river just after half past six. By then there were three more trout in my creel, and the heaviest weighed one pound twelve ounces; he was a lovely fish with full fins and a golden belly; he was probably a stock-fish that had spent two or three years in the river and I was not certain that I did not prefer the smaller fish that were sharing the creel with him. The biggest of them was almost a pound and was perhaps a year older than the day's first; he was undoubtedly one of the river's fish and he had made the mistake of feasting on the river's flies.

It had been a difficult, low-water hatch and my trout had all been taken on different patterns: one on my own version of the BWO (which is probably no better than anyone else's but sometimes works), one on a little parachute olive and one (inevitably) on a Greenwell Klinkhamer. It had been a difficult hatch, which was probably to be expected with blue-wings in a thin river; it had also been a wonderful hatch and I knew, at the end of my part in it, that the worms in my tin would be returned to the compost heap without one of them ever being impaled on a hook. It had been a wonderful hatch and, in its own way, it had been a wonderful day. Blue-wings are very beautiful; along with all the duns – except for mayflies – their beauty is of the subdued sort that so perfectly suits a cloudy day with a soft flow of silver-white water.

The sight of trout rising to eat olives on such day is a beauty of incomparable subtlety. It is a pity that those little marks and patterns on the river's surface interest only fishermen; our response to them is less purely contemplative than the beauty of them demands. We cannot just stand and stare and lose ourselves in wonder; but something that we can do is to acknowledge that fishing with a worm is a poor thing compared to casting a fly into those beautiful marks and patterns and then suddenly finding that we have hooked a trout.

The next day there were very few blue-wings, although there was a big trout of two pounds five ounces that swallowed a bushy palmer from a slow corner of the river in the shadow of tall trees; he was a dark

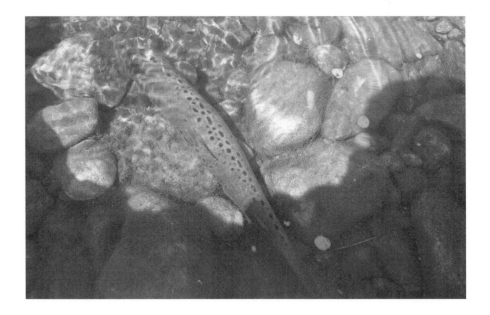

fish with a huge tail; he was in very fine condition though he was not beautiful. Still, he was very welcome, coming perhaps ten minutes after a trout almost as big – perhaps every bit as big – had swallowed the same fly and had seemed, after vigorous and sometimes savage resistance, at last ready for the net; he was lying on his side and I was moving my net – very correctly – underneath him, when a slow, tired circle took him round one of my wadered legs and trapped the line and set him free. It had never happened to me before. I just stood there and watched it all happen, until I saw a very tired trout, no longer attached to my line, lying in the water and then suddenly pushing away from me.

The dark two-pounder was a sullen fighter, a sulky hanger on the line and a stubborn head-shaker. He was slow to give in and he was a great comfort after the comical loss of what was possibly as big but most certainly a much lovelier trout. I got another fish of almost two pounds to the palmer. It was one of those days when big flies work; it was a good day but it was not a special day. The next day was a blank day; I finished early and drove home and gave my worms back to the rich earth from which they had come. I think it is very unlikely that I shall ever again trouble either them or their descendants with a fork. I think I have urged forward my last worm.

CHAPTER SEVEN

Out of Sorts

The rain did come at last, but not until we were deep into September. It was wonderful to be standing by a full river again, looking at the water and drinking in the exuberant vigour of its flow, the layered shine of its currents and the sense that something weary and enfeebled, something reduced to a dribble and a creep, had at last won back its vitality. I had not seen water like this for more than three months. And the sound as well as the sight of it was a deep pleasure to me; it was a rich mixture of all the sounds that water makes when flowing in fullness between the banks of an upland river. It is a beautiful sound that lifts a fisher's heart and fills it with the hope of trout.

It was Sunday afternoon and I was standing by the Wharfe at Yockenthwaite, standing on my favourite river at the bottom of the beat that I love best; at least I think the Yockenthwaite water is the stretch of the Wharfe that I love above all others. It may be because I can only go there when the river has been lifted by recent rain, which means that I never go there as often as I should like. There is no danger that I shall ever have too much of Yockenthwaite; even in a wet season I rarely manage it more than seven or eight times; in a dry summer whole months pass without a single day at Yockenthwaite, although you could find me driving along the top of the river, heading downstream or heading home; but in whichever direction I am heading, I will almost certainly be looking dangerously away from the road, praying for rain as I catch glimpses of the trickling remains of my favourite trout stream.

Parts of the high river dry up altogether after three or four rainless weeks. You can often stand on Yockenthwaite bridge beneath the sun, staring down at a rough basin of rock covered by nothing but dust and shrivelled strands of moss. Only a day or two later you may catch a brace of big trout from the same basin. I do not know what happens to the fish when the water disappears, but they are always there when the river is flowing and they are very rarely small.

There are more serviceable beats on the Kilnsey water. I have just written of four day's fishing at the end of August, most of it spent between Watersmeet and Kettlewell, four days which, in spite of low water, were full of interest and even sent me home with a few trout. It is on these four beats that I have spent most of my Kilnsey days, fishing a river that is in so many ways on the perfect scale for a fisher of flies, a river where every rising fish is within your range, a river small enough to seem intimate and welcoming, but big enough to fish when the last rain is almost a month away. And the Wharfe between Kettlewell and Kilnsey is very beautiful and it is full of trout and fewer of them are stock-fish than was the case five or six years ago. It is also water that is full of memories, which matters a lot to me, and I go there again and again to make more of them. Now that I think about it I am no longer so certain that the mile below Yockenthwaite Bridge is my favourite portion of the river Wharfe.

I once thought that the stretch winding up the valley from Kettlewell was the equal of anything above or below it, being beyond the immediate range of each season's stock fish, being much smaller than the river below the village and yet still in good order for the fly when the river at Yockenthwaite has already fallen too low for sport. I ought not to have changed my mind for, in its own way, and on the right day, the Kettlewell water is very fine. But it has not been so kind to me of late; just recently I have often struggled there – even more than in other places – with smutting fish and I have left it more than once in recent seasons with the feeling that, after more than thirty years filled with fishing, I am still no good at it.

Difficult water and difficult days should breed determination. I should revel in the challenge of scores of trout smutting down those long glides, and in all those pools and runs, and on all those corners of the river between Kettlewell and Starbotton. I should go back to the same fish again and again until I discover its weakness and learn how to exploit it. The problem with this approach is that I am not sure how much humiliation I can take on the road to final triumph. The beat above Kettlewell is superb trout water; but at present we are rather out of sorts with each other.

The Wharfe above Kettlewell

CHAPTER EIGHT

Autumn Shadows

I find it very difficult to decide which bit of the Kilnsey water I like best. I know that my favourite beats are all above Watersmeet and that I have never had quite the same feeling for the tributary Skirfare, which is probably wrong of me because it is a very graceful river flowing through a valley of exquisite loveliness. The water is brighter than the water of the Wharfe. When the Skirfare is full and settled there really are places where the flow is gin-clear, as pure as the water of any chalkstream flowing close to generous and unplundered springs; in other places there is a shining tinge of yellow that comes from the rock and is, I think, even lovelier than the gin-look. It is like the exquisite tinge of yellow that shines out from a glass filled with fino sherry. I prefer sherry to gin, which may explain my preference for the Skirfare's yellow moments. Anyway, whether its water turns my thoughts to Tio Pepe or to Gordons' Export, it certainly flows with startling clarity and whenever I move from the Skirfare to spend the afternoon on the Wharfe, always I am struck by a slight brownness in the water of the main river, by a faint stain of peat that would probably have passed unnoticed without experience recent enough to force comparison.

The Skirfare is the river of Charles Kingsley's revolting water babies. I do not think the thought of them, or the fear of perhaps catching one of them, has put me off their river. I have had some great days on its banks, and some of the Skirfare beats should certainly make me wonder whether I love them as much as anything on the Wharfe; but for some reason they do not; it is one of those strange affairs of the heart and there is an end of the matter.

I am devoted to the upper Eden, which is without doubt a richer and even finer trout stream than the Wharfe. I should feel bitterly deprived if, for some reason, I found that I was fishing the Eden for the last time. But the wrench of farewell would be nothing like a final parting from the Wharfe, nothing like walking away from Spout Dub in the knowledge that I should never be there again, nothing like driving away from Yockenthwaite and realising that I could never return. It is on the Wharfe above Watersmeet that I come to places with associations stretching back almost to boyhood. Everywhere on those high beats of the river I keep rediscovering little bits of myself: it may be when I am sitting on the bank, enjoying the unhealthy pleasures of pipesmoke and half-wishing that I had never started smoking all those years ago; often it follows the catching of a trout, when I suddenly remember that the same spot brought me a trout of very similar size the first time I ever came there; it happens in all sorts of ways and it is only occasionally the result of deliberate recollection. I do not go to the Wharfe in search of my younger self, I go there to fish, but continually I find that some event, some coincidence or repetition or some trick of the mind, something or other at any rate, strikes a chord of memory and suddenly calls up an experience from the past. There is rarely much of a response beyond acknowledgment, but in its own way it adds to the pleasure of a fishing day.

In autumn, things are sometimes different. In autumn middle-aged fishers other than me are perhaps in the habit of sitting by a river and, under the compelling influence of the season, giving themselves over to a flow of memories that takes them back to their earliest days on the same river. In autumn we sometimes do it deliberately and in autumn, by the way, I have no hesitation in declaring which beat of the upper Wharfe is nearest to my heart; in autumn I know that, if the river is flowing full, and if the breeze is light, I want to be at Yockenthwaite, where the quiet intensity of a September afternoon, gathering slowly like an invisible mist between the steep and narrow sides of the valley, affects me very deeply. And there are fewer walkers high up on the river in September; by five o'clock, anyway, they have gone home, leaving the steep fields to the browsing sheep and leaving the river to a middle-aged fisherman and a dipper or two, to the robins in the willows, to the flocking swallows in the sky and to the slow fading of the light.

By five o'clock this fisherman, assuming that he drove over from Sedbergh after mass and did not start fishing until two or three in the afternoon, will probably have reached the loveliest stretch of the

Memories of other rivers: here on the banks of the Ribble

Yockenthwaite beat: three or four hundred yards of water where the river is open to the sky and passes through a quick succession of little pools and glides, spilling over yellow limestone slabs, pushing through constricting channels of rock with a smooth and strong and muscled sort of flow, then spreading itself out into runs and glides that seem wide and leisurely in comparison with its more frequent confinement. There are trout everywhere; some of them are big and they are all, except perhaps for some of the really big ones, very beautiful. Perhaps the three-quarter-pounders are the best of all.

These observations are, of course, leading up to something; which is that, when at last the rain came, and after starting fishing down by the little barn about a mile below Yockenthwaite at two o'clock on a Sunday afternoon, I had by five o'clock reached the part of the river that I have just described so inadequately. The afternoon had started well. Fishing two wet flies I had caught a trout of a pound within five minutes of my first cast. Smaller fish followed, five or six of them: fish of six and seven ounces that did not even tempt me (a man who, by modern standards, is undoubtedly a killer of small trout) to knock them on the head.

The afternoon was cloudy and still, with browning or yellowing or stubbornly green leaves hanging from the branches, unless they were scattered over the grass or floating down the stream where from time to time they caught my flies. Withered grasses drooped along the banks; the river murmured and gurgled and splashed, gleaming with a thousand cloudy reflections of white and grey. There was a touch of dampness in the earth and on the air. It was the sort of September afternoon that is most inclined to encourage autumnal thoughts in a fisher, the sort that invites him to sit down on the bank every twenty minutes or so and light his pipe.

The invitation was often accepted, usually just after the unhooking of another seven-ouncer, and more than once, as I sat and watched the river flowing on its way, more than once I remembered how gratefully I had killed half-pounders when I first fished the Yockenthwaite water something like twenty five years ago. There were other memories; most, but not all of them, were similarly trivial. What mattered was the long association stretching back through many seasons, and the familiarity of every feature of the river and its fields; for this brought the feeling that I was moving through a place that was a part of my history. There is little power to autumn unless it is working on a sense of the past.

Perhaps surprisingly, mixed in with this stream of recollection, there was also some thought for the future; for I told myself, in one of these interludes, that the time was coming to break with the past in yet another way, by starting to fish with barbless hooks. Once I had fished with rods of split cane and thought never to change; now I fished with two Loomises and two rods by Sage; now, although I still thought of myself as a fisher of the upstream wet, I spent at least half my time fishing Klinkhamers and parachute flies.

This had all happened within four or five seasons; and now on a soft and cloudy autumn afternoon I saw that more change was on the way but that next season would be soon enough; the beginning of a new season would obviously be the right time for innovation; I would cling to my barbs for another week, saving new things for next spring. But the recognition, prompted by those five or six small fish, had at last been made: that trout, especially small trout, are often badly damaged by extracting embedded hooks from their jaws; that every fisher who makes a habit of returning some part of his catch should fish with hooks that come easily from a trout's mouth. It is a wretched business giving back to the river torn and bleeding fish that are almost certain to die.

There were frequent rests for tobacco and reflection. I also spent more time than I should have chosen sitting on the bank and not just smoking and thinking, sitting there with no memories of the past and no thoughts for next season; for it turned into one of those days when every fish that took the dropper wound my cast into a maze of knotted coils that took at least five minutes to sort out. I do not know why I so rarely look at a tangled chaos of nylon and tell myself that it will be best to cut it all away and tie on a new point or even a new leader. It does happen, but usually only after I have lost my temper wasting what seems half an afternoon failing to sort out a confusion with which any sensible fisher would have dealt much more brutally and much more effectively and in about ten seconds: with a pair of scissors.

I am, as it happens, rather good at untangling nylon; over the years I have developed an eye or perhaps even an instinct for it. I suppose I have come to enjoy the challenge of a really serious tangle, and I can usually sort them out. On Sunday I grew sick of the challenge. I was spending as much time intricately involved with nylon as I was casting flies onto the water or sitting quietly by the edge of the river. The solution, of course, was a Klinkhamer, just one of them, which was tied to the end of a new point when, sometime after half past four, my instinct let me down very badly. It happens, however clever you think you have become; it makes you wish that you had never bothered trying in the first place; it calls for rude words, a few snips and for a single fly.

Fishing the lower half of the Yockenthwaite water always brings some sense of confinement. The river has suddenly realised that it wants to get down to the wider valley below; it falls rapidly between steep banks, with steep-sided fields on one side or the other and with trees, mostly ashes, clinging to those high banks and stretching their branches out over the water. One or two bits of the lower beat are almost gorge-like, in a miniature sort of way; always in shadow from the rising land or the overhanging branches, with lots of churning and foaming and gushing water, and with a few quieter places where the river moves smoothly over unmoving rock, dark places where big fish move when the urge takes them. There are short open stretches where the sky gets a clear view of the river; more usually there is something in the way, something that shuts out the sun and often leads to one of those long struggles with ravelled nylon.

Small trout rather than careless casting were the reason for Sunday's struggles, but it was still a relief to leave the trees and the shadows and the dark pools and come to that part of the river which flows between level fields, level at least for ten or twenty yards on either side of the water. There are still trees, ashes and sycamores, but now they are well spaced so that you can admire the shape of them, or they stand in groups of two or three with, only in one place, perhaps half a dozen of them clustered together on one side of a deep rock pool.

Before you reach this pool you fish a delightful stretch of water where you will be very lucky to catch a trout. The river flows over tilted slabs of bedrock, pushing the current along the far bank and with two or three little pools where the slack water is always covered with a rocking scum of foam. Over the years I have caught a few small fish from this stretch, but I never expect to rise a trout here; it is a surprise when a rise comes, even without one, it is a delight to be in the open again, walking along water-shaped and mossy rock and flicking my little brown Klinkhamer into the edges of the river, conscious with every cast that I am getting closer to the best and most beautiful part of the Yockenthwaite water.

I move upstream and the river widens; there is a long glide over shelving limestone, with all sorts of sliding colours and drifting patterns of colour that draw their inspiration from the changing sky above. Beyond the glide there is a gravelly pool with a neck of water rushing into it through a narrow channel carved down into a yellow slab of rock. There is a single ash tree on the bank, across from which a large boulder, out almost in the middle of the river, marks the point where I begin to fish the faster water of the pool. It is one of my favourite places; it is a place where I expect to catch fish. On Sunday I sat and smoked on the grass beneath the branches of the ash-tree, hoping that the autumn calm of a cloudy sky and a gleaming river would soothe away the knotted tensions of those struggles with tangled nylon. They had dispelled the late-September serenity and it took me at least ten minutes to recover.

Then it was time to fish and within a minute the little brown Klinkhamer had disappeared; within another minute or so I had put a fourteen-ouncer in the creel. A few minutes later I had returned a similar fish from the top of the run, relieved that the barbed hook had come away so easily from its jaws.

Catching nothing beneath the ashes of the rock pool I passed on to the straight and open stretch beyond, where the water flows smoothly over the rock, with seams and ripples of flow mapping out the ridges and hollows of the bed. It is, I think, of the whole Kilnsey water, the place where water and light and limestone combine most subtly and most marvellously to create infinitely varied beauty. For many years an ancient bath-tub, the enamelling all cracked and streaked yellow or black, lay on its side by a willow bush on the far bank. I suppose it came there as a cattle trough and doubtless, lying abandoned on the edge of the field, it was an eyesore. I rather liked it; it was a feature of the place and I was sad one spring to find that it was no longer there. The Klinkhamer rose two trout from this most beautiful glide; one I missed and the second came off the hook after just a few seconds. Neither of them was big.

For about half an hour, fishing through the little pools and runs, I did not see a rise and did not rise a fish. The trout, it seemed, were all drowsy or asleep; it was as though the grey and cloudy afternoon was too still and too quiet for anything more vigorous than inactivity. It was, of course, nothing of the sort, but that was how, for a time, it seemed to me as I moved very slowly and cast my Klinkhamer and did not stir a fin.

If you are heading upstream towards Yockenthwaite and fishing the left bank of the river, which is the only bank that you can fish, since the right bank stands high above the water and is often obstructed by trees, you will find that, about a hundred yards below the bridge, you have to clamber over a confusion of wire that fills the gap between the end of a stone wall and the edge of the bank. This loose structure certainly used to contain an old bedstead; but, although I was there less than two days ago, I cannot remember whether it is still where it used to be. Anyway, once you have got over the wire and the bedstead, assuming that it is still there, you are back on the open moor (on your own side of the river), with the land climbing steeply to the road above and with, across the water on a much gentler rise of ground, a huddle of sheep pens and an old barn. The river flows between steep banks of smoothly shaped rock and the current sets along the far bank,; it is here that the trout rise, all along the current, right up into the turbulence at the top of the pool where the water foams over a deeply-grooved shelf of limestone.

I was not expecting any rings on Sunday; I was convinced that every trout in the river had gone to sleep. I was delighted to find that I was wrong, for a trout was rising now and then under the far bank about half way down the pool. The little brown Klinkhamer floated over him; he took it gently, weighed just under the pound and went into the creel. Fishing on up into the faster water, although I saw no rising fish, I caught two more trout and kept one of them. Both of them came very quietly to the fly; there was a movement round it, an almost casual absorption that seemed only slowly to turn into a taut line. And with both fish the fight seemed predetermined, it seemed there was never any doubt that my net would at last reach under them and lift them from the river. All this seeming was, of course, an illusion produced by the quiet and darkening air, which made it seem that everything was happening with a slow and a very soft inevitability.

By now it was almost six o'clock and, under the cloud, the light was thickening fast. Swallows were the only restless things, swallows and the river in those places where the bed shaped it into rapid motion. Everything else was still or moving slowly. Nothing made a loud noise. There was no bright flash of colour to be seen anywhere, only browns and faded yellows, only shadowy greens and sliding reflections of grey and soft white.

It was impossible to resist the mood of the evening. I sat under the

bridge and gutted my trout, tossing their entrails rather solemnly into
the water, watching the ripples of their fall. I was full of the feeling of
late September: a feeling that comes to fishers (it comes to me at least)
when, at the end of our fishing, we sit by the river on a still evening with
the last day of another season barely a week away. It is, like most other
feelings, a compound sort of experience and there are evenings when
one element of the mixture dominates; there are also evenings when
we explore different strands of the feeling and see where they take us.
It was not like this on Sunday evening beneath Yockenthwaite Bridge,
for my response to the autumn mood was more or less inarticulate, was
simply an acknowledgement of possession by it, with the simultaneous
recognition that it was a possession for which I felt very grateful. And
there was, of course, in everything round me, a symbolism too obvious,
too compelling and too profound to be expressed in words that would
inevitably seem both conventional and inadequate.

I did not want to put my feeling into words; I did not want delve
into it in search of some fresh angle or insight. And so I sat there as the
shadows deepened and the water dimmed, knowing that the bracken
was already brown above the roots, that the leaves were turning and
that the swallows would soon be gone. It was a very powerful feeling
and it was much better left unharassed and undisturbed. After about
ten minutes I took it with me up to the Land Rover; I felt it all the
time that I was stowing my tackle; then I climbed into the driver's seat
and decided to drink a last cupful of tea before driving home. There
was only half a cup left, tepid and with the grey taste that belongs to
the dregs of a thermos flask. The taste did not matter: what mattered
was sitting there with the window open, looking down at the river
and listening to the small sounds of the evening. They were faint and
muffled sounds, drifting through dim gleams and stronger shadows;
they worked on the feeling inside me to produce an intensity so soft
that it seemed an irreverence, when the last cold drops of tea had finally
been drunk, to turn the ignition and turn on the lights and then drive
noisily away.

Chapter Nine

In Praise of the Ordinary

The Sunday afternoon at Yockenthwaite was not the end of my fishing for the season. I was there again the next Thursday, although I went up above Deepdale for the last hour and finished in dead calm and near darkness, with fields spreading out dimly and with slopes rising like shadows all round me, while the river gleamed white and grey in the last remains of the light. I had caught nothing down at Yockenthwaite; a few smutting trout had refused my patterns and then the fish had stopped rising altogether. But in those little pools so near the river's beginning there were a few fish stirring as the light failed. I caught and killed a brace of them, striking when something moved somewhere near where I thought my fly was, striking three or four times and twice lifting my rod into the splashing weight of a twelve-ounce trout.

On Saturday I slipped away from school at lunchtime, to spend a last weekend on the Wharfe. Again the afternoon was still and the air was warm. I fished up from Watersmeet and almost every minute of it was a blessing. There was a trout of one pound nine ounces to a wet Coachman; some time before it there had been a trout nine ounces smaller to a parachute Pale Watery. Not long afterwards I hooked a big trout in fast water and thought that he was well hooked until he was no longer hooked at all.

Up in the calm air there were swarms of great red spinners. I was hoping that they would fall and that the trout would start eating them; it can happen at any stage of a September afternoon, but it was slow to happen on this particular one. And then, about six o'clock, a sudden chill came onto the air as soon as the sun slipped behind the high sides of the valley; the sky turned pale and the light turned dim and there was no rise to the spinners. I confess that I was almost relieved. I was meeting a friend for dinner at *The Falcon;* I did not want the rise to start and then to find that I had to leave it before it had properly begun. On warm September evenings under cloud trout will sometimes rise right into the darkness; cold does not always put them down but it puts paid to the spinners. And so it meant that I could leave the water, already deep in shadow and with all the bright seams and wrinkles of its flow smoothed out into a blurred impression of moving water – I could leave the river and walk back slowly to the Land Rover, knowing that there would be time for a glass of wine before food with more wine, knowing that I had left the river at the right time and not abandoned it, thanking God for the calm that had filled this autumn's fishing days and found its way into me.

My friend was, of course, a fisherman and it was of fishing that we talked all through our wine and our food and our coffee. It was good fishing talk; it was not about huge trout rewarding incomparable skill; there was nothing boastful about it, although I am sure we both mentioned the best trout that the season had brought us. There was, I am sure, some talk of two-pounders, but it was mainly fly-talk, water-talk, and there was this difference between it and the similar talk that has passed between us in recent years in the dining room, or at the bar, of the same pub: that this time it was talk of bigger hatches of fly and better breeding by the trout. It was hopeful talk and it was good to speak and good to hear.

The next day, my last fishing day of the season, was a Sunday and so I went to mass in Grassington before I went to the river. I lit a candle at the end of it, said a prayer and then left the candle burning there in honour of Our Lady of the Riverbank; it was in thanksgiving for all the blessings of the season so nearly past.

Then I went fishing in the quiet sunshine, starting above Kettlewell because all the lower beats were full. It was still, it was warm, it was very beautiful, shining and serene: as always on those days of radiant autumn calm, there was the sense of fragility that touches things with sadness, but it was very beautiful and by one o'clock I had killed two trout: one on a little black gnat (he weighed fifteen ounces) and the other (a pounder) on the little brown Klinkhamer.

In the afternoon, knowing that the beats above Watersmeet would now be free, I finished the season there, unsuccessfully and with no bitterness at all. I pricked a good fish; then a big one broke me almost in the same spot from which I had taken the two-and-a-half-pounder just about a month ago. Perhaps ten minutes afterwards a third trout – certainly over the pound – threw the hook when I was thinking that he would be mine. On another day these lost trout, one after each other, would have frayed my temper; on this day, on the last day of the season, although I should have preferred to catch all three of them, their escape seemed almost appropriate; for perhaps it is a good thing to end the season by relearning the great truism that no trout is truly yours until it is helpless (and perhaps also dead) on the bank. And only a week ago those trout in the dim evening light at Yockenthwaite had seemed fixed to my line by a soft and invisible potency from which no fish could possibly detach itself. It was good for me, anyway, to acknowledge all over again that knots slip and that hooks come suddenly away. I admit that I reviewed my prospective commitment to hooks without barbs and I am proud to confirm that it still held firm.

I lost those three trout and looked for more; and then the sun went and again the chill came as soon as the sun was gone. I sat down on the bank and realised that I should not cast another fly on the water until next April came along. It was only this, I suppose, that made the day special. In most other respects it had been a typical sort of day, with a brace of trout killed and a few fish lost and a few small ones returned to the river.

It had been a piercingly beautiful day, with sunshine and quiet air, with the slow and silent falling of leaves, with swallows and dippers and wagtails and shining water; and my response to it all had been touched by something of the solemnity that belongs to ends and farewells. But, as I sat there smoking, there was no self-indulgent surrender to autumnal sadness; it is true that change and decay were to be seen all around me; it is also true that I had been looking at the evidence of it for about six hours and thinking how delightful it all seemed.

The big autumn experience had come at Yockenthwaite the

Sunday before. Now, at six o'clock in the evening, I sat by the river at
a place I call Two Barn Flats and acknowledged that my fishing was
over for the season. There might, late in October, be a day or two
after grayling on the Ribble; it would depend on the weather and, if it
happened, it would almost certainly be enjoyable as long as the water
was right and the sun shone and the grayling rose to my flies. But I am a
trout fisher; everything else in fishing is incidental. Sitting there at Two
Barn Flats I acknowledged that my real fishing was over for the year. I
felt sad and grateful at the same time, and I also felt that my fishing was
finishing at the right time, for one of the great beauties of trout fishing
is that it ends with the fading of the year.

I thought that I would drink half a bottle of claret with the lamb
steak that was waiting back in Sedbergh for my supper. Half a bottle
of something or other – almost always French and more often claret
than anything else – accompanies almost every supper that I eat; there
was nothing distinctively autumnal or end-of-season about deciding to
drink half a bottle of *Cissac '93* with my lamb steak. I have sat by Two
Barn Flats in the middle of July and wondered which half-bottle to
open when I got back to Sedbergh in an hour or two.

There have been some last days of the season that ended in resentment at the prospect of the troutless months ahead; there have been last
days of wild wind, with the air full of impatient leaves and me full of
frustration; there have been last days of flood that were fishing days in
name only and left me feeling cheated of my last sport. Unsatisfactory
last days breed transient bitterness, but a day of calm sunshine or a quiet
day under cloud somehow make the end of trouting seem appropriate as
you sit quietly by the river and realise that it is almost time to go.

Sitting by Two Barn Flats I felt sad and grateful at the same time
and I sat there for about quarter of an hour, smoking and drinking tea.
Then it was time to walk back to the Land Rover, along the bank and
up the short steep slope and then through the loose gate and across the
road. I cut the fly from my leader and reeled in the line; I took the
reel from my rod and then took the two pieces of the Loomis apart; I
took off my waders and put on my shoes and it was all done without
the usual sense of impatience. Before I drove away I stood on the edge

of the road above the river, smoking again and drinking more tea, standing there to look at the line of the Wharfe between Knipe Dub and Black Keld, conscious that I would not be fishing anywhere along it for almost half a year.

And then I drove away. I drove through Kettlewell and along the road to Starbotton; I drove on to Buckden and then up towards the beginning of the dale. At Yockenthwaite I stopped near the bridge; I stopped to light my pipe, but then I walked down to the bridge and stood there above the running water for a minute or two.

I drove up to Cam Houses, with the sloping shapes all round me still dimly visible and all the more affecting because they were dark and indistinct forms. On the way down towards Gayle and Hawes a sudden insight came to me. In the middle of all these impressive shapes of folded land I had, of course, been thinking fishing thoughts, which had taken me forward to the early weeks of next year, to the beginning of February when I knew that, with the shooting over, I should begin to feel urges to be fishing again; now, at the end of a season when I have tried to examine the specialness of certain fishing days, I saw that when these February urges came to me, I should not be longing for any such special days, though they would be memorable when they turned up: I should be longing for the ordinary experience of the fisherman, for running water and my presence beside it, for the sight of a few rising trout and the skill to catch one or two of them, for all those central and incidental beauties that feed fishers in the course of a fishing day and for all those feelings that grow out of our presence on a riverbank or transmit themselves to us through a rod and a line.

It is too neat a conclusion for the record of this season, discovering right at the end of it that the whole enterprise has in a sense been a waste of time, since it has suddenly become clear that all those ordinary fishing days – those days that make up most of our fishing in the course of a given season – are just as important, just as representative and just as precious as days of unusual events or some extraordinary significance. It may be too neat; it may seem contrived and you may suspect that it was predetermined, which it was not.

It is what I felt, anyway, as I drove to the head of Wensleydale, now invisible beyond the glare of my headlights, and then headed down Garsdale on my way home. I tested it with the claret and the lamb steak and it still held true. By the time I had washed up and taken the dogs out and settled down for a glass of whisky before going to bed, by this time I had decided that it did not matter a fig. I had not wasted my time at all; for if all fishing days were special it could scarcely matter which ones I decided to write about; it was all a question of teasing out the specialness of whichever days were chosen. I have, anyway, finished with this year's selection; I must now turn my thoughts to shooting and wait to see what next year brings along.

CHAPTER TEN

The Shooter and the Fisher

It is the third of October, trouting is over and pheasants are now in season, although I shall not be trying to kill many of them until October is almost past. There will be an afternoon or two over the road on my rented land, well away from this year's poults, afternoons that may bring a few old birds to the bag if I manage to shoot straight. I shall flight my pond for the first time very soon. Meanwhile trouting is over and it is something of a relief to wake up without immediately asking myself what the river will be like or whether the wind will be blowing upstream. I did, in fact, wake up this morning wondering about wind and water, and then I realised that it did not matter. I need to start thinking like a shooter, for shooters and fishers, even though they are often the same person, think very differently.

During parts of the trout season there is some conflict between the shooting and fishing sides of my life. There is no problem in the spring and there is no problem in high summer when rivers and trout are all that matter. But, once August comes along and my poults arrive at High Park, then Catlow the fisher and Catlow the shooter are no longer always in agreement with each other. The fisher feels resentful that every day is spent faffing round with young pheasants rather than casting flies onto running water; he knows that the evenings he is promised along the edges of the Eden almost never happen, because the shooter-keeper, once he gets back from High Park, is usually too tired to do anything but pick his vegetables, lie in the bath, drink his sherry, then cook and eat his supper before finishing his wine and so to bed.

The shooter and the fisher also find that the weather comes between them. One of them wants plenty of rain to keep his rivers full; the other, knowing that poults like nothing better than sunshine, prays for weeks of settled weather with blue skies and dusty earth and trickling streams. He hates hot weather almost as much as his *alter ego*, but he makes the sacrifice, praying fervently for a whole month of blazing sunshine. This summer his prayers were answered and already you have read how, when he turned back into a fisher at the end of August, he almost did it with a can of worms.

The August drought, anyway, was good for my pheasant-poults and, now that October is here and my fishing is over, I am glad that it happened and glad that summer is past. Autumn has arrived, the days are shortening, the leaves are turning and fat men have put away their bellies, so that I no longer need to turn my eyes from huge expanses of wobbling flesh, flushing pink as they parade down the street or lounge outside the pub or spread themselves over the grass in some otherwise inoffensive public place.

The bellies have been covered up for the winter. I can look back to the August drought now and tell myself that it was a good thing and that on the whole I enjoyed it. At least I enjoyed the evenings, when the sky turned pale and the air at last turned cool. Earlier in the day and out at High Park under the midday sun, although I was usually drenched in sweat and even took to daubing exposed bits of myself with sun-cream – anyway, the shooter in me relished the sight of his contented poults getting bigger every day and showing no signs of weakness or disease.

And there were no wobbling stomachs out at High Park, and there was midday rest in the shade of the trees where it seemed to me more than once, while chewing a sandwich and drinking tea and then lying back in the grass to smoke for a while, that the fields all round me had come as close to silence as ever happens in the summer daytime. There was no breath of wind, there was no bird in the sky, the sheep were all lying in the shadows of banks or hedges or walls, feeling far too hot to baa, although sometimes an old ewe would produce one of those dry and deep and rasping coughs that you also hear in the throats of men who smoke fifty a day. Now and then a willow warbler sang half a faded song from somewhere in the branches; now and then an old cock pheasant cleared his throat; there was the occasional squeak from one of my poults; there was the intermittent buzzing of flies up in the leaves: but there were whole seconds on end when it seemed that there was no sound at all, when it seemed that every living creature at High Park had finally yielded to the heat and found some shady spot in which to settle down for a nap. It was a good idea and once or twice I did it myself.

On the whole I disapprove of hot weather. I find it sweaty, uncomfortable and exhausting. I think it burns away the beauty from the countryside and, of course, it means that swollen male bellies feel compelled to advertise their pink and flabby horror to the whole world. I have a thing about naked male bellies; they make me feel sick. Pheasant poults do not care about bellies (not that there were any to be seen out at High Park) and, this August, they clearly loved every minute of those blazing days more typical of Naples or Athens than of Kirkby Stephen. They arrived looking big and fit and within a day or two they were looking bigger and fitter. In less than a week, even though they had arrived with their flight feathers pulled, I realised that it was going to be impossible to keep them in the pens for much longer since, even deprived of their primaries, most of them seemed capable of something very similar to flight.

Beyond doubt they were flapping up to roost much higher than the top of the wire, or I should not have been finding so many of them on the wrong side of it every morning. Most of them, of course, stubbornly refused to return to safety, scuttling off into bramble or blackthorn thickets rather than walking obediently round the fence until they found a gate offering them re-entry into a protected world. I normally try to keep most of my birds in the pens for about three weeks.

This August, after fewer than ten days, all the pens were open and, on either side of the wire (but mostly outside it), there were pheasants soaking up the sun, dusting themselves contentedly and occasionally getting to their feet to eat a few turkey pellets or take a few sips of water. And there was no trouble from foxes and the four mink that turned up all turned up obligingly in my traps. There was a brief problem towards the end of the month, which I shall leave for the next chapter, but undoubtedly it was a good August for the shooter who rears pheasants and, all the while, the fisher in me was appalled by the sight of the river Eden, which had turned into a thing of dry rocks and waving slime rather than an eager flow of bright water.

As a shooter I am now blessing an August full of heat and still air and glaring sunshine. At the same time I am hoping that, when the shooting starts, the days on which it happens will be days of wind. From April until the end of September the wind, except in the form of a gentle upstream breeze, is my enemy; but in November, December and January a lively blow adds challenge to a shooting day. You do not want a gale, which makes birds unmanageable; you may prefer the wind from a particular direction, but on the whole you prefer some sort of wind to no wind at all.

Shooters and fishers think differently, and so far I have just been playing round the edges of this difference. I love both sports and there are times each winter when all that I want to do is to spend the short days of a brief season out under the sky with my gun and my spaniel. I love the few formal days that the season brings my way, always provided that I shoot well enough to avoid feeling ashamed of myself; I love the days at High Park when I try to produce sport for myself and a few of my friends; I love tramping the margins of my shoot with just a dog for company; perhaps I love sitting by a flight pond best of all, sitting there as day turns almost imperceptibly into night and wondering whether the duck will come.

I love shooting, drawing from it a deep and innocent and absorbing pleasure, but at the same time I acknowledge that fly-fishing for trout involves a subtler, a more complex, more intricate, more beautiful and more binding involvement with the life of nature than does swinging a gun at a bird. There is, moreover, a delicacy about flyfishing which does not belong to shooting; there is a world of difference between a fishing rod and a shotgun. Fishing is not accompanied by loud bangs; the two sports are as different as the music of Mozart and Shostakovitch and they appeal to different people or to different sides of the same person.

Think of their seasons too and how different they are. When I think of fishing I think of soft days in May, of still days in September, of sleepy afternoons in June and July, of shining high-summer evenings. When I think of fishing I think of quietness and the sound of running water. I do not always get them but they form my vision of the ideal. But now that October has come and my thoughts move towards shooting, they fill me with the hope of restless days, with the wind in the trees and pheasants rushing impatiently through the sky, while some of them, with a brutal sort of beauty, collapse out of it and splash or thud onto the ground. I think of pheasant days or of evenings by a flight pond, and the wind is there too, blowing to muffle the sound of gunshot and to keep the birds coming in.

I think of hard earth, with rutted gateways; I think of ice along the edge of water that flows shrunkenly and with a black shine; I think of cold skies and steaming breath and mittened fingers. I think of weather when the frost grips and when, after a shivering and foot-stamping start, warmth and exhilaration drive out the cold as I tramp up and down frozen or snow-covered fields. I am not sure it matters that my shooting days are more frequently damp days or wet days of mild air, full of mud and squelching earth. The ideal days come along from time to time and are recognised as such; there is very little to connect them with their equivalents from trouting months.

Fishing and shooting are very different activities. Fishing is usually a solitary affair whereas shooting is very often a sociable business; and while fishing is essentially a sort of contest between one man and nature, most forms of shooting are a cooperative activity with different men performing different and complementary roles. And even the lone shooter, the rough shooter along hedges and ditches, relies for his sport on the presence of his dog.

Perhaps dogs are the heart of the difference. They have no place in fishing and there is no form of shooting – except for shattering clay pigeons – that does not more or less depend upon them. And shooting not only depends upon dogs; they also provide a great part of the pleasure of our shooting days. To watch a spaniel quartering a rushy field, with his tail beating out a wild rhythm of delight and a sense of urgency quivering through every muscle of his frame; watching this, or watching the gorse shake above him as he hunts through it in contempt of discomfort or pain, is always a delight. A difficult retrieve performed by your dog, whether the bird fell deep in tangled cover or set off for the next county as soon as it touched the earth, and especially if the retrieve is the result of a long search when hope was almost gone, often brings more satisfaction than the shot that kills a bird stone dead.

And the pleasure that our dogs take in their hunting is itself infectious and extends itself to all round them. Their eagerness, their enthusiasm and their energy make half the mood of a shooting day. And all this dog-talk is a good excuse for me to start rambling on about my own dogs. It will help me to chase fishing thoughts from my mind; it will help me towards the right frame of mind for writing about shooting and, if you have read my earlier books that dealt with autumn and winter sport, it will bring you up to date with the dogs in my life.

When I started writing about shooting I had two spaniels. One of them is now dead; he died this year and it seems almost a necessary act of piety to take a formal farewell. I shall not give you a long eulogy extolling his many virtues and ignoring his few faults. I shall say that he was a big spaniel, liver and white, and a fine one, that no cover was too thick for him, that, in his prime, no day was too long for him and that he was the apple of my eye. When he was eight he began to be troubled by arthritis, although it never stopped him working; when he was ten he began to go deaf, so that bad Digby, my second spaniel, took on more and more of the work and did it in his own way (disobediently).

It was at the end of the August of his twelfth birthday, on a Friday to be precise, that Merlin went off his food. The vet thought it was an infection and gave him what seemed the appropriate jabs, but there was no noticeable improvement over the next two days and he vomited up the bits of food that he swallowed. On the Monday there were more jabs, but he did not brighten and I could barely drag him round his nightly circuit before putting him to bed. Next day he was badly dehydrated and stayed with the vet. He was put on a drip and it was time for blood tests. On Wednesday I was hoping to take him home, but he had weakened further and the tests had revealed advanced kidney failure. I did not take him home. I held his head in my arms while the needle performed its fatal work of mercy. Such was the end of my old spaniel, Merlin.

In the surgery I had managed – more or less – to hold back my tears. Once I had bundled Digby into the back of the Land Rover and driven out to High Park, and while I was going round the pens, feeding and watering my poults and doing whatever needed to be done, out there in the gloomy privacy of my little kingdom, out there under a grey sky with spots of drizzle blowing on the wind, out there at High Park I wept for old Merlin just as often as I felt the pressure of tears. It would, it seemed to me, be callous to hold them back, especially in the place where he had worked for me so tirelessly over the seasons, and especially when I remembered that High Park and Merlin had both come into my life in the same year.

I had to sit down and dry my eyes outside the old pen when I remembered how Merlin used himself to sit there, snapping at flies in the dusty August sunshine while I got on with my work. Almost every patch of gorse that I passed produced more tears, because every patch

Merlin, tireless worker over the seasons.

of gorse had shaken to the power and the drive of Merlin in his prime, as he flushed out pheasants or rabbits, as he plunged into the thickest and sharpest tangles in search of fallen game. The meadow-gate, where I ate my sandwich, was full of sadness because, as I sat there eating it and throwing Digby a morsel or two, my mind went back to all those shooting lunches when, spiked with gorse and caked with mud and wet all over, Merlin had lain there, steaming and panting and waiting patiently for a crust from my bread or a scrap of pastry from my pie.

There were memories of him everywhere demanding the willing tribute of tears. They were not the sort of tears that come with human loss, the sort that are held back because we are frightened that, if we let them flow, they will engulf and overwhelm us; they did not fall with that same anguished sense of incomprehension and hopelessness. They were less important tears; they were much softer and they came more easily, filled with sorrowful and sentimental longing for the strong companionship that grows up between a shooter and his spaniel.

Perhaps the saddest place that I came to was the strip of land where my third pen – known incidentally as the West Pen – now stands; it was the saddest place because I knew that it was the last place from which old Merlin had put a pheasant into the sky. It had happened in December when, with the horrors of foot and mouth disease finally over, I decided that the time had come to see if we could find a pheasant or two out at High Park (there was no release that season). I took Merlin along, determined to find the opportunity to give him a bit of work. He was profoundly deaf by then and far too stiff in the joints to be given the freedom of the gorse. Bad Digby and my friends' dogs did most of the work; bad Digby, in fact, was in one of his more amenable moods, behaving for whole minutes on end like a half-trained spaniel. Old Merlin spent most of the day, a day of only four pheasants and five rabbits, sitting on a lead in the company of a standing gun. He looked for a fallen bird or two and I seem to remember that he came back with one of them.

But his real moment came in the afternoon, when he hunted out the narrow strips below my northern boundary. They are securely fenced and so I thought that his deafness would not matter too much, and the cover, mainly blackthorn and thick rushes between tangles of benty grass, would not be too punishing for his arthritic old joints. The whole manoeuvre, moreover, would not last much more than ten minutes. It would be just right for him and I wanted Merlin to make his contribution to the day's sport.

He loved his last little drive. There was no point in blowing a whistle at him; he set off and went about his business in a private rapture, sniffing and snorting and advertising his delight with a mighty thrashing of his old tail. I confess that he pegged two rabbits, though I was inclined to blame the rabbits for sitting too tight rather than Merlin for pouncing too eagerly (the truth is that he was always inclined to peg game). There were no pheasants in the first strip, but about thirty yards into the second, when Merlin pushed his nose into a thick tangle of dead rushes, a startled hen came out of them and climbed steeply above the trees. I promptly missed the bird with both barrels but my friend, Austin, brought her down to earth with a single shot and it took Merlin no time at all to deliver the dead pheasant to his master's hand.

The place where this happened, the place where Merlin flushed and retrieved the last pheasant of his hunting life, was the saddest place I came to on the day that he died. I did not linger there. I did not linger at High Park beneath the weight of the cloud and all those memories. As soon as I got home I went to the deep freeze and took out the one pheasant that was waiting there. I did not know that it was Merlin's last retrieve; very probably it was a different bird, but I nevertheless proclaimed it the old spaniel's final triumph and such it became for me. Then I went to my store of wine and chose the best bottle of claret that I could find. I had decided to hold a feast, a very private feast, the next evening.

In the morning I buried old Merlin, down by the meadow gate at the heart of my shoot. In the evening I held his wake. Bad Digby was the only guest. He got none of the wine, though he was given a slice or two of roast pheasant and a couple of roast potatoes. Digby did not howl out his grief, though he had been doing it in the morning when I went to collect him from his kennel. I decided to keep him in the flat overnight. At the end of Merlin's funeral feast, at least at the end of the semi-formal part of it, with tears spilling from my chin into the last drops of *Pichon-Lalande '83,* I lifted my glass from the table and, in between putting it to my lips, pronounced the solemn words of parting: 'Farewell, old Merlin! Old spaniel, farewell! Mighty hunter, king of the gorse, rabbits' bane and pheasants' terror, gentle friend, dear old Merlin, hail and farewell!'

It is right to grieve for the loss of a dog, but you must acknowledge the shallowness of your grief, and acknowledge at the same time that it is transient pain and will leave no lasting scars. I mourned Merlin's death and then spent the season shooting over bad Digby, which brought its own pleasures and its own frustrations and was on the strenuous side. Digby is unpredictable – too unpredictable to take on other men's shoots – but for a whole season he worked his heart out on my own, flushing game, retrieving it after a fashion, chasing rabbits, killing cats

Merlin's last retrieve

and behaving, on the whole, like a disobedient spaniel. But there were days when he was different, just a few of them: there were one or two days which Digby approached from the start in an almost cooperative spirit. I treasure the memory of them and, now that he too is old and slow and deaf, with his hunting days almost over, I should like to share with you his day of glory, the one day in his career as a shooting dog when he did very little wrong, did many more things right and so filled his master's heart with wondering gratitude.

It was as near a Christmas card scene as you will get, although it was much more beautiful, even with my presence somewhere in the middle of it all, and it was also early January rather than December. Over all the fields there was a thin cover of fresh snow, criss-crossed with the tracks of rabbits and pheasants. On Beck Bank rose the sombre green of the firs, with ice all along the dark edge of the running water beneath them. There were straight columns of smoke rising from the surrounding farmsteads, down in the valley or half way up the fells. Dense beds of rushes poked brown stalks above the snow; bare trees were very sharp against the blue sky and, all round the horizon, the white hills were shining in the sun. I was sitting by the meadow gate with bad Digby for company. It was ten o'clock in the morning and I was wondering where to go searching for the first pheasant of the day.

After smoking for a few minutes I took Digby up to the rushes below the Well. Now Digby usually behaves himself after a fashion for about ten minutes, until the excitement goes to his head and provokes an incident. He had been in the rushes for less than a minute, hunting with commendable spirit but rather more independence than you look for in the best trained spaniels, when a cock clattered out of them into the bright air. He was not a difficult bird, he was a rough-shooter's pheasant and I pulled the trigger gratefully. Digby obligingly retrieved him for me, dropping him somewhere near my feet, and I can remember that, as I held the bird in my hand, his red and copper feathers glowed against the snow. The incident came a minute or two later after two rabbits – they would have made a splendid right and left – had been left to run on because a wild spaniel was only inches away from their hind legs.

The incident itself – a traditional blend of ear pulling and roaring complaints loud enough to unsettle every pheasant in the parish – lasted no more than thirty seconds; then Digby and I continued on our way through the sunshine. In spite of the incident I was expecting more pheasants up in the high pastures, in the Hag and the Faraway but in spite of my expectations Digby, now in a compliant frame of mind, drew blank.

It is, of course, all part of the pleasure of rough shooting: the sudden moments of excitement with the sound of a flushing bird and the sight of him in the air, then the intervals between them when nothing much happens for ten minutes or for half an hour. Unpredictability is the essence of such sport. This particular interval lasted rather longer than half an hour. We had doubled back through the Hag, we had worked our way all along the boundary fence where those little patches of gorse so often hold a bird or two. They should have been there on so bright a day. Perhaps the incident really had warned them of my approach and sent them running away to safety; stealth is a part of the rough-shooter's armoury and bellows that would make an angry bull feel proud of his efforts have little to do with stealth.

I told myself that in future my demonstrations of disapproval would be closer to silence and then went down the steep ground to the sike. It was cold down there beneath the trees, but soon I had climbed onto the level and open ground above them. And it was there, up there in the sunshine and the snow that, as soon as Digby plunged into a thicket of brambles, a cock and a hen leapt out of them and rose very steeply into the sky. They were my one and only right-and-left of the season. Digby retrieved them rather sloppily; I laid them shining in the snow together with the day's first bird, sat down on my game-bag and smoked a pipe of triumph and delight.

It was almost time for lunch, but there was another cock before the time came, which meant that there were four birds hanging outside the hut as I sat on a bucket in the sunshine, sipping a measure of damson

Bad Digby: not always responsive

gin, generously allowing myself a second measure as a reward for straight shooting, eating a meat and potato pie and feeling just about as happy as any man deserves to feel in this imperfect old world.

The morning had been wonderful but in the afternoon there were marvels. The first of them came almost as soon as Digby had plunged into the gorse. He seemed to have forgotten the morning's incident. He seemed no longer to be haunted by the booming terror of his master's voice or by memories of tweaked ears; at any rate he was hunting a long way ahead of me and not responding to the frantic summons of my whistle. I had just decided that the time was approaching for a second incident, which would of course be quieter, when, right from the top of the gorse, a hen broke back towards me with the sun in her feathers. She was a fast crossing bird, she was dipping as well and I was full of self-satisfaction when she collapsed into the thickest tangles of the gorse. Almost immediately I realised that she was very unlikely to emerge into the light between the jaws of a spaniel, because Digby's version of searching for dead or wounded game is to rush wildly to and fro, changing from one scent-line to another and sticking to none of them for more than a few seconds at a time.

It took Digby perhaps a minute to reappear on the scene; it took him perhaps another minute to dive back into the gorse and come out of it again with a hen pheasant held very proudly between his black jaws. The incident that followed was the opposite of the sort for which I had been preparing; it was full of tender affection; ears were stroked rather than pulled, words were soft and filled with praise for a good and faithful spaniel; as its climax Digby was presented with the Mars bar that I had forgotten to throw to him while I had been eating my meat and potato pie.

The second marvel came almost immediately. Another hen rose from the gorse; she was a high going-away bird and I could not clearly mark her fall. She had come down somewhere over the beck and I also thought that she was most likely a runner. Digby was still questing in the gorse and there was no chance that he had seen the fall. Even if he decided to turn up some time in the next ten minutes and even if I managed to get him onto her scent, there seemed little chance that he would bring her in. His record with runners was not encouraging.

At last, in response to my desperate whistles for help, Digby emerged from the gorse, half covered in snow. I waved him over the water; he bounded up the hill, bounded down again, stuck his nose to the ground, disappeared into the trees on the edge of the beck and returned almost immediately with my bird. There were no more Mars bars in my pocket; he had to make do with the display of tender affection and the words of praise. And that, as it turned out, was more or less it for the day. Digby pushed ahead of me and flushed one or two birds way out of range. I did not care much and I was, of course, still feeling far too grateful even to think of staging one of my incidents of the more usual sort.

The sun was low by now. The evening chill was creeping onto the air and very soon the frost would begin to bite. It was time to finish before Digby forgot himself in a way that would tarnish his glory, time to smoke for five minutes before hanging my pheasants on a stick, shouldering my burden and plodding down the meadow as the snow turned blue in the surrounding fields and pink on the hills above. It had been a most marvellous day. The sun had shone and from time to time a pheasant had risen into the sky; and two birds that I had thought lost had been brought to hand by the best spaniel in the world. And there was a marvel even greater than Digby's two great retrieves, which was the fact that I had pulled the trigger of my gun six times and was now trudging on my way beneath the weight of six birds. You will hardly need telling that, as the sun set over High Park and as I climbed into the Land Rover and sat there a minute or two before heading off home, I was, for once in my shooting life, feeling pleased both with myself and with my spaniel.

Undoubtedly it was Digby's greatest day. His hunting days are now almost over though. At the age of eleven, he is still fit enough for at least half a day in the field, but he is deaf now, deafer than Merlin ever was, and it is now impossible to exert even partial control over him. Our last full day together was in February and there was a special reason for taking Digby rabbiting. We should have gone anyway, for it was one of those February afternoons, with soft air and singing birds, that look forward to the spring of the year and, given that it is still at least a month too soon for trouting, turn a sportsman's thoughts to rabbit stew. Even without a special reason for it, Digby and I should have gone rabbiting together and we thoroughly enjoyed ourselves.

Digby rampaged through banks of gorse and through beds of rushes, more like a wild spaniel of three or four than one that had already lived out his first decade. I toiled after him, keeping more or less in touch, while rabbits fled ahead of us, except for those less sensible ones that came out to one side or those plain stupid ones that came back towards me and my gun.

Many were way out of range, others vanished into a hollow of the land, or down a hole, before there was any chance of getting my gun onto them. A few were less fortunate and, of the seven that came my way, remaining above ground and visible for long enough to offer a shot, six of them ended up in the bag at a cost of ten cartridges. There were pheasants showing themselves among the rabbits, at least a dozen of them. Most of them were cocks; it was only the first week in February and two or three of those cocks, I feel obliged to admit, birds with long tails that rose suddenly and sharply and defiantly from cover, were a temptation barely resisted. The pheasant-shooter – remember that his sport does not properly begin until the very end of October

Digby (front) and Merlin

– has only three months to enjoy it. This particular shooter cannot understand why he is not allowed to get on with it through most of February, until, say, the twenty-first, and then he would have less than a month to wait before going in search of his first trout.

Anyway, I resisted those magnificent cocks, keeping my fire for rabbits, and every quarter of an hour or so I stopped for a smoke. Keeping up with Digby has always been an exhausting business; every rabbit, moreover, made the bag on my shoulder heavier. I needed those frequent rests but I should have sat down almost as often with no rabbits in the bag and in the company of a spaniel willing to hunt at my speed rather than his own; I should have sat down to breathe in the mild air as well as the nicotine, to listen to the mistle thrushes and the robins and the dunnocks, and to look at the land all round me, climbing up to the Pennine fells and gleaming in the pale sunshine: gleaming softly with its irregular pattern of dark walls, with its brown streaks and patches of rushes and bracken, with the blurred green of distant banks of gorse and with the hazy shapes of little woods and plantings dotted over the rising slopes. It is one of the delights of shooting alone that you can pause and look round you just as often as you choose; it encourages the contemplative approach.

I was a happy rabbiter, anyway, when I plodded back to the Land

Rover at the end of two or three hours' sport. I stopped at a friend's farm on the way home and demanded a pot of tea in return for a couple of rabbits. I got my pot of tea and left with an enormous fruit-cake under my arm. Back in Sedbergh I fed Digby, paunched and skinned the four rabbits left to me, splashed round in the bath for half an hour or so, did one or two bits of schoolwork, got my supper ready, drank a glass of sherry, stroked Digby a time or two, drank another glass of sherry, ate my supper, stared at the ceiling, took Digby out before bedding him down rather ceremoniously, stared at the ceiling again while finishing my wine and beginning to think about bed. And through all this I kept wondering whether I was making a mistake and, though I was alone and sober and not, as far as I could tell, doing anything abnormal or eccentric, I was haunted by a feeling that came close to fear.

There was really nothing, I kept telling myself, to feel frightened about. Merlin had died in August and I had decided at the time that the New Year would be soon enough to start looking for a young spaniel. I had enjoyed my sport with Digby over the winter but there was no use pretending that he was a model gun-dog and he was getting old anyway. I needed a young spaniel; I needed one that was better than Digby at doing what he was told and at finding wounded game. I could think of at least half-a-dozen runners lost in the course of the season that a better spaniel would have been likely to bring in.

There had, of course, been Digby's day of glory, but that had been an exception; he was, rather like his master, an enthusiast rather than an expert, and his master had felt throughout the season a growing need for more expert assistance in the matter of finding game, not so much on those days when he shared High Park with his friends, for then his friends' dogs could usually make up for Digby's shortcomings; it was more on those occasions when he roamed the fields with Digby alone that he was forced to acknowledge Digby's deficiencies, and he hated leaving ungathered birds at the end of the day and he knew that this season there had been too many of them. And so, when finally the New Year arrived, he knew that the time had come to start looking for a second spaniel.

I shall not bother you with details of the search; it is the end that matters and he is called Ross. All that staring at the ceiling happened on the night before I drove to collect him from Colin Myers, his owner and trainer, who had brought him out to High Park a few days earlier. I had bought him on the spot and what clinched it had not been his perfect obedience or his disciplined relish for the roughest part of my gorse, it had been the cock brought out of the gorse, a cock with a broken wing that I felt certain was a bird shot on the last day of the season and never found in spite of all Digby's manic eagerness.

Once this bird had been delivered to Colin's hand, once we had examined it and both spotted the fractured wing-bone, there was no longer any chance of me rejecting the magnificent Ross in all his black-and-white glory, no chance at all of me looking for a cheaper but still serviceable spaniel. I was already dreaming of a season at High Park when not a single bird would be lost to the bag, when runners would elude the best efforts of every dog on the shoot until finally Ross found them and bought them in. I announced my eagerness to buy, Colin confirmed his willingness to sell a near perfect spaniel to a very imperfect spaniel-handler and, since I was to be away for a few days, we set a date for me to drive over to Colin's kennels and collect him.

And why did I feel almost fearful as I studied the limited interest offered by the ceiling of my flat, noticing very little but the brown stains of at least ten years' exposure to tobacco smoke? What could have been more sensible, following Merlin's death in August, than to wait for the end of the shooting season before replacing him? It would give all spring and summer for me to get used to Ross and for him to get used to me. In a few weeks I should be able to take him rabbiting and see how we were getting on together. And, if there were any problems, I should certainly not be too proud to consult Colin, so that he would be able to tell me where I was going wrong and iron out any problems before the pheasants came round again.

I had behaved with admirable good sense. I had not rushed in to a new dog as soon as Merlin had died. I had bought what seemed the right dog at the right time; I was going to collect him in the morning and somehow the thought of this inspired a feeling close to fear, unless it was a feeling nearer to embarrassment. The reason, in fact, was that I could not help wondering whether bad Digby's owner and trainer deserved a field-trial winner as the next dog in his life. Merlin had been a fine dog when I bought him, but he had certainly developed bad habits with me for his master. Was I on the edge of a terrible mistake? Would Ross, in six months, be chasing rabbits and running into shot and ignoring the whistle and making me feel like the prince of fools for spending a lot of money on a dog that I lacked the skill to handle?

It has not turned out like that. I have had Ross for eight months now. We have done a fair amount of rabbiting together and he is still behaving like the dog I bought in February. He is, like almost all spaniels, an affectionate creature and I have not regretted buying him for a moment. He is fast and obedient and we seem to get on well together. And Digby has not been completely ignored. I have found time for an hour here and there with him running riot through the gorse and the rushes while I stumble and sweat behind him and usually manage to take aim at the few rabbits that for some reason flush within range of my gun. Digby's pheasant days are over; but he is looking at me as I finish this chapter and I have just promised him that he will be given the chance to chase rabbits somewhere in front of me for just as long as his strength allows.

Undoubtedly the best way to get into the proper mood for writing about shooting is to write about dogs. I have done it now. October has started and I am ready to go duck-flighting with Ross for the first time.

Chapter Eleven

Flighting with Ross

Yesterday evening Ross and I went for our first flight together. It was also my first flight of the season and very soon I shall tell you about it; but I am looking forward to reliving the experience so much that I am going to delay the pleasure for a page or two, building up to it by telling you one or two other things first. Think of them as a sort of prelude to the main event.

Before describing the great flight I shall look back into September and the afternoon when I took time off from rivers (and feeding pheasants) to do a bit of shooting. Now it so happened that, until that September afternoon, there were only three species of bird at which, in the course of many year's sport, I had managed a right-and-left. I had managed it (amazingly) with grouse, on a dark November afternoon, after I had spent the morning missing the few chances that hurtled past my butt.

It was the last drive of the day at the end of my first day on a grouse moor. I was sitting there feeling incompetent and depressed. I had watched the men on either side of me killing a fair share of the birds that came their way but I could do nothing with them, with those brown shapes that appeared out of the brown heather and were so suddenly past me, disappearing into the brown slopes behind me almost as soon as they had been seen. I was sitting there in my butt, brooding over bitter thoughts, when the sudden appearance of a small covey momentarily chased reflection from my mind. I swung the gun through a crosser, turned to fire at a bird behind me and found that I had suddenly been transformed into the happiest shooter in the world.

I have killed a few grouse in the years following that first day but there has been no second right-and-left.

With pheasants I have done the deed six or seven times, a time or two more with mallard, although I have never watched two birds, stone-dead in the air above me, descending to the earth together from a great height. My achievements have been of a humbler sort and sometimes one half of the right-and-left has reached the ground with most parts of its body in good order, sometimes it has needed an eager spaniel to plunge into cold water or to hunt along gutters and hedges in order to bring in the second part of my triumph.

There have been one or two hybrid versions of the double-kill. There was once a pheasant and a woodcock, which I thought rather distinguished; there was also a pheasant and a rabbit – very clearly a rough-shooter's sort of right-and-left – and, one sunny evening years and years ago, I shot a rabbit with my first barrel and, even as he tumbled down the steep bank in front of me, a fox flushed from a bed of rushes and, as soon as the second shot rang out, he fell dead almost at the rabbit's feet. It was a strange and memorable sight and it made me very popular with the farmer whose land I was shooting; with the fox gone he thought that his two surviving geese might make it through to Christmas and their destiny on plates.

Half-way through September, anyway, I added another species to the list. You will probably be thinking of partridges. It was, in fact, much less grand: it was an afternoon out at High Park and I was up at the West Pen, lurking on the edge of the blackthorns, waiting for the enemy with a loaded gun and looking at the green sloes thick on every branch, looking at the clustered fruit and gloating over the prospect of gallons and gallons of sloe gin.

Before long the enemy started arriving in ones and twos; they turned my thoughts from winter booze and I found that I was on fairly good form. Half a dozen birds had already fallen before the supreme achievement of my right-and-left. They were not carrion crows (I wish they had been), they were jackdaws; and unfortunately this latest right-and-left entitles me neither to an exclusive tie nor to an annual dinner in the company of others who have managed the same feat. Perhaps I should make myself the founder member (and President) of the Jackdaw Club, which would, of course, avoid anything that might smack of pretension: there would be no black ties or speeches or fine wines. Moleskins would be more appropriate for men who spend afternoons knocking down jackdaws; moleskins would be just about perfect, with hot-pot and pints of bitter beer to spill over them in some corner of a smoke filled tap-room. I like fine wine and fine food, but I also like bitter beer and hot-pot and tap-rooms full of smoke; and I always feel awkward and uncomfortable when imprisoned within my dinner suit. I am beginning to think that the Jackdaw Club is a splendid idea.

An odd feature of this season's release has been that crows and rooks and jackdaws, which usually descend in hordes on all three of my pens once they have realised the presence of easy pickings (this rarely takes longer than a week), have confined their depredations to the West Pen. On the afternoon of the right-and-left I shot twenty four of them and hung up their corpses round the pen. This kept them away for a week or two, then I deployed my giant scarecrows, which are still filling their black hearts with dread. But my giants will not scare for much longer; the crows will realise the fraud and then, admitting defeat, I shall feed legions of corvids through the winter as well as the pheasants I want to feed. Next year I must get some traps.

For the time being, at any rate, my birds can scratch round in the grass, pecking at the hoppers and filling their crops in the polite company of tits and chaffinches and a few pigeon. They have never done better. I have declared the release a success and am looking forward to my pheasant days with mounting expectation. When things have gone well, early October is a good time for men who release pheasants. In September we begin to breathe a little easier; in October we begin to relax.

The only blemish on the best release I can remember was half a dozen birds killed towards the end of August. I found them in ones and twos in the course of a week, and they filled me with vicious thoughts about the buzzards (sometimes three or four of them together) that spend the whole summer circling, soaring and mewing over my land. I was angry with the buzzards; I was angry in a murderous sort of way and, if the law had allowed it, I should have waved my gun at them with intent to kill. Then one morning I spotted a half-grown kitten dozing in the sunshine on Pheasant Hill; he looked a satisfied and full-bellied kitten and I cursed myself for coming out to High Park without a gun (it had been left behind just in case buzzard-hatred should tempt me to sin). Half an hour later the curses were redoubled when suddenly there were two kittens in front of me, bounding playfully through the long grass.

Traps were moved up from the beck and baited with sardines. Within a week they had caught six kittens and their mother. They were all very beautiful, barred on the body with black and gold between the white; each time I pulled the trigger of the air rifle I should have preferred to be doing something else; but feral cats, however affecting they seem when seen through the mesh of a cage-trap or in the limp helplessness of death, cannot be shown mercy, and I have found no dead pheasants since I pulled the trigger for the last time. I have taken to waving friendly greetings to the buzzards as they wheel and screech above me.

Perhaps it is time for the flight now, perhaps it is time to get back into the month of which I am meant to be writing, time for the middle of October and my first evening of the year by Low Park Pond. In the afternoon I had fed my pheasants and gathered sloes beneath the sun, purple masses of them far beyond my need. Greed had taken over, stripping branches of berries that should have been left for the fieldfares and the redwings, although there were so many left that there was no need for guilt. I am the same with blackberries: once I start picking them I find it difficult to stop. Perhaps it is the thorns that prick me to anger and goad me on, perhaps it is because both brambles and black-thorns offer sharp resistance to the man who would harvest them, but mushrooms surrender without a struggle and I am even greedier in a field of mushrooms than along an autumn hedge dark with blackberries or sloes. It must be, I suppose, that I am prone to excess.

I had fed my pheasants, anyway, and filled three plastic bags full almost to bursting with sloes. Then I sat smoking above the old pen, watching a chaffinch busy beneath one of the hoppers, looking for and finding a few of my birds skulking on the edge of the brambles, and wondering whether to stay for flight. It was still and warm and the sky was clear. Conditions would not be those most flighters relish, but then I am an eccentric flighter: I love the wait as much as the flight itself; I love quiet evenings that sink very slowly into the night; and if, when night eventually comes and it is time to go, if I leave then with fewer duck than wind and racing cloud might have put in my bag, I do not care a fig. On a rough winter evening, with teeth on the edge of the wind and with ice all along the edge of ruffled water, flighting is a sport for the hardy. It is wild and exciting and it is good to feel that you are a tough sort of a man. It is even better, with flight over and half a dozen duck brought home, to sit by your fire, chewing mouthfuls of stew, gurgling mouthfuls of rich, uncomplicated red wine and listening to the howl of the wind against your windows.

There was no prospect of this sort of flight as I sat in the sunshine above the old pen. Waiting by your pond in the softness of a warm autumn evening, waiting there as the light fades imperceptibly into a soft autumn night, is more like the favourite pleasure of a refined hedonist; it should, of course, be followed by a glass of *fino,* by three scrambled eggs scattered with smoked salmon and Parma ham, and then, after the eggs and a cup of coffee, by an hour's reflection with a glass or two of burgundy.

It was thoughts such as these that determined me to stay and try for the first duck of the season, and the afternoon was so beautiful that I knew there would be no difficulty in spending two hours before the time came to sit down on my upturned bucket and wait for the mallard. I wandered through the wood, with pheasants scurrying ahead of me and with dry leaves under my boots. I sat down by the beck in the shadows and watched my smoke curling up towards the coloured trees. I saw a grey squirrel, hating him for his cunning and his agility and wondering if I should ever again see a native squirrel on my own land.

Then I strolled back to the Land Rover and stood on the bridge for ten minutes, looking at the water and thinking of fish. My beck runs into the Bela and the Bela runs into the Eden a mile or two above Kirkby Stephen. My beck also flows within a few yards of Low Park

Pond, and I remembered a November evening some years ago when, to the more usual sounds that come to my ears as I sit there waiting for the sound I have come to hear, there was added the loud splashing of trout in the water behind me. It was a sound that at first puzzled and then almost thrilled me; for I realised they were fish running the beck to spawn, squirming and lashing their way over the shallow banks of gravel, and there was deep satisfaction in the thought that, while I was sitting there waiting for winter sport, behind me were trout filled with the urgent desire to produce another generation of my summer prey.

Before long it was time to leave the bridge and take old Digby for a run in the fields, explaining to him that he was now too old and too deaf to go flighting and that soon he must return to the Land Rover while Ross and I went off to see what came with the darkness. I had brought the gun along with Digby, who now rampaged slowly through a field full of rushes and straggling patches of gorse. I was hoping for a rabbit or two, and one or two showed, but with Digby so close to them there was no chance of a shot. Then it was back to the Land Rover for a cup of tea and a smoke.

By now it was almost seven o'clock and I was able to persuade myself that it was not too early for the bucket, and so I took it from the back of the Land Rover before taking both bucket and spaniel to the edge of Low Park Pond. The sun was sinking towards the hills, the light was golden, the air was warm. I was at least half an hour too early, but half the joy of flighting is the waiting and the peace as you sit by the water, listening and watching while the light fades and the darkness refuses to come.

My bucket was really quite comfortable. Once settled on it, anyway, I sat smoking with the old Webley resting broken and unloaded over my knees. Less than a fortnight ago I had been filled with the sadness that belongs to the end of things. September had seemed deep autumn, with rivers carrying their cargo of withered leaves and with dead or dying grass all along their banks; now I was sitting on my bucket and feeling impatient, not for the duck to come – it was so pleasant sitting there that I was happy to wait – but for the first frosts and for drifts of black leaves beneath the birches and the ashes, with bare branches for pheasants to fly through and to help shooter see them. Less than a fortnight ago I had been contemplating ends.

Now I was at a beginning and it was good to think of what lay ahead. I also thought about wine, which is a constant preoccupation. I had forgotten to think about it before I left Sedbergh and so there was no half-bottle waiting for the evening. It was my first flight with Ross. It was a beautiful evening; if a few duck showed up, and if I shot efficiently, and if Ross retrieved as well as I expected him to, then perhaps it would be the proper occasion for something better than usual; and perhaps, rather than some of my better burgundy, it would be time for half of my last bottle of *Clos des Papes '90;* and if duck came and I missed them all and gave Ross no chance to prove himself, I would have to make do with some of that Chilean stuff I had bought from the Co-op.

One of the incidental benefits of shooting and fishing, by the way, is that they are always providing excuses for celebration. I never need an excuse to drink; as soon as the time for supper approaches it is time for a glass of sherry; and a supper without wine would seem as incomplete to me as a hotpot without potatoes. I never need an excuse to drink, but I am somewhat inclined to hoard my better wines. I like to gloat over them, telling myself that they will be better next year. I get them out to share with fellow wine-snobs but, except on those occasions when the deep and grateful satisfaction of a fishing or shooting day demands special recognition, I rarely sit sipping them by myself. Thank God such occasions happen about once a fortnight.

Meanwhile, among the usual sights and sounds of an October evening by a flight pond, the light began to thicken at last. A heron croaked over on primevally stiff wings. A robin sang softly somewhere behind me. A few woodpigeons flew past. Cock pheasants shouted and jackdaws flocked to roost, forcing me to admit that even they, as they wheel and tumble and cackle through the sky, bring their own restless and noisy sort of beauty to the end of an autumn evening. It is also a revelation to see how many of them there are, flock upon noisy flock of them heading for their dormitories in the trees. As I sat on my bucket a few squadrons of the uncountable host came right over me. I was tempted to try for another right-and-left, but I reminded myself that I was waiting for mallard and that if, on nearby streams and splashes, any of them were thinking of flying into my pond, the bark of my shots might warn them to think again.

There are, of course, stages to the coming of darkness. Once the sun has gone the dusk sets in, but on a clear evening the brightness stays in the sky far longer than you ever expect; it is like a memory that refuses to fade. It seemed to me, anyway, sitting on my bucket and smoking my pipe and filling my mug with yet another dollop of tea, that, in the immediate surroundings of Brough Sowerby, the processes of nature had been changed, that the sun had sunk but not with its usual result; for a time it seemed that night would never take possession of the land, that visible darkness was become a thing of the past and that some new order of creation was unfolding in a small corner of south Cumbria. It is a fancy that accompanies almost every wait by a flight pond.

And then I saw that the ash tree ahead of me, some sixty yards beyond the far edge of the water, was no longer a form of dim colour

Waiting for the dusk at High Park pond

and circumference; it had become a silhouette, flat and black against the western sky, with the tapering rise of the trunk, with the intricate patterns of the branches and with the fingered leaves, recently vague impressions of leaves, now very sharply defined. The evening was moving on; the darkness would arrive and it was time to slip two cartridges into the breech of my gun, time to put my pipe in my pocket and my flask in my bag, time to start listening for the sound of wings.

Ross heard it before I did. Suddenly he stiffened and sniffed, and then the rhythm came to me from the air above, circling and throbbing through the sky. The gun was ready, the rhythm was louder and nearer, there was muttering talk mixed in with it, and then I saw two dark shapes planing in towards the water, wings wide and cupped, legs already stretched out for water-contact. The first barrel produced a loud splash; the second duck flared into the sky and the second barrel was followed by the thud of his crash into the rushes.

Ross was as taut as a bowstring but he had not stirred. I waved him into the water, he sprang at the sign and returned with a duck; I sent him to the rushes and in less than a minute he had brought back a drake. I told myself that a right-and-left at mallard, appearing in the dramatic intensity of dying light and gathering darkness, was more satisfying than three at jackdaws in the warm stillness of a September afternoon. I also recognised that a drake and a duck were better than a pair of ducks or of drakes; just as, with pheasants, an afternoon's rough sport that ends with a cock and a hen in the bag is a little more satisfying than two hens or two cocks. There is something complementary in the drake and the duck, in the cock and the hen. Perhaps this could be developed into an argument against same-sex partnerships; and perhaps it would be better if I left the development for someone else.

Just at that moment I was more interested in my swing. There was something abnormal, or at least untypical about it because, whenever it went into action, it brought a bird dropping from the sky. A single mallard was suddenly high above me; a second later he had splashed into the rushy pasture over the fence. I left him for the end of flight and waited for more. I caught the pulse of wings again and a second pair were dropping in from behind. One I shot, but lost sight of the other in marking the fall of the first on the far side of the pond. Before I could send Ross, a mallard crossed to my right and dropped on the edge of the water. Five duck were enough and I decided to finish, giving more birds time to come in and feed undisturbed. Ross had the two near birds in no time at all. I slipped him under the fence and told him to get on. There were the splashings of a spaniel bounding through a marshy field in the darkness, there were sniffs and snorts from his eager nose, until there was no sound for a second or two and then the sound of steadier movement with more laboured breathing. I knew the bird had been found and very soon Ross was trotting up to me with a drake in his mouth.

As I left Low Park Pond, with two mallard in my bag and three in my bucket, the air was full of wings and grunting duck noises. In three or four weeks I should be back with Ross as the night came. But now it was back to Sedbergh for a glass of sherry, for three scrambled eggs with smoked salmon and Parma ham (eggs do not do justice to fine wine and so they were eaten with a glass of the Chilean stuff); there was time for a coffee before taking the dogs out and then it was time for the half bottle of *Clos des Papes,* which smelt and tasted of at least a dozen delicious things; and, with every sniff and every swallow, I told myself that I owned the best spaniel in the world and that I loved flighting duck very much indeed.

CHAPTER TWELVE

Pictures in the Mind

It was late October and the evening of my first full day at High Park. There had been five of us shooting and we had ended the day with eighteen pheasants, which is a record for my first day. I was feeling pleased as I sat by the fire and looked back over things, pleased not only with eighteen dead pheasants but with almost everything about the day. The weather had been soft and bright; High Park had shone out in a glory of yellow and gold and orange leaves. The birds had flown strongly and we had left the low ones. Those eighteen pheasants had not been flappers, they had been worthy birds, easy birds to miss. I had missed three and shot seven, which is good enough for me and better than usual. I had enjoyed the company of my friends and, beneath the noonday sun, our lunch by the meadow gate had been more like a summer picnic than a break for whisky and sandwiches in the middle of late-autumn sport. It had all been very enjoyable and it was delightful to be sitting by the fire – the evening was just cold enough for one – drinking sherry and going back over it all.

But you know how it is with an organised day in late October: however well it goes you always feel that you are doing it a fortnight too soon. There is still too much leaf on the trees; it is the end of autumn rather than the beginning of winter and, although well-grown birds of the year are by late October more or less ready for the gun, they do not fly with quite the speed and determination that comes as the season advances. There had been two birds on this particular first day that had given me real pleasure: there had been a hen – the first and only bird of the first drive – that had flushed high over the larches on Beck Bank and fallen dead to my single shot. She was the first bird of the day and she was also my first driven bird of the season; she was a good beginning. Several drives later there was another hen: a long crossing bird that flushed from the Whins when I had just missed a moderately high cock. I was pleased with these two hens but I could not help thinking that, in December or January, I might well have missed them both, for in a month or two the first of them would almost certainly have been faster, while the second would also have been rising more steeply as she crossed in front of me.

I have a main day in October because I cannot have one in November; if the law allowed me to shoot pheasants on Sundays, I should wait for the second Sunday of the month; I should go early to mass and be less attentive than I should be, and then I should go pheasant shooting; but the law will have none of this. It is happy for me to slay ducks and rabbits on the Lord's Day, whether or not I spend any portion of the day thanking him for providing them, but on no account must pheasants be made to work for their living on the Sabbath. There is, of course, no sense to this, but there it is: one of those absurdities that will never be changed. Saturday mornings find me in a classroom and so I cannot have a main day in November. I therefore have one in half-term at the end of October. I always enjoy it but always feel that it is happening just a week or so too soon.

Anyway it was the evening of my first proper shoot. It had gone well and, after the sherry, I ate one of the mallard from my first flight, thinking how good it tasted while continuing my contented review of the day's sport. I tried to remember each little drive, where the birds had risen and how they had gone over the guns and which of them had fallen; and gradually my mind moved from a particular day's sport to more general considerations, for it struck me how a shooting day always leaves pictures in the mind. Now that I think about it, I suppose most days do, although the images of commonplace experience fade and disappear almost as quickly as they are made.

What really struck me was that a shooting day does it differently from most other days, by stamping on the memory the experience of a split-second in deep and lasting relief. I can still see with perfect clarity and, I believe, with perfect accuracy of recall, moments from shooting days that took place years and years ago.

I can, for example, still see myself standing at the back of a spruce plantation, standing half way down a slope which ends, perhaps ten yards below me, in a dry ditch with a few patches of gorse spreading along its length. It is an afternoon between Christmas and the New Year, raw and cloudy. I have been put at the back of the wood as an experiment, because a few birds have broken back on earlier shoots and the beaters have said that they have flown well. A hen has already flown back over the far corner of the wood, making me wonder whether that is where I should have placed myself.

A few shots have rung out from the guns surrounding the front of the covert and I am beginning to think, without much disappointment, that my shooting is over for the day, until a voice from the wood cries 'back'. It is not a loud voice for by now the beaters are well forward in the covert; it comes to my ears like some faint warning or distant encouragement and, just after it, comes a hen, very fast and very high, pale buff against the grey sky, inspiring an instinctive swing from the gun and the sudden collapse of the bird, which falls dead thirty yards on the other side of the ditch, lying there a pale shape with a few feathers stirring, until Merlin is sent to bring her in. Now it is the moment of collapse that is now the heart of the memory, so strong and so vital that it keeps alive all those surrounding details; without it everything would have gone within the course of a few weeks or a few months.

Further back still there is a moonlit picture from an October duck flight. I am sitting in the angle of a dry-stone wall, about ten yards from a small pond that sometimes draws surprisingly good numbers of mallard and an occasional teal. It is a calm evening and the daylight has almost gone. On my left is an old planting of ashes and sycamores, black shapes of rising trunks and intricately spreading branches with the shine of the full moon now lifting itself above them. It is the moon that has persuaded me to stay on for ten minutes longer. I have one duck in the bag, but he has cost me five cartridges and I am out of sorts with myself for shooting badly and for coming flighting at all on so unsuit-able an evening: one with a clear sky and a full moon and almost no

The Whins, High Park

wind. I know that it is really time to finish, because birds will now be almost impossible to pick out against the sky, but the irrational hope of a successful shot keeps me waiting by the water. Perhaps ten minutes pass, and then suddenly I hear the beat of wings and, a second later, I see the silhouette of a single mallard, crossing the silver moon and turning to come in. The gun swings and the shot rings out and the mallard falls in the field behind the wall. Flight is over; it has turned to glory and that image of silver light and a shadow beating across a silver disc and then falling into the darkness, is an image that will never fade.

Then there is the probably the highest pheasant that I ever killed. I was a guest on a shoot in North Yorkshire and had shot tolerably at demanding birds on the first two drives, although I was uncomfortably aware that I was surrounded by guns who seemed to shoot with effortless and elegant efficiency. Their birds had fallen dead, one after the other, and very few had survived the raising of their guns; I had hit something like one bird for every three cartridges, but at least half of my dozen or so birds had needed prompt action by the pickers-up to stop them running away. I told myself that the men round me did this sort of shooting three or four days a week, that I was a rough-shooter who was just a little out of his depth; I also told myself that if I could manage to keep shooting at the standard of the first two drives I should be able to go home feeling that I had done my bit.

On our way to the next drive one of the guns said that I was about to see some really high birds and that my peg, number five, would have fewer birds over it than the lower numbers but those few would be indisputable skyscrapers. When I got to my peg I saw why. In front of me was a steep bank, running up about thirty yards to a road. Over the road, I was told, and running parallel with it, there was a cover crop; it was from this long strip of kale, and from the covert behind it, that birds would be sent over the guns. To the left of me, on my side of the wall, a planting of mixed conifers ran down the bank and then curved round into the field behind. On my right was another gun (there were only six of us shooting) and an open expanse of rough pasture. The other guns were on pegs in the wood, where there was also a pen, and it was clear that most of the birds would head for cover and home. That was fine by me, for they would obviously be high and fast and it would be the sort of situation where I easily get flustered, especially when surrounded by the spectacle of birds falling on both sides of me to other men's guns.

Out in the field, something like twenty yards from the edge of the plantation, I was unlikely to have an endless stream of birds over me; those that came my way would be the ones that caught the breeze and headed for the back of the covert on the rising ground behind me. They might easily be birds at or beyond the limit of range and there would be little shame in missing them. You will see that I was not adopting an entirely positive approach; I felt intimidated by the pheasants up in that cover crop even before I had seen any of them in the sky.

In the early stages of the drive I began to think that I might just get away with it. Plenty of pheasants flushed. They started almost thirty yards above the guns; some of them dipped down the slope but more rose as they flew and crossed the line at least forty yards up in the sky. They were dramatic and very difficult birds, often with a curl in their flight; they were frightening birds but every one of them went over the guns in the wood.

Many of them fell dead from the sky, although I was relieved to see a fair number flying on after two shots had rung out beneath them. At least my fellow guns were not all infallible. I can remember wishing that I was not standing there with a gun in my hand waiting to miss any pheasant that came my way. It would have been good just to watch the spectacle, because I was witnessing a finely controlled drive sending a succession of tall birds in ones and twos and threes over a line of expert guns.

It seemed to me an almost perfect exhibition of driven shooting, and the fact that some of the birds were too good for those expert guns seemed somehow part of the perfection. There was a blue sky; beneath it was the dark spread of the pines and spruces, and up in the light there were the pheasants, burnished cocks and shining hens. Some of them rose on their long tails, others glided on spread wings; some spiralled in death, some collapsed in the sky and fell like feathered stones, others folded their wings and planed steeply down. And there were those that did not fall, those that defied the guns beneath them and went flying and climbing on their way in high and shining contempt. It was dramatic and beautiful to watch and I should have preferred to be just a spectator rather than someone who at any moment might be obliged to play his own incompetent part in the proceedings.

Above me the cover crop extended perhaps fifty yards to my right, so that towards the end of the drive, birds started coming towards me and filling me with dread until, almost without exception, they curled back into the planting. A cock refused to curl, came straight over me, and flew happily on his way. There was no disgrace in missing a single bird. Even the best shots often missed their first bird on a difficult peg; but then a hen sprang into the sky and came on through the sunshine, shining and rising all the way.

I waited for her to curl and suddenly realised that she preferred the straight path and that I should have to take her on. The swing that greeted her was not smooth or elegant, it was not a little masterpiece of precise and fatal timing: it was a wild and despairing swipe and it brought her diving out of the sky with the unresisting grace of a dead bird. The gun on my right shouted his approval; the horn sounded and,

a few minutes later, the keeper apologised to both of us, explaining that
a different wind would have sent more birds over our end of the line.
I did not say that, as far as I was concerned, more birds would almost
certainly have been too many. It is that single hen, and the fraction of a
second that changed her movement from flight to fall, that is engraved
indelibly upon my mind and has preserved a clear memory of the scene
surrounding it.

I mention these memories in the first place because, while chewing
my mallard and drinking my burgundy on the evening of High Park's
first proper shoot, I realised that the day had made a new memory.

It belonged to the last drive, which was North Bank and for which
I decided to stand since Ross was already exhausted and it needed a
spaniel with energy to work the gorse above the trees. I stood as a
sort of back gun, with my friends up in the wood and with me down
below it on the edge of the gorse, looking at the bright sky, looking at
the coloured leaves and the red berries on the hawthorns and feeling
pleased with the way things had gone. There was a shot or two from
the forward guns and I wondered whether the bag would reach twenty,
which would be a fine round figure for my first shoot. Then there was a
double bang followed a second or two later by another double bang, and
in another second or two the reason for all the commotion flew over me,
a high fast hen which was undamaged by the single shot I managed to
let off at her. I had been daydreaming, thinking end-of-shoot thoughts
and looking at the slow drift of the white clouds above me; that hen had
caught me unprepared and she was not the new memory.

I was ready for birds now and before long I heard a cry of over
and saw a cock coming down the valley. The other guns cannot have
seen him soon enough, for he flew over at least two of them without
provoking a shot. The leaves still thick on the trees may have helped
him, and those stands up in the wood call for quick sighting and quick
shooting even in midwinter when the branches are bare. I saw him,
anyway, as he came down the valley over the trees, and some trick
of the light made him seem almost black. There were red berries and
yellow and golden leaves, and there flying above them was a dark shape
heading towards me, a shape which seemed to be skimming over the

trees as the dark shape of a grouse skims over the heather as he heads towards your butt. No pheasant has ever made the same impression on me or seemed in such contrast with everything about him. He was a dark and purposeful bird; he crossed to my right and I shot him into the beck. Ross brought him out of the water and I saw that he was a commonly coloured cock, a handsome cock with a white collar and a long tail and long sharp spurs. He was one of last year's birds but he was no darker than your average cock and the shot that killed him, though sporting enough, had been an average sort of shot. Somehow the light had transfigured him and made him memorable, and it was not, as it usually is, the moment of his fall that would preserve the scene for the rest of a lifetime; it was his approach as he came down the valley over the trees, where his presence in the sky seemed almost menacing, seemed driven by some sinister and private purpose that had nothing to do with spaniels disturbing the place where he had been hoping to spend the rest of the afternoon.

He was also the last shot of the day and you have probably noticed yourself how important such shots are and how often they stay with us. They may not in themselves be memorable but they can put the seal on a good day when you have shot well or they can bring hope at the end of a dispiriting day when you have shot little and missed plenty. Then you somehow manage to shoot a decent bird with the last barrel of the final drive, which persuades you that you can still do it and may even do it consistently the next time you stand in a line of guns.

There are memorable shots; there are also memorable retrieves. I remember a January day with my little syndicate shoot near Settle. Birds had been thin in the morning, as they usually are on this shoot once January comes along, but it had not bothered me. At lunchtime I had shot two pheasants with four cartridges. They had been good birds; I had enjoyed seeing them fall; I had enjoyed the company of my fellow guns and felt throughout the morning how glad I was that I had stayed in the syndicate when it had been reformed with a different captain and a different team of guns after the old syndicate had broken up in the wake of foot and mouth disease. Every syndicate creates its own atmosphere and the atmosphere of my little syndicate shoot near Settle is an atmosphere of which I thoroughly approve. Perhaps this was the day on which I realised how much I relished my days there, determining that, in future, I would not accept invitations for grander shoots which put more pheasants in the sky if they clashed with my syndicate days. To shoot a few pheasants with friends is much more enjoyable than to shoot, or shoot at, scores of birds in company that, however affable, is mostly strange to you.

Anyway on this January day with my syndicate we had our sandwiches in the barn, as usual, and then went to the first of the two afternoon drives. It is perhaps the most dependable of all our little drives; even late in the season it usually puts between a dozen and twenty birds over the guns. My peg was a good one at the bottom corner of the wood. I probably told myself that I should be surprised if I did not have two or three birds over me and probably expected them to be good birds, for it was a peg well beneath the level of the wood and pheasants usually rose into the sky as they came over it.

The early birds crossed the guns on either side of me. Some fell and some flew on and then my chance came with a high crossing hen that was even higher and was still crossing when I had let off two barrels at her. I was disappointed, because those two cock birds in the morning had convinced me that I was on form. If another bird came and I missed that as well, then two kills for four shots, which means satisfaction, would suddenly have turned into two for eight and nagging discontent. The next pheasant was a cock, another crossing bird with a particu-larly striking white collar. The hen had crossed on my right; the cock came to my left and the first barrel hit him so hard that I forgot about the second and just watched him, waiting for him to fall dead to the ground, but he staggered on through the sky and disappeared over the wall behind me.

My syndicate shoot does not have pickers-up and I knew the drive was nearly over, for I could see one or two beaters at the end of the wood. I did not wait for the horn, which is a freedom more or less permissible on my little syndicate shoot; I put down my gun and set off after my pheasant, expecting to find him dead somewhere over the wall but anxious to get after him in case he was a runner and managed to

'It was time to finish'

run beyond discovery before a dog got on his scent. He was not lying dead in the field and Ross did not find him in the rushes along the beck. Before long there were three or four spaniels busy with the search and at least one labrador as well; but it was all in vain. There was no sign of a dead or wounded cock. Men who had been on higher ground during the drive and had been better positioned to see where he had come down pointed to the area where he was most likely to be found and the search was renewed, but it had to be abandoned after five minutes or so because it was time to be moving on to the next drive.

I did not expect a shot as number five on the last drive and I did not get one. We went back to the barn and I announced that I was going to spend a few minutes looking for my bird. You know what is going to happen or there would be no point in me telling the story. Ross went to work again and he covered all the ground that had already been covered by half a dozen dogs; once or twice he seemed very keen indeed, once or twice he buried into the rushes and the brambles as though on the point of a find and, each time this happened, hope leapt up within me and then died again when Ross turned towards me with nothing in his mouth.

It was time to finish. We all hate leaving stricken birds but you cannot search for ever. The moment must come when you curse yourself for not killing your birds in the air and gloomily admit that this one must be abandoned. I had almost reached this point. Ross and I had gone further and further from the corner of the field where my friends had told me that the bird had fallen; we had moved at least a hundred yards down the line of the beck and were not too far from the edge of the next wood. It was here that Ross pounced; it was down by the rushes on the edge of the water that I saw his head go down and knew immediately that he had found a bird; and then I saw that it was a cock and, when Ross had brought it in, I saw that it was dead and, on the neck above the hanging head, I saw a broad white collar. It is difficult to describe the satisfaction of moments such as these, except to say that it is very great indeed and brings one of the deepest pleasures that come to shooting men in the course of a day's sport.

I went back to join my friends, waving a cock pheasant at them in proclamation of my pleasure and my pride. The shoot-captain grumbled that I had spoilt the neatness of his shoot record, because now he would have to change eighteen pheasants to one more; but he was glad the bird had been found and I drove home exulting in the prowess of my spaniel and reliving the moment when I had seen Ross pounce and seen that white-collared cock held firmly between his jaws.

Ross and Digby were both lying on the carpet as I let my shooting memories take me where they wanted. For a time they turned to Digby during the years of his active, and often uncontrollable service. Digby came up to me for a stroke and I remembered how his retrieving had never really been first-rate. In early days he was inclined to eat rather than to deliver, although, to be fair to him, this unfortunate practice was soon abandoned; I doubt if, in his career as a gun dog, Digby molested more than three or four pheasants and perhaps a couple of mallard. Once the temptation to make a meal of a retrieve had been successfully put behind him I used Digby more and more as old Merlin became deafer and stiffer and was then finally put down.

Digby was never a polished retriever and he was never very good with runners because he was easily distracted by intervening smells. But he did have his moments, even his whole days, and I have already told you of the winter day out at High Park when I shot six pheasants with six cartridges and Digby found and retrieved them all in more or less exemplary style. As I sat by the fire and looked at the old spaniel, now too deaf to be taken shooting and with much of the muscle now gone from his thighs, another Digby memory came to me, a memory of the time when Digby confounded and delighted me with his greatest retrieve. The moment at the heart of this memory was still very sharp and clear, but I reached for the game book to rediscover the incidents on its either side.

It happened at High Park at the end of a January afternoon. There had been three of us shooting and we had killed a few birds, which had flown strongly and shone brightly in the sort of pale silver January sunshine that is already beginning to look forward to spring. By now the light was fading and I was thinking that North Bank would be our last little drive. I shot a couple of birds, which had flown as dark and sudden shapes against the reddening edge of the sky. They were both hens, and then I saw a cock fall to one of the two boys who were shooting with me. I guessed he was a runner and a strong one too; he had come down in the wood over the beck and I remember thinking that already his legs had probably carried him beyond the reach of Digby's inconstant nose.

It took some time to get Digby out of the gorse which spreads above the trees along the top of North bank. I met up with the two boys, who had seen the wounded cock come down and take to his legs immediately. I waved Digby in his direction and settled down to be disappointed, wondering how long I should let Digby search for a pheasant that he was very unlikely to find before setting off myself in search of Digby. I think I lit my pipe and explained to the boys that Digby's quest was unlikely to be successful. Digby, by the way, had completely disappeared and I could not hear the sounds of a rampaging spaniel anywhere in the wood. I have always been nervous of giving Digby too much freedom as night approaches, fearing that he might melt into the darkness and never be seen again. I was beginning to think that I should forget about the runner and try to find my spaniel, when suddenly there he was, splashing across the beck and trotting up to us through the deepening light with a cock pheasant held in the classic fashion between his jaws. I think it was Digby's most glorious achievement, even if the bird was found by chance in the course of a wild riot through the wood, and half the glory of it was that the boy who had brought down that runner had missed the few chances that had come his way earlier in the afternoon. It was a bird that mattered and the sight of Digby, splashing through the water and sauntering up to us with that bird in his mouth and his head held high: that sight is one of the most deeply imprinted memories of my shooting life.

And something now struck me, as I sat by the fire and gave old Digby a pat or two in commemoration of his finest exploit; it struck me, as I stroked an old spaniel and took another sniff and gurgle from my glass, that shooting memories are different in kind from memories of fishing days.

A shooting memory is of a moment: a pheasant throwing back its neck, dead in the air: a mallard tumbling through the darkening sky; the sudden appearance of a spaniel with a missing bird. It is a moment,

Gorse on The Whins

frozen and preserved, and round this moment of sharp and perfect recall adhere, in greater or lesser detail, impressions of the circumstances that preceded or surrounded it.

Fishing memories, my fishing memories at any rate, are not like this: they are softer and more diffuse; they are often recollections of mood and atmosphere rather than of incident. Perhaps memories of failure are an exception to this general rule. Certainly the great trage-dies of my fishing life still haunt me with a clarity of vision that keeps fresh in my mind the horror of a brief moment.

I remember hooking a sea trout off the mouth of a burn on a loch in the far North of Scotland; I remember the silver of his leap and the strength of his first run; but much more clearly than these I remember the sudden slackness of the line and the blankness that came over me in the knowledge that he was gone; and I can still see the yellow gleam of my rod in the pale sunshine, the gleam of a rod rocking gently with the motion of the boat, the gleam of a rod that was stiff and straight and no longer bending to the power of a great fish.

I can remember a big trout high on the Wharfe just below Yockenthwaite bridge. It was the end of May; it was soft, warm and sunny and the black fly was thick on the water. I hooked him on an August Black and, if he was not a two-pounder, I am not a fisherman. He was not a brief encounter: I fought him and tamed him and held him in the net. And the moment that haunts me still is the splash of his return to the river, as he slipped through a hole in the mesh, snapping the nylon and swimming free. I watched him as he slid with the current for a few seconds before sinking out of sight. And then I trudged out of the water and sat on the bank; I put my fingers into the hole and stretched them wide to see how big it was. I felt foolish and depressed.

There are one or two similar moments from years ago that I can recall in all the sharpness of the hurt they brought me. But when I look back on the great days it needs the record of my diary to bring back much more than blurred impressions of satisfaction and delight.

My first trout ever came long before I kept a fishing diary; he is no more than a dim gleam on a September evening. I can see no more than this, but I can remember that he was a sacred thing, an object of reverence and worship and that I knew, having caught him, that it was my vocation to catch more.

About ten years ago came the greatest afternoon of my fishing life when, during a huge hatch of blue-wings on the Eden, I caught four trout over two pounds in little more than two hours. It is an afternoon to which I like to return; as I lie on my death-bed I should like to visit it for one last time, for it will help to persuade me that my life has not been entirely wasted. I am revisiting it now because, without searching out its written record, what remains to me from it is almost incidental to its main events. I remember the blue-wings, great drifting masses of them beneath a cloudy sky. I remember the swifts, the swallows and the martins swooping among them over the amber shine of the falling water; I remember the damp air and the hanging grass and I know that I caught four great trout, with one or two lesser but worthy trout in between them, but I cannot see a single one of them.

What I remember most deeply is that, after three of them were caught, I paused in my fishing to let the dogs out of the Land Rover, and I can still follow Merlin and Digby as they run to and fro, exploring the edges of the old bridleway to Soulby, pushing and sniffing through brambles and through thorns to investigate the excitement of the rabbit holes beneath them; I remember the wild roses in the hedge, the sweet cicely all down the verge; I remember the red earth beneath my feet and how Merlin wreathed himself with an unofficial garland of cleavers and white parsley.

All this I remember but what I remember most of all is a feeling of unqualified gratitude for the profuse and untidy beauty of a damp afternoon in high summer, accompanied by a sense of profound thankfulness, welling up from deep inside me, to the river which I had left for a short time and to which I should soon return. And I do, after all, remember those four fish: I remember the shape and the gleam of them on the front seat of the Land Rover, where I laid them so that I could feel their presence and glance at them as I drove home to Sedbergh and dinner with friends.

Sitting by the fire I compared these surviving impressions of fishing days with the sharply graven images of instants from my shooting

life. I also poured myself another glass of wine and threw a log or two
on the fire. Then I left the wine and took the dogs out, so that I could
settle down for half an hour to think deep thoughts and reach profound
conclusions. Back in my chair I decided first of all that burgundy was
incomparable, the subtle and silky beauty of it, the infinite suggestive-
ness on the nose and the palate.

You will have guessed that I was in one of my more pretentious frames of mind. Someone, by the way, some wine-expert once
pronounced that good burgundy smells of excrement. He was wrong
but I know what he means; there is always a whiff of decomposing
matter in the smell of mature burgundy, but it is closer to the mould-
ering and wholesome smell of autumn leaves than to the stench of shit,
for somehow the smell of decay has become a heavenly fragrance with
lingering memories of the earth from which it came.

I may, at this point in my reflections, have begun to wonder if I
could make money as a wine-writer, contributing articles to *Decanter*
and the weekend supplements as well as to *Trout and Salmon* and *Shooting
Times*. I may even have toyed with the idea of a regular series, called
something like 'Reflections in a Glass', which would find me sitting by
the fire, or sitting outside on a summer evening, with half a bottle at
hand and some of it already in a glass; I should set the scene, telling my

readers whether I had been fishing or shooting during the day and how
the day's events had influenced my choice of wine; and then I should
describe my evolving response to the half bottle and it would almost
certainly be full of nonsense and not worth reading. I decided to stick
with fishing and shooting, which allow me plenty of opportunities to
bang on about wine, and at last I managed to steer myself back to
memories of shooting and fishing days.

Between sniffs and swallows of burgundy it now became clear
to me that the difference between my fishing and shooting memories
reflected a fundamental difference between the two sports. Shooting
is a succession of almost unrelated moments: each bird is a different
drama and success in shooting is a split-second up there in the sky.
Notable successes stamp themselves very sharply on the memory:
lonely, unconnected images that survive our general memories of the
day to which they belonged. Catching a trout, as opposed to shooting
a pheasant, is a process rather than a single act: you have to rise him
and hook him; you have to play him out and bring him to the net and
lift him from the river; and this process produces memories with less
focus upon a fleeting moment of fulfilment, less clarity of definition,
but more power to bring up from the past the mood of a whole day,
that sense of benediction that rises from the currents of a river, filling
with gratitude the hearts of the fishers who have managed to catch a
few of the river's trout.

Fishing memories are also more deeply connected with the
landscape that helped to produce them, with the lichened trunks of
the trees around the margins of a pool, with a clump of blue harebells
shining out from a crevice in the white rocks, with the September
glow of the hawthorns all along the banks. There are, of course, similar
visions in my shooting memories, but they are less essentially a part of
the experience that produced them; fishing is somehow more bound
in with the beauty that surrounds it. In our recollections of shooting
days, moreover, there is nothing as subtle, as soothing and as pervasive
as the sound of running water. Fishing is a gentler sport than shooting:
its climaxes are less sudden and less savage; its sounds are softer and it
makes softer and gentler memories. You know that I think fishing is a

more intricate and more beautiful sport than shooting. I think a fishing rod is an instrument of connection in a way that a gun can never be; I also think that the memories growing from it are more beautiful and, for all their impressionism, more powerful than the isolated images of a shooting day.

There was still a whole glass of burgundy left, smelling of earth and black cherries rather than of animal waste. I decided to treat it with reverential slowness, at the same time trying to recapture my most precious fishing memory, which must be there somewhere and which I knew was not the afternoon of the four two-pounders, because on either side of it there were much darker memories of a father's and then a mother's death.

There was the day of my first big catch at Kilnsey, a late September day on the edge of my return to university in London; it was the last fishing day of the season. It was a day when the blue-wings came in numberless droves; the day when, having never before managed to catch more than a brace of fish in the course of a day's sport, I went home with seven dead trout; undoubtedly it was a great and a happy day, but it now seemed to me that there had been something of frenzy about it, both in the wild wind with which it ended and in my frantic dash from pool to pool as I revelled in the hatching blue-wings and the rising trout and the excitement of fishing a long stretch of the Wharfe that I had never fished before.

There was a Sunday in August, again at Kilnsey, when the upstream wet had for the first time caught me an indisputable bagful of trout, but all day the cloud had sagged low and the water had been thick; it had been a day of triumph, a day of fulfilment but it was not the day for which I was looking. When I found the day I knew at once that it was the right day, but, although quite certain about this, I recognised its pre-eminent status with something almost of surprise.

It was a September day more than twenty years ago, the first day of a week's fishing on the Wharfe before the beginning of another school term. I could remember the slide and the shine of the river, which was full and falling from recent rain; it was a clearing water and the bedrock shone through its bitter-beer glow to create fluid seams and patterns of brighter shine. Above the water, impressions of yellowing leaves hung in my memory beneath a grey and white sky; there was a deeper impression of windless calm with the damp air suddenly full of the feel and the smells of autumn.

I knew that I had caught fish from the beginning to the end of the day, but that was all I knew about them, except that they made me happy and that ten of them were in my bag when I finally called it a day. I could not remember a single trout and I refused to go to my diaries to search them out. I could remember my beat, which was Black Keld to the Stepping Stones, and I could remember sitting under the sycamore on the edge of Knipe Dub at the end of my fishing, possessed by the quietness of everything round me and by a feeling of deep and unquestioning contentment. I can remember trudging up the steep bank from the river to the road and looking back down the line of the Wharfe with a feeling of profound thankfulness for the series of accidents that had brought me to Kilnsey; and I can remember sitting in the bar of *The Falcon* before dinner, drinking gin and tonic – I knew no better all those years ago – savouring the crude taste of the spirit while, on the chest in the hallway, ten trout were lying on a broad platter, lying there and gleaming softly through the quiet evening air.

In these impressions of a distant fishing day all the excitement and the mounting elation that had certainly been there, as fish followed fish – there were many more than ten of them – had now disappeared beyond recall. There were no surviving pictures of tense struggles between a fisher and his trout; I rather thought that at some stage in the day I had hooked and lost an enormous trout but there were no memories of savage regret. All that remained was yellow leaves and flowing water and a sense of gratitude very close to worship; it was all that mattered. It had not been a day that had marked a new beginning or an end; it had possessed no significance beyond itself and most of it had been lost to the memory. But what survived told me that it was beyond doubt the day when, without any internal voice of qualification or dissent, I had believed what the river and its fish and the surrounding landscape were all telling me about the glory of creation and its power to bring peace. And there was nothing rapt or mystical in this apprehension of the nature of things. It was as matter-as-fact, and as wonderful, as flowing water and it made me deeply and quietly and unreservedly happy.

The burgundy was almost gone, but the memories it had unlocked also seemed to have revealed an important difference between our experience as fishers and shooters, particularly in our response to success. I wanted to follow this train of thought for a time and wondered whether a glass of whisky would help its development. You are lucky that I decided against it or this chapter, which is now nearly over, might still have pages and pages to run. Anyway the ascetic in me said no to a glass of Glenmorangie and half an inch of wine in the bottom of a glass only gave me time for about another ten minutes' reflection.

During this ten minutes I compared shooting and fishing memories, deciding that I most definitely preferred the fishing sort. I liked their blurred edges and the moods drifting through them like smells that bring strong and sudden associations. And it seemed to me that they preserved precious states of mind, calm and contemplative states of mind that had brought insights of lasting beauty and important truth; whereas my shooting memories were no more than records of performance, snap-shots of great moments in my career as a shooting man. It seemed to me, by comparison, that those memories of notable fishing days had no pride in them at all and were full above all of gratitude to the Eden or the Wharfe, or whichever river it was, for being kind enough to give me a few of their trout.

But those high pheasants falling through the sky were images of self-congratulation; they were icons of pride. We lose ourselves in fishing in a way that never happens while we are holding a gun in our hands: when fishing we are absorbed into things beyond us; out shooting we are too often preoccupied with ourselves. When I shoot well I feel pleased with myself; I feel other things as well and among these feelings are a sense of wonder in the beauty of the landscape from which birds flush and of the air through which they fly, but always in my response to a day when I have shot well, and in the memories that come from it, always at the core of it there is the pleasure of self-satisfaction.

When I catch loads of trout it is different; then my heart goes out to the water from which they have come; I may feel pleased with a neat cast or a well-timed strike or well-chosen fly, but always I praise the river much more than I praise myself.

I put the glass to my lips and swallowed the last drops. The thought of the whisky bottle tempted me once more but, in an admirable spirit of self-denial, I put the thought behind me and went to bed, where I lay awake for a while, wondering whether my mental ramblings over half a bottle of burgundy had been the purest drivel: the intellectual equivalent of what some say the smell of burgundy brings to the nose. I was still, of course, under the influence of burgundy and it may have been this influence that took a broadly favourable view of the ramblings; their conclusions had probably been overstated but there was something in them and there was something in fishing that made it a more complete, a more enriching and self-effacing activity than shooting can ever be. Reaching this conclusion in no way lessened the thankfulness I felt for my first main day at High Park and the gentle autumn sunshine that had filled it. I was not longing for winter to come and go so that spring could return me to my rivers.

The time for shooting had come round again and I was happy that the next few months would be full of it and full of the beauty that belongs to it. I suddenly realised that fishing is sometimes very boring, whereas shooting is almost always full of hope and expectation. Then I thought of the calm and contented weariness that often comes over me at the end of a rough-shooting afternoon when, with a spaniel beside me, I trudge back to the Land Rover through the thickening November shadows; I thought of the peace that enfolds me as I sit by some still water waiting for the mallard to come; and then I drifted into sleep through visions of flying and falling pheasants and, just before sleep claimed me, I think I decided that the next evening would find me by Low Park pond.

Chapter Thirteen

November at Last

I like November and this chapter is in praise of it. I like it because it brings the start of serious pheasant shooting, which is something to which I start looking forward as soon as my poults arrive at the beginning of August. Pheasants, of course, are legal quarry a whole month earlier than November and this year, as in most other years, by the time that November finally arrived, I had already shot a few birds out on the edges of my rented land. The last chapter dealt in part with the season's first day of the sort that is my rough and ready version of organised shooting, but all October sport with pheasants is a sort of prelude: it is in November that the real action begins and it is this, of course, that recommends the month to shooting men.

People with no interest in pheasants groan about the darkness and the damp and the cold and the thought of the whole winter stretching gloomily ahead of them, but you and I hear the clatter of wings and see pheasants springing from the gorse, or flying down the wind, or rising over the trees, we see spaniels hunting their hearts out and caked with mud at the end of the day. With the mind's eye we see all this and we thank God that the time has properly come to start seeing it all again in the reality of feather and flesh.

I like November for the sport it brings. I also like November for its own sake, although this year I had to wait for half the month until it stopped pretending to be something else; for it began, not in dank greyness, not with wind and wetness or with leaf-stripping frost but with days of serene and glowing stillness, with quiet, warm days of soft air and shining blue skies. They were very beautiful days. They lay over the earth like a blessing, they shone in the last glory of the leaves and they showed off the strutting splendour of cock pheasants in all its burnished magnificence. In their own way they were wonderful days but they were not real November days, they were leftovers from autumn at a time when I wanted the season to be getting on with it. The unbroken succession of them seemed abnormal and they seemed like some sort of warning; they were a very beautiful warning and I enjoyed them, but I kept having to remind myself that it was November.

The change came after almost a fortnight, with three or four days of wind and rain, plenty of wind and not very much rain, but enough of both to do their job and leave branches bare. Suddenly it was winter and I was out at High Park on a real November afternoon: an afternoon of spotting drizzle and sagging clouds, with the damp earth deep in fallen leaves, with brown light in the woods and with the air moist and smelling of decay. I was not there with a gun. I was there with a bucket in my hand and a sack of grain over my shoulder, trudging from hopper to hopper and sitting down to smoke in between most of the trudges. There were scuttling pheasants all over the place, although quite a few of them were ready to stop scuttling and get on the wing, weaving their way through the stripped branches and then setting off through the sky as though they meant business.

I like November days for their own sake; I like the dampness of them and that sense of richness rotting down into the earth to make another spring. Put pheasants into them and, whether I am trying to shoot them or pottering round attending to their needs, I enjoy them almost as much as anything that the year brings, for the sight of November pheasants always reminds me that their time has arrived at last and that, brief though their season is, there is lots of it, and all the best of it, still to come.

Another reason for liking November is that it brings me the annual ritual of my boundary day, which does not take place on the boundaries of my shoot and must not be confused with October outside afternoons which (rather confusingly) do. There is a bit of history to all this and perhaps I should unravel it before proceeding to an account of this year's boundary day.

When I first started shooting at High Park, almost twenty years ago, it was a shoot of about seventy acres. There was my own land and there were one or two bordering fields where I had permission to walk with a gun. Now you will probably understand that it is difficult to have a boundary day on a shoot of seventy acres; you will find, if you try it, that your boundaries are more or less in the middle of things. In spite of this obvious drawback, there were several successive seasons when I was determined to give it a go; once October arrived it was never much more than a week or ten days before I put on a shabby pair of breeches, drove out to High Park and then, accompanied either by old Merlin or by bad Digby, set off rather solemnly round the margins of my seventy acres, telling myself that this was my boundary day.

The sun was always shining because, with only myself and one of the dogs to organise, it was possible to fix the date of my boundary day on the morning of the day itself. There was a ritual drinking of sloe gin before sport began, a ritual marking the fact that the season to which sloe gin belongs had come round again. Then I would shoot three or four pheasants, feel unusually pleased with life and drive home. My boundary day rarely lasted much longer than a couple of hours.

Suddenly it was winter: leaving The Hag

The Stackhole with Ross

After a few years I realised that, however enjoyable it might be, my boundary day was far too early and a foolish thing anyway; I realised that I had been carried away by the freedom of having my own shoot, which meant that I could go shooting whenever and as often as I chose. It is a marvellous freedom but it needs to be exercised with restraint and this was what I acknowledged after those few years, realising that I was shooting birds of the year before they were properly ready for the gun, realising at the same time that I was disturbing my pheasants on ground where, in early October, they should be spending their days eating and drinking and pottering round the place in perfect peace. My boundary day was abandoned and my pheasants were not asked to fly for their lives until October was almost gone.

Things changed again when I began to rent the shooting on about eighty acres of land just to the south of my own ground. The boundary day was reinstated, but it was now early in November, a week or so after my first shoot at the end of October. It was in fact a boundary afternoon; it was restricted to these eighty acres and, as well as being intended to provide some enjoyable sport and a bag of perhaps half a dozen birds, it was designed to send my pheasants, which have always been inclined to acknowledge the pull of the south, back to the little valley where they belong.

In recent years my rented land has grown and now covers more than three hundred acres, all of it south of High Park. A narrow road, winding its way up into the Pennines, rather neatly separates the eighty acres next to High Park from the later and more extensive addition to the shoot, which is where you are likely to find me on one or two Saturday afternoons in October. This new ground is full of gorse-covered ditches and gorse-covered banks and thick beds of rushes. Not many birds of the year get there until they have been disturbed a time or two elsewhere and in a good year for rabbits the gorse and the rushes are full of them. What all this adds up to is almost the perfect place for October shooting. The pheasants there are mainly old birds and, if they are few or have all run off on their wise old legs before a spaniel gets anywhere near them, there will usually be rabbits enough for sport, and it will be testing sport on such steep and folded land.

There you have the history of my boundary shoot: how it began and ended and then, moving both its time and its place, began all over again; how it has kept its name though it no longer happens on my boundaries and how it is now preceded by one or two outside after-noons, which do take place on or somewhere near my southern bound-aries, over that narrow and winding road which climbs up into the bare hills above Brough.

I am meant to be writing about November and my boundary day. I shall come to it before long, but mention of outside afternoons has persuaded me to go back in time and describe the first of them, which belonged to a Saturday in mid-October and found me, at about one o'clock in the afternoon, walking up that steep Pennine road with a gun over my shoulder and with Ross at heel, obediently at heel but very impatient for sharp gorse and soggy rushes and all the thrilling smells that he was longing to find there. There was drizzle on the wind but already there was blue on the edges of the sky and it was much better than it had been twenty minutes earlier, with me sitting in the Land Rover and drinking a measure of sloe gin, drinking it in a moody sort of way while a savage onslaught of hail battered the roof above me and lashed the windscreen so furiously that it no longer provided much of a view. The storm had come suddenly after a morning with broken cloud and a lively breeze, a morning that had convinced me as I sat in a class-room, feeling almost as impatient as a springer spaniel at his master's heel, that it was definitely the day for my first outside afternoon.

It had seemed, as I was sitting there in the Land Rover, that I might have to wait another week, but the storm passed in about ten minutes and I decided to get moving. I had soon set off up the road, feeling more cheerful with each step, and by the time I climbed the gate into the first of my southern fields, I was strangely confident that the weather would be kind to me and that the afternoon might even end in sunshine. I was not looking for much in terms of edible results (one of the pleasures of an outside afternoon is that satisfaction comes easily); a rabbit or two would do very nicely and a single pheasant would do fine. I was in search of spectacle as much as food and, as far as spectacle was concerned, I should be happy with a few rabbits bouncing over the rough ground and a single cock pheasant: just one cock pheasant clattering out of the gorse, lifting himself indignantly into the October sky and then falling to my shot. I should be happy with a runner, because then I should get Ross onto his trail and he would hunt him down and bring him back to me, filling me with pride in my spaniel – not that I should have much reason for pride – but filling me, anyway, with deep pleasure that pheasant time was here again and only just beginning.

Almost as soon as I was through the gate, and before Ross was given permission to plunge into cover, I heard a cock shouting from somewhere in the field. He stirred my hunter's blood and every second, as Ross tore through the gorse, I was expecting the sound of his wings and then the sight of him; but it did not happen. No pheasant rose into the sky, although I missed a very sharp chance at a rabbit, and another at the top of the big forty-acre over the wall.

I tend to hit rabbits or miss them, which is a statement of the obvious. We all hit them or miss them; what I should have said is that some days I very rarely miss them and other days I am virtually incapable of killing, or even wounding, a single one of them. Those two shots without a rabbit in the bag were thus a bad omen for the rest

of the afternoon; it looked as though
it would be pheasants or nothing.

The hunting, anyway, was
now unexpectedly interrupted by a
few minutes' gathering, for the grass
between the rushes was dotted with
the shapes of late mushrooms, most
of them looking white and fresh
enough to convince me that they
would be delicious additions to the
evening's rabbit stew (cooked the day
before). When the hunting started
again, now under a sky that was
more blue than grey, three rabbits
had soon bolted from cover and
joined my mushrooms in the game
bag. Those two missed chances had
been, for once, a false sign of things
to come.

One of the pleasures of rabbiting is the variety of shots that it
brings. The first of my three had been an easy target, running straight
away from me over level and open ground. I should have cursed myself
if he had not dropped dead. The second was a much greater satisfaction.
He was obviously a rabbit in training, for he showed an impressive turn
of speed; he was a quick and crossing rabbit, racing down a steep slope
of the field. He was already at least twenty yards away when I pulled
the trigger and, running no longer, he tumbled down the slope and lay
still against the trunk of a hawthorn, with clusters of dark red berries
hanging from the branches above him. Number three was a fleeting
chance between a tangle of gorse and a bed of rushes. I was not sure
that I had hit him, but I sent Ross to investigate and back he came with
a dead rabbit between his jaws.

Often I wish that I did not smoke. About a year ago I gave up
for a whole morning, but then I went fishing in the afternoon and lit
my pipe every time that I caught a trout and needed to sit down for a

minute in grateful contemplation. You have already read how, in May this year, I gave up again for an afternoon, although this was only because I had no choice; I started again just as soon as I could. There were now three rabbits in my bag and it was heavy. I had been walking up and down steep fields for something like an hour, and walking with a gun – even without the weight of three rabbits on your shoulder – is for some reason that I do not properly understand much more strenuous than plain walking.

A rest was therefore necessary and a pipe of tobacco was essential. The occasion somehow called for mouthfuls of smoke, half-inhaled and then blown out onto the autumn air as I sat on top of a rise of the ground and felt contented. The sun had come out and the whole valley below me lay in golden October light. There was still the hope of the season's first pheasant and I felt almost certain that there would be a bird or two hiding in the banks of gorse all along the bottom of the field. I felt completely certain that I was already satisfied with my first outside afternoon and that it would not much matter if I did not fire another shot; it might even be better if I had to wait another week for the season's first sight of a cock pheasant rising angrily into the sky.

With thoughts such as these I re-shouldered the burden of my bag and sent Ross back to work. No bird came from the gorse along the field-edge; three or four rabbits bolted out and then back into cover without the chance of a shot. I smoked again, paunched my rabbits and almost, but not completely, abandoned my hopes of the autumn's first pheasant. There was not too much disappointment in this. I had enjoyed the unexpected crop of mushrooms; I had enjoyed the rabbits even more and I had delighted in the possibility of a pheasant wherever I had gone.

And that, after all, was really the point of my outside afternoon: an afternoon at the beginning of the season celebrating the fact that pheasant time had come round again and would begin in earnest within a few weeks. It scarcely mattered that I had still to lift my gun at the season's first bird; what mattered was that the hope was real once more and would be there, on all sorts of days and in all sorts of weather, for almost four months.

There was one field left to me and it showed no sign of a pheasant. I wandered back down the road, with Ross now happy to walk slowly at heel. I went to feed Low Park Pond, where the litter of feathers all along the edges of the water told me that it would soon be time for the autumn's first flight. Then I drove home with my rabbits and my mushrooms and a dirty spaniel. Even without a pheasant I most certainly drove home a happy man. The mushrooms, only slightly bruised from their time in the game bag, were briefly fried in olive oil and then went into the stew; undoubtedly their hour simmering among the meat and the juices made it a better stew than it would have been without them.

Between this outside afternoon and the boundary day I did shoot the first pheasants of the season. In the last chapter you read something of my first High Park day; there was also the first of my syndicate days near Settle, which was a good day and I shall tell you nothing more. They were both good days, though on both of them it seemed strange to be out after pheasants beneath skies so blue and in air so warm that late October felt more like June.

By the time my boundary day came along it was half way through November and it no longer felt like June; it felt like November and, as always, I myself felt the special sense of release that comes to me when I set off shooting after spending the morning in a classroom. I had, as it happened, enjoyed the morning, though part of the pleasure had been knowing that, within an hour or two, it would turn into something completely different. At noon I was pulling on a pair of breeches in the flat. Five minutes later I was putting Ross in the back of the Land Rover, together with gun and game bag and a flask of tea and a sandwich. Then there was a dash back to the flat to grab a dog-whistle and a box of cartridges; and then it was time to go.

One advantage of shooting over fishing, by the way, is that there is much less to forget; and there is also much less to lose in the course of a day's sport. You need a dog, a gun and some cartridges to put in it. There are lots of other things that are likely to prove useful or enjoyable, such as dog-whistles and sandwiches and flasks filled with tea or coffee or with sloe gin, but you can cope perfectly well with the three items first mentioned. It is difficult to forget them and, if you do manage to set off without the cartridge-bag that you put out the night before, you will almost certainly find a box or two hiding somewhere in the back of the Land Rover.

I have gone fishing without a rod; I have gone fishing with a rod and come back without one; I have gone fishing without a reel; I have gone fishing without waders; I have set off with a landing net and returned netless; I do not think I have ever gone fishing without any flies, but over the years I have lost at least four boxes full of them, sitting down to change a pattern and then getting up and leaving my box somewhere on the bank. Two or three times every season I find, after deciding to take off a fly and tie on a different one, that the box with the pattern I want is no longer in its pocket, that it has not been carelessly shoved in a pocket where it does not belong, that it is not in my creel or my bag or anywhere at all where I can put my hand on it. It is always a dreadful moment, and always it is followed by a desperate search as I head off to revisit every place where I can remember sitting down to change flies.

Finding the precise spot is usually difficult; one rock often looks much like another; rocks are a feature of rivers and riverbanks and often there are twenty or thirty very similar rocks within a few yards of each other. And you might not have sat on a rock. Perhaps you sat on the bank, in which case the search will be no easier; it is not always a simple matter to recall on which bit of a grassy bank you decided to park yourself; and fly-boxes, especially on cloudy days, are able to merge with their surroundings, or they can slip cunningly out of sight. Usually the search results in a glorious moment of recognition and a joyful act of repossession, which is always followed by the resolution that, in future, I will never change flies and start fishing again without first making sure that all my fly boxes are where they are meant to be.

Usually the missing box is found but three or four times it has stayed hidden and it has been a sort of bereavement. It is a dreadful thing to acknowledge that all those flies you tied so skilfully, and then so proudly admired, have gone out your life for ever. And, almost inevitably, the flies that have gone will be the flies the trout would have taken if only you could have tied them to your cast. You will

end the day feeling certain that every trout you failed to rise would have weighed two pounds and gone in the creel had you not left your favourite box of flies among the rocks and the moss and the gravel and the tangled grass that spreads itself along riverbanks, with dark holes and crevices everywhere in between, all conspiring to hide from sight whatever a fisherman carelessly abandons somewhere among them.

Shooting, thank God, is less prone to disasters of this sort: dog, gun, cartridges. I have always set off with them and I have always returned with a gun, with a collection of spent and unused cartridges and with a spaniel; although, when Digby was in his prime, there was a time or two when the urge for freedom took such complete possession of him that I thought he would not be joining me in the Land Rover at the end of the day. I have never, by the way, run out of cartridges and had to go begging. In predicting how many cartridges a day is likely to demand I tend towards excess. I have forgotten my sandwiches, which does not matter much because it means that I eat my friends' sandwiches instead. I have forgotten my whistle, which did not matter at all in the Digby-years because he never took any notice of it. Once I forgot my wellingtons, but that did not matter either because I found a pair of leather walking-boots in the back of the Land Rover. I have gone fishing and found, two or three hours from home, that I do not have the means to fish; I have never gone shooting without being able to get on with it. Once or twice my gun has let me down. There was the day when a firing-pin broke off, which meant that I spent the rest of the day missing birds with one barrel because I knew that the second was unavailable. On another occasion some part of the ejecting mechanism disappeared into the grass so that I could not remove the spent cartridge; this happened at flight and I finished immediately rather than wasting the rest of the evening with a half-crippled gun.

There was the time when the metal contraption on the underside of the barrels, the thing into which the fore-end stock fits came suddenly loose and then fell off altogether, sending me to spend the rest of the day among the beaters. I now always take two guns with me to the few formal days that a season brings. My boundary day is not such a day and I took the risk of taking just one gun (the old Webley) and one dog and a single box of cartridges. I cannot remember what led me from the point of this chapter – my boundary day – but I seem without trying very hard to have wandered back to where I was meant to be and now I shall get on with describing it.

It began at one o' clock. There was no ritual drinking of sloe gin because I thought my hip-flask was in the Land Rover and found that it was not. Instead of sloe gin there was a slurp or two of tea, as I sat in the driver's seat and planned my route through the traditional eighty acres, deciding unsurprisingly that it would be the same as always, it would be the traditional route through the traditional ground. There was a quick sandwich and a quick smoke and then I was off, rather pleased that this time my boundary day was for Ross and me alone. Often I have taken a couple of boys along with me but this time the two I might have taken were both busy with games. Sometimes my friend Austin has joined me, but this time his wife had claimed him for a shopping trip, and so this time my boundary day was all my own.

It was a good afternoon for a boundary day, with sunshine and broken cloud and sharp air. There were fieldfares and redwings among the berries, and the few leaves left on the trees were bright. It was a good afternoon for a boundary day because it was beautiful, but I also thought that the sunshine would have brought birds out into the fields and that Ross would flush me a few. I told myself that I should stop at half-a-dozen, although any mallard or woodcock would be regarded as a bonus.

The traditional first manoeuvre of my reinstated boundary after-noon is stalking the flight pond. Sometimes, especially early in the season, mallard rest there during the day. I do not think disturbing duck beneath the sun deters them from evening flight and, although walked-up mallard rarely offer challenging targets, I allow myself the chance of an easy duck or two once or twice a season. This time there were no mallard on the water and I was not much disappointed. There were no mallard, but there were feathers and droppings all along the edges of the pond, telling me that it would be time for a second flight before too long.

Behind the pond, and over the beck, a bank rises steeply about twenty yards. On it stand two or three mature Scots Pines and a few larches, lifting themselves out of a tangle of briars and brambles and blackthorns. Right at the top of the bank there are two or three patches of gorse. Pheasants always roost in the trees and sometimes they lurk in the scrub. It is really a place for at least two guns. It needs one man and his dog on top of the bank to push birds over another man and his gun down by the pond. But it can work with only half this team; you can put a dog in from the bottom and sometimes he will flush a pheasant back over you as you stand waiting on the edge of the water. I stood there waiting while Ross went hunting. Very soon there was the sound of wings, but the pheasant they belonged to took a prudent departure, flying from the top of the bank away from Low Park Pond and over the road.

And so, for me, it was over the fence into the marshy pasture beyond, which is a very marshy pasture indeed. Even in the middle of a dry summer there is standing water in the marshiest bits and once the autumn rains have done their work, you pick your way carefully between oily pools of water and it is very easy to get a bootful. I should feed it and make it an additional attraction for the duck that flight into the pond; one of these seasons I shall but it will not be this one. Anyway, as I was squelching through the less marshy bits of the marshy pasture, a snipe rose ahead of me, climbed very steeply with a screech or two and was soon a distant, shining speck. The gun was never raised, for I seldom bother with snipe these days. They offer wonderful sport; they taste every bit as good as woodcock (which means that they taste as good as any meat known to man), but you need half a dozen of them to make a meal, and I very rarely see more than a couple in the course of a day or an afternoon at High Park. It is true, I suppose, that I could store them in the deep freeze (which is what I do with woodcock), but I cannot be bothered and so, since snipe are fairly infrequent visitors to the boggier bits of my shoot, I usually suppress predatory thoughts and enjoy the sight of them. Just to be inconsistent, there are times when I surrender to the impulse to have a go; it is an impulse that usually results in a miss.

The snipe flew on. A few seconds later the cock pheasant did not; he rose from a patch of short rushes where you would not have thought that a cock pheasant could squat without being seen; he rose with the typical clatter and commotion of his kind. I waited until he had risen into the sunlight and was flying over the trees along the line of the hedge, and then I pulled the trigger. Ross brought him in to me and I put him in the bag; he was a bird of the year but he was well-grown and well-fleshed.

The traditional route of my boundary day now crosses a stile and takes me over ground reserved for my main days, along the top of my meadow where traditionally I admire the light in the larches on Beck Bank, while resisting the traditional temptation to put my spaniel over the beck with orders to get to work among the pheasants that will certainly be hiding there. Then I go through the meadow-gate, cross the beck and climb Pheasant Hill, go over the stile above the old pen, telling myself, as it wobbles beneath my weight in the traditional fashion, that I must knock in the posts more firmly, telling myself at the same time that I should also wire the plank to make it less slippery and treacherous. My spaniel does not have to face the traditional hazards of the stile, he watches nervously until I am safely over and then joins me through a gap in the bottom of the fence. We are both now on the ground where my boundary day properly belongs.

It was fine and sunny up there on this season's boundary day and there was time for a rest and a smoke. All the ground that I was about to work is also the afternoon ground of my three or four main days, so it may seem to you that it is foolish to disturb it in-between them. You have probably got a point, but you should remember that it only happens once and, more importantly, you should acknowledge that most of the pheasants found there on my main days have been put there, from Beck Bank and the Rise and the Strips and the south side of the wood, by the morning's sport; most of the birds, moreover, that I flush on my boundary afternoon fly straight back to my own land, so that I can tell myself that I am doing more good than harm. The boundary day is a splendid institution.

One of the delights of working a properly trained spaniel is that, just before you send him into cover, you can keep him sitting for a few

Snipey terrain on The Hag

seconds as you make sure that you are ready; you can keep him sitting and feel the tension of his gaze, the tension of his whole being in those eyes fixed on you unshiftingly and longing for the sign that will unleash the quivering tautness of his frame into the rapture of the hunt. There is, I suppose, something of the pleasure of power in this, but there is also something of beauty in the stillness of it all and in its frozen strength. It is like those Greek sculptures that somehow manage to capture latent energy in motionless stone.

The gorse above the Old Pen tapers to the east, running parallel with the fence that divides my own from my rented ground. It is a long thin wedge of gorse and its eastern extremity is no more than a few bushes straggling along a natural furrow of the land. It was on the edge of this long finger of woody gorse that Ross sat for a few seconds, with his head raised and turned towards me, with unmoving black eyes. Then the signal was given and the gorse began to shake.

Almost immediately a hen flushed low and flew over the fence back into the wood. Even a few years ago I should have lifted the gun and pulled the trigger, but now I have almost trained myself to leave low birds, especially on my boundary day and especially when they are heading back home. Ground-hugging birds, by the way, are not necessarily simple birds for the rough-shooter. It is very easy to shoot over the top of them; they are unsporting birds because they are unbeautiful and it seems to me at any rate that what divides the sporting from the unsporting shot is very largely a matter of aesthetics. I left that hen, but only a few seconds later Ross put up another, which rose almost vertically into the light. My gun followed her because she seemed a challenge as she rose and she was undoubtedly beautiful with the sunshine in her feathers; there was something of beauty too in her steep fall through the bright air. That first hen, if I had shot and killed her, would just have flopped onto the ground; the second was a satisfying but not, to be honest, a difficult shot.

From the wide end of the gorse, two or three cocks flushed with a clatter of wings on the far side of me. They offered no chance of a shot, but from one of the two patches of gorse on top of the sloping field another cock emerged and crossed to my right, long-tailed and accelerating on the wind. It was the second barrel that killed him and he fell with a splash onto a patch of wet ground.

I am not very good with names. There is a Gully and Gutter on my land and sometimes I get confused about which is which. There are the Patches (we are there at the moment) and there are the Strips on the other side of the valley. These are not resonant names. Already we have walked through the Marshy Pasture; shortly we shall be going to the Rushy Pasture and I shall not blame you if you get mixed up. Frequently I have to remind myself that the Marshy Pasture is down in the valley next to the flight pond, whereas the Rushy Pasture is up on the breezy heights of my shoot and that the top of the Gully runs into it.

I have stood at pegs on other men's shoots and hit or missed pheasants on drives with memorable and distinctive names. I remember a shoot near Wooller where there was a Jubilee Wood and a Coronation Planting. I remember a small stand of larches not far from Penrith, on a steep knoll and how the pheasants that came from it were high and fast: it was its owner's favourite drive and it was called 'Little Gem.' And once I waited for birds, with a river behind me and a line of jagged rocks in front, at a drive called 'Hell's Teeth.' The names I have given to my own bits of cover are feeble compared with these and it must be that, at least in the naming of things, I am short of imagination. I have never managed to come up with a title for any of my books; someone else has always had to do it for me.

It was the Rushy Pasture that inspired this little digression, unless perhaps it was the Patches; it was to the Rushy Pasture, anyway, that I went next, a field that rises gradually as it runs due south from my own land. It is about fifty yards wide with a stone wall on the higher eastern side and a fence along its western margin, where a few hollies and hawthorns and the remains of a ditch mark the line of an old hedge. Parts of the Rushy Pasture are almost as wet as the Marshy Pasture; it is undoubtedly much rushier and the thickest and driest of these rushes grow near the wall, which is also where pheasants love to lurk, and you never know which way they will flush.

There are places where the direction that a pheasant will take is predictable; even these places spring surprises but every bird from the Rushy Pasture is a surprise. It may jump over the wall; it may fly either way down its line; it may cross to either side or fly straight back over your head; and it might rise swiftly into the sky or skim the top of the rushes. The wind will channel them if it is strong enough, although even in a strong blow the occasional pheasant will perversely head off into it; the wind may carry them and lift them and turn an ordinarily respectable rough-shooter's bird into a pheasant of which the most selective driven shot would be proud. The wind on my boundary day was no more than a breeze; pheasants would do with it whatever they chose, which is why I approached the thickest spread of rushes near the wall with all the expectation that comes from short cover on open ground. There might, of course, be no birds in it at all, in which case I should go looking for them somewhere else.

Ross was very eager. Four or five times he seemed on the point of a flush; the snout went down, and pushed, and then he froze as though in surprise that there was nothing on the wing, that there was no shot to tell him that he might soon be searching for a bird. Then he turned and came back down the wall and I sensed that a pheasant would soon be in the air. It was a hen bird and she crossed towards the fence. She crossed and she rose and she fell to the first shot. She fell like a stone but she ran as soon as she came down; it took two or three minutes to find her in the ditch back on the northern edge of the field. Three or four birds flushed during the search. I had unloaded my gun in case temptation should prove irresistible, for you should never shoot while looking for a runner. You should not shoot again until the runner is found or until the search has at last been abandoned.

My runner had one broken wing. It is good to kill birds dead, but especially when shooting over a dog you will inevitably wound a proportion of them. It is good to kill birds but the relief and pleasure of finding a runner is very great indeed. The hen was the fourth bird to go into the bag and I would allow myself only two more. Now, the Gully runs up into the Rushy Pasture and just half way along the field there is a deep ditch, a natural ditch with steep sides and a trickle of water running through it in all but the driest times of the year. The upper half is almost bare, but below it the gorse is thick on both sides.

This is the top of the Gully, above the fence and the beeches that stand along this fence; over the ditch there are more rushes and there is more gorse, a thick square of it that very often holds birds. On this boundary afternoon there were four or five and I did not see a single one of them till it was on the limits of range. I heard the snorting of a spaniel and the sound of wings, and then each time I saw a pheasant flying down the Gully and heading back towards my valley. They flew over places where guns would have been if this had not been a solitary boundary afternoon, and they would have been proud guns if they had brought them down, curling and climbing as they flew. All I could do was to watch them and admire the beauty of their flight.

It was time for a rest now. Time to get the weight of four pheasants off my shoulder, time to get out the flask (of tea) and get out the pipe (after getting over the fence). And what, in the name of English, is wrong with getting over things and getting them out and getting them off your shoulder? I could have slid the strap of my bag from my aching shoulder, after leaping or perhaps even negotiating the fence; I could have extracted the flask from my game bag before pulling the pipe from my pocket, and all this might have pleased a third-rate teacher of English. I did it more plainly and then I sat with my back to the fence, with four pheasants lying in the grass beside me, smoking and drinking and looking at the view.

It is a fine view on a sunny afternoon in November towards the end of your boundary day; further south you can see the rough ground over the road where you may go next Saturday afternoon; up on your right you can see the spiky tops of those two patches of gorse where you shot a cock forty minutes ago. Beneath them the land falls quickly and then rises to a wall on the left; ahead of you it drops steeply, for you are sitting on the upper rim of a rough half-bowl of a field, and running down it is the long line of the Gully, full of gorse and brambles and the hope of pheasants. Beyond the Gully, two flat fields away, you can see the Scots pines and the larches where your boundary afternoon began, and you can just catch the gleam of water from the flight pond next to them. It is a fine view and it is improved by the shadows of the folded land, by the presence of a dirty spaniel sitting panting at your side and by the sight of four dead pheasants, two cocks and two hens, lying in the grass with their eyes closed and their feathers stirring very faintly in the breeze. It is a traditional view, enjoyed on most days when I am out shooting alone, but especially on my boundary afternoon. On this occasion it was as enjoyable as it has ever been and it lasted for about ten minutes.

I have to admit that it almost a waste to shoot the Gully by yourself. It is a place to put two or three friends down its line; you put them there even before you work the Rushy Pasture with another friend and two dogs; you tell them to be ready and to enjoy the wait. Now those birds from the Rushy Pasture may go anywhere (which is why, in spite of your waiting friends, you take your gun); if they go the right way they will be high and curling when your friends have a go at them. The birds from the rushes are unpredictable, but those from the gorse in the Rushy Pasture usually fly over the beeches and straight down the Gully or out over its northern rim; they often rise steeply; they have time to get moving and they are sometimes as fine as the view they are flying through. I only shoot the Gully by myself on my boundary afternoon and again in January; it is perhaps my favourite drive and, in the season's prime, I like to share it with my friends.

If you do shoot the Gully by yourself the important thing is to get below your dog, unless you are full of tasteless pomposity and prefer to make certain that you descend the slope in advance of your canine friend. Get beneath your dog on the south side of the gorse, for most birds will fly back towards the pens, unless they fly straight down the Gully before at last curling over the trees at the bottom of the field. In Digby's day there was no hope of staying below him. He set off and I followed and if, for some reason, he turned back the way he had come, then perhaps for as long as a minute I was further down the slope than he was. With Ross it is simple: he comes when I call him; he stops to the whistle and he goes where I tell him to go; with Ross you can work the Gully exactly as you choose.

I walked twenty yards or so down the slope with Ross at heel, then I sent him back above me into the gorse. A rabbit ran from cover, too long for a shot, from the far side; I moved down a yard or two as

Ross began to work his way towards me. And then a commotion in the gorse told me that something was about to flush. Seconds later a cock was in the sky above me. He was not very high but he was fast and dramatic, glowing darkly in the level light of the sun. I pulled the first trigger and there was no fall or stagger; I pulled the second trigger and he flew on, rising down the Gully and then curling as he turned towards High Park and flew higher still before he began to glide.

Ross continued to work as soon as I told him to get on. There were no more pheasants, not even a rabbit, until we had almost done, but right at the bottom of the Gully two hens flushed and rose to fly over the trees along the fence. I waited till the first was just over the branches; when she had been dealt with, the second was a few branches away from where the first had been and she fell as well. Ross was sent for them; they were both brought in and so my boundary day ended with the season's first right-and-left, which may also be the season's last. It was a good way to end, and the end of a day's rough shooting that has

Pausing at The Hag

gone well is almost the best part of it, with its laden trudge though the thickening light of the late afternoon, with a grimy spaniel plodding wearily beside you, with thoughts of when next a similar afternoon will be coming your way and with that feeling of weary contentment that is always deepest and fullest when the shadows fall softly and the evening gives only soft sounds.

I fed the duck pond with bad Digby and then drove home. I hung my birds and had a bath and drank the traditional two glasses of sherry before a whole mallard and a half bottle of claret complemented the quiet sense of celebration that traditionally belongs to the evening of my boundary afternoon. I very rarely drink port, because I think that, when the time for port comes, I have usually drunk enough already and, if you are hovering on the edge of over-indulgence, port is the worst possible drink to take you stumbling over it. If you must have more, have something clean and wholesome, have an inch of Glenmorangie and take your time with it. In spite of these misgivings I relish the taste of good port and there is little harm in the occasional treat. There is no danger that deep draughts of port will turn into a daily feature of my drinking life and, when you have spent the afternoon toiling up and down steep fields with the weight of a few pheasants over your shoulder, filling your lungs (between the pipe smoke) with deep draughts of tonic air, when you have spent the afternoon in this way and have then drunk only two glasses of sherry and half a bottle of wine in the course of a long evening, on such an evening at the end of your boundary afternoon, a glass of port is almost a necessity, which is, I suppose, why it is also a tradition. It was good, not great, port, *Calem* LBV; there was one glass of it as the fire burned low to the accompaniment of warm and comfortable and drowsy thoughts. Then it was to bed, where I listened to the late weather-forecast, decided that I should enjoy hopper-filling in the morning sunshine and just had time to think how much I had enjoyed my boundary afternoon before I fell into a sleep of the soundness that traditionally belongs to its end.

Chapter Fourteen

Hosting the Shoot

It was Monday the 15th December; it was a high and solemn day and, for once, it looked as though the weather was going to recognise the dignity of the occasion. I had been up at six o'clock (two hours later would have been quite early enough). I had been up at six, anyway, peering through the window to make sure there was no rain falling through the darkness. I had got back into bed and drunk half a cup of tea, but it was no good. I was far too restless, far too impatient for the day to begin and, although I had slept several fewer than the recommended eight hours, I knew that I should not feel tired until the evening; and, when at last the evening came, then I should want to feel tired, I should want to sit by the fire, drinking a glass of sherry and looking back over the day, then drinking another glass of sherry before eating a steak with half a bottle of red wine, leaving most of the wine until the food was finished, until the dogs had been out for a brief run and it was time for the rest of my wine and for a last half hour by the fire, with the possibility of a small dram before an early night and a deep sleep.

I always feel restless and nervous on the morning of a High Park main day, which should, of course, be called something else. Mention of a main day will make you think of pheasants crossing the line in hundreds rather than one or two here and two or three there. My main days are very small days, but they are as big as any of my days get, and the approach of such a day always fills me with anxiety. How men in charge of grand shoots sleep at all during the height of the pheasant season is something of a mystery to me.

In preparation for a day's shooting at High Park I have virtually nothing to do, except to invite four or five guests, make sure that I tell them to turn up on the same day at roughly the same time and then make sure that I turn up myself. My beating team consists of a friend and his dog, with help from me and Ross and from those of the guns who like to work their dogs for some part of the day. There are no pickers-up or stops or flagmen. There is no blanking-in to be done before we meet at ten o'clock. Lunch is under the sky and everyone brings his own.

Apart from the invitations all that I have to organise is myself, making sure that I put my dog, my gun and some cartridges in the Land Rover, together with my sandwiches, a bottle of sloe gin for mid-morning comforts and some whisky for a lunchtime dram. That is about it and still I get out of bed at a quarter past six and gaze mistrustfully into the darkness; I fret about the weather as I shave quickly and carelessly, which means that I usually cut myself and spend at least ten minutes messing about with bits of cotton wool to staunch the flow; then, with my chin de-stubbled but lightly scarred, I turn my attention to the day's clothes: some sort of checked shirt (worn collar permissible and no need for a tie on my own shoot), a pullover (a plain one unadorned with images of pheasants, a few holes here and there perfectly acceptable), my second-best pair of breeches with green stockings beneath them and wellingtons on my feet from the start of the day. While all this is being assembled and while I put myself into it all I will be asking myself what needs to be done before I drive off at half-past nine. The answer is not very much, although I never acknowledge this, and by eight o'clock I will be sitting in my study with two boiled eggs in my belly and with everything ready; I will be drinking a third cup of coffee and wondering whether the Land Rover will manage to make it all the way to High Park.

I am always anxious on the morning of one of my big days; often the fretting begins whole days before the morning itself. While out feeding I decide that the hoppers are much fuller than they ought to be, that pheasants seem fewer than last week, fewer and much jumpier than I have ever seen them before. Then I waste half an hour examining the ground beneath roosting trees and muttering gloomily that all the droppings are at least a fortnight old. The conclusion to be drawn from all this dark evidence is obvious and depressing: that poachers have been in my little valley and helped themselves to most of my birds. It seems almost pointless to bother filling the feeders in the wood, but I do it anyway. My heart leaps up when I find that two of them are half-empty, but then I find the tattered remains of a pheasant's wing, which immediately convinces me that foxes have pounced on the few birds that the poachers had so generously left behind.

Some time later I see two or three birds fully provided with legs and wings, but they are in the air just as soon as they are spotted and over the boundaries of my shoot within seconds; this confirms every suspicion that the afternoon has inspired and makes me certain that I have no more than a handful of birds left, a handful so harried by nocturnal predation of various sorts that they are as wild as hawks and will, on the day of my shoot, be off my ground before we have lined out for the first little drive.

I leave High Park thinking that my guests will be lucky if they pull their triggers at all on what had been advertised to them as a shooting day. Once home the prospects for the weather turn into an obsession that almost always fills me with despair, for the prospects are almost always bad, suggesting that my friends will not only go home from my supposed shoot without having fired a single cartridge between them; they will also go home shivering and soaked to the skin.

It has never turned out as badly as I have feared. We have certainly all gone home wet through, and once we abandoned the first shoot of the season at lunchtime. But there have always been birds; usually there have been more than enough of them – no one comes to High Park with great expectations – and it has only happened once or twice that I have finished one of my main days without feeling profoundly thankful for the sport that has filled it. But it makes no difference: however often things go well I cannot stop fearing the worst.

On the morning of Monday December 15th I was ready to leave by eight o'clock and was sitting at my desk drinking my third (unless it was my fourth) cup of coffee. There was nothing to do but sit there feeling anxious, although the appearance of things suggested that there was little cause for anxiety. It was almost fully light by now and the weather was exactly as it had been the previous day: the ground was hard, the air was cold, the sky was clear and there was no prospect of any change. It is true there was virtually no wind – one from the east is perfection at High Park – but it would still be fine weather for a shooting day, above all because it would be beautiful. It would be the sort of day when we should stamp our feet to begin with and feel grateful for mittens and a thick coat; by lunchtime the sun would have got to work; by then we should have got to work ourselves and we should all be sweating beneath those layers of clothing that the bite of the morning air had told us to pull over our bodies.

A coat or two might come off at lunchtime, for even in December the hedge by the meadow-gate is a warm spot on a sunny day at noon; but, however warm we felt at lunchtime, the chill would be back on the air by three and frost would set in with the darkness. All in all the weather looked good for shooting and I think that, as I sat there drinking coffee and already smoking the day's second pipe, I gave it nine out of ten (a stiff rather than strong easterly would have meant full marks).

There was nothing to fear from the weather and, for once, there seemed no reason to fear a shortage of birds. I had been out feeding the day before and the hoppers had clearly been well used (even in spots where the crows never troubled them). There had been indisputably fresh droppings under all the roosting trees, there had been no obvious signs of predation and there had also been plenty of birds, running from hoppers as I approached them, scuttling into cover ahead of me and sometimes leaping from the rushes as I trudged across one of my fields. Unless poachers, or a whole army of foxes, had struck during the night, there seemed every possibility that the day would, by my modest standards, put plenty of pheasants into the sky.

I did, of course, find something to worry about as I sat smoking and drinking coffee, wondering whether I should leave early and finally deciding not to. I had flighted Low Park Pond on the Friday just gone, on the first evening of the holidays. It had been the third flight of the

Pheasant Hill from across the sike

season and it was intended to be a celebration but I came home from it in a filthy mood and full of shame. For, although I had fired fourteen cartridges, I had not managed to hit a single bird. It was true that on Saturday, on the rough ground over the road, I had shot two woodcock and a cock pheasant with six cartridges, missing two very sharp rabbits that anyone might have missed. But now, with nothing to do but sit and smoke and drink coffee for another half-hour, Friday evening came back to haunt me with visions of duck in the sky and me beneath them, poking a gun at them and missing every time.

I had missed the first duck with both barrels; I had not heard its approach (because I had not been listening); it had come suddenly out of the shadows and I had told myself to be ready next time. Next time I did hear the pulse of wings and the muttering duck-talk above me, so I was ready for the two shapes circling in the sky and then planing in. The first of these shapes flared up when I missed with my first shot. I missed with the second as well, and you know how it is: once you have missed a time or two you expect to miss when the next time comes, you shoot with a sense of predestined failure and almost inevitably your destiny is fulfilled. Ten cartridges later I crept away from Low Park Pond with a spaniel that could not believe he had been given nothing to do. There were still duck coming but I thought it was a good idea to finish early, before fourteen wasted cartridges had turned into twenty or more. When I got home I put away the end-of-term claret and made do with some stuff from Chile. I should have gone to *The Spar* and punished myself with a bottle of *Blossom Hill*.

Sitting at my desk, with the coffee now finished and the day's second pipe half-smoked, with the day now bright and the weather set fair and with every hope of enjoyable sport, I began to doubt my ability to hit any of the birds that the day might send towards my gun. Friday's flight seemed a clear indication that I was on the edge of one of those dark and incompetent periods of my shooting life. I told myself gallantly that today would be a day when my own form scarcely mattered; that the purpose of today was to provide sport and pleasure for my friends. I saw the point of what I was telling myself and recognised it as true, but I still knew that, even if all my friends were on top of their form and were given pheasants to shoot and enjoyed themselves enormously, I should go home feeling discontented if I had shot like a fool.

I thought of wine and immediately got out Friday's cancelled claret *(Grand Puy Lacoste '93);* it was a bold and defiant gesture, expressing my sudden determination to deserve it. Then I remembered that the steak was still in the freezer and got that out as well. Then I checked that the fridge contained the makings of a salad and found that it did. Then I did a bit of washing up, cleaned and laid the fire and very soon it was time to go.

In spite of the cold the Land Rover started immediately. There was a High Park morning years and years ago when one of its predecessors refused to start at all: it took desperate phone calls to my guests to find one who had not yet left and could pick me up on his way. The turbo-diesel engine, anyway, sprang into life just as soon as the key was turned and kept going right up the valley past Cautley Spout and beneath Harter Fell; it kept going the whole way over Raven-stonedale Common, chugging comfortingly between the frosty fields, then it dipped down past Tarn House, where the water in the tarn was blue beneath the sky except where it was frozen silver along the shallow margins. Ash Fell, with its little grouse moor spreading out on my left in a patchwork of deep rime and dark heather, presented my Land Rover with no problems at all. Then it purred down through the sunshine into Kirkby Stephen, where it found that it was waiting behind one of my friends at the lights in the middle of the town. Soon it had taken me past Winton and Eden Farm Supplies, and it did not let me down, it kept moving more or less smoothly forward until, at five minutes to ten, it drew up outside the Black Bull in Brough Sowerby and was given a brief rest.

Most of my guests were waiting for me and, within five minutes, we were all gathered apart from Austin and Phil, who both knew their way to High Park and were meeting us at the shoot. There was a bit of hand-shaking, there were commendations of the weather, there were no introductions because everyone already knew everyone else. There were one or two questions about the prospects for the day and a few comments on recent sport, but very soon it was back into our vehicles and off to the farm – about two minutes away – where Austin and Phil were waiting with their dogs.

Perhaps I should take this opportunity, as dogs sit waiting at heel or sniff inquisitive greetings to each other, as their masters fill cartridge-bags or belts and pull on boots and take out their guns and shove their lunches into pockets or game-bags, perhaps I should take this opportunity to run through the participants in this particular day's little drama.

There were Austin and Phil, to begin within. They often shoot with me at High Park, but today they were beating with their dogs, with Holly the Labrador and Pearl the cocker-spaniel. It was, in fact, the first ever shooting day at High Park with two full-time beaters to send pheasants streaming over the guns; and there were six guns, which is one too many for my little drives and would mean that I should spend most of the day as a beater myself, but as a beater with a gun, leaving birds that flushed the right way and having a go at some of the pheasants that flew away from my friends.

There were two boys, John and William, with their fathers, Kyle and Tim. Both boys had helped me keep my pheasants fed throughout the term and this was the day of their reward. There was also Neil

McKerrow, the school bursar who, in spite of being a bursar, is a good friend: a fisher, a shooter, a stalker of deer and a most generous host.

And so there were eight of us when, after ten minutes' talking and getting ready and warming ourselves with a few mouthfuls of coffee, we set off across the fields, laden with guns and bags and with dogs in impatient attendance, tramping over the hard earth, crushing the stiff grass beneath our boots and with a cold bright sky all above us. It should, I kept telling myself, be a good day, because it was almost Christmas and it was only the second time that my main drives were to be disturbed by the commotion of a shooting day. In the past I have always had a main day in the middle of November, but this year I decided to leave it, to shoot once right at the end of October and then wait for December and the end of term, with nothing in November but little half-days out on my rented land. I want to see if this policy of restraint produces more birds in December and January when pheasants are at their best.

High Park's first shoot of the season

I hoped, anyway, that Beck Bank, my first drive, would be holding a few birds. I stopped the guns at the gate into the meadow and we waited there, talking in whispers, while Austin and Phil walked forward very quietly, crossed the beck and crept up the back of the bank. Only then was it time for us to move. Beck Bank is a problem. Pheasants like to run or fly out at its top rather than doing their duty and heading over the beck and the meadow above me and my guests. I have tried putting guns in the pasture beyond the ditch at the top of the bank, but the birds that come to them are too low to shoot. Once Beck Bank has been beaten out two or three times, most of its pheasants have sought safety somewhere else long before we get anywhere near them. But, since this was only the second time through, there was hope that a fair number would wait for our arrival and that some of these, rather than legging it along the ditch, would cross the meadow or rise over the larches and shine in the bright light before shots rang out and they fell steeply from the sky. Seven pheasants is the record for Beck Bank. When finally in position at the end of the line, I told myself that five would make a good start to the day.

I was nervous; any host should be just a little nervous as he stands waiting and looking round him at the beginning of his first drive. There was still thick frost on the grass of Pheasant Hill up on my left. In front there was an orange glow to the top of the larches in the sun; there was ice gleaming along the edges of the beck and the water flowed almost black beneath clusters of red holly-berries shining out from their surrounding of darkly polished green leaves. It was beautiful, but I was waiting anxiously for what, given the time and the situation, would seem the better beauty of a pheasant flying through the blue sky.

I love watching pheasants fly. There are the hens that shine; there are the cocks that glow; there are birds that rise higher and higher on proud wings; there are birds that set their wings and glide; and some fly straight and fast, while others wobble and curl as they go. I did not see much from my stand below Beck Bank. There were no pheasants near me, but I heard cries of 'over', I heard at least a dozen bangs and I saw one hen pheasant climb high over the larches and keep climbing in defiance of two shots.

My stand was through the meadow-gate, round the corner and down by the beck, which was why I saw so little; and then Austin declared 'drive over' from the top of the bank and I took Ross with me back through the gate to see how many birds had fallen and whether a spaniel was needed to find any of them. There were two pheasants down, both had been gathered and I was disappointed. I thought my team should have done better. I did not say so, but I still thought it and the thought was unfair. I have stood beneath other men's birds and missed them one after the other; and now here I was complaining to myself that my guests were not doing their job by bringing down a respectable proportion of the pheasants that came over them. I was beginning to fear that the sun would shine and birds would fly, while my friends waved their guns at them and put little or nothing in the bag; and then I should drive home feeling that six or seven, even a dozen birds had been a poor reward for such a day and all the effort that had preceded it; and I should sit brooding over my supper, asking myself despondently what was the point of releasing pheasants if no one could manage to knock them from the sky.

The second drive was worse than the first. It is called the Rise and it faces Beck Bank across the meadow. I fenced it off seven or eight years ago before planting it up with ashes and oaks and hazels and wild cherries. They have done well; aspens have seeded themselves every-where, blackthorns are spreading out from the hedge on top of the Rise and brambles are creeping over the slope of the ground. There is plenty of cover on the Rise now and there are days when it is full of birds.

It looked beautiful in the sun today, with every branch sharp against the sky, with the undercover still thickly rimed and catching the light. I lined out my guns in the meadow, left Phil and Austin by the gate at the western end of the Rise, going with Ross up through another gate into the square pasture that runs down to the hedge. As soon as the beat started two or three birds flushed the wrong way, almost my way; then a trickle of pheasants went out over the meadow. I could hear the sound of their wings and could see them as they rose into the sun, perhaps half a dozen in all.

With a couple there were no shots to greet them and I felt almost angry that my birds were being ignored; then shots did ring out but nothing came down. The Rise added no more to the bag and at the end of it I was depressed. How on earth were we going to shoot something like twenty birds if my guns left good pheasants alone or bungled every chance that flew over them? I was beginning to think wicked thoughts. I was beginning to hope for a few unsporting pheasants, for a few low birds and a few slow ones to provide a few easy kills. I was beginning to think that when, in later drives, Ross flushed pheasants that headed off in the direction of my guests, I would shoot them myself before my guests had the opportunity just to watch them fly or to waste another two cartridges. I had forgotten that I was uncertain of my own form.

Obviously it was time for comforts. I might not be feeling like a generous host, but I needed to behave like one and, anyway, I was in need of the consolation of sloe gin. One of the good things about shooting, by the way, is that you can have a drink at half-eleven in the morning without feeling that you also have a problem; tradition almost demands a tot of something or other at the end of the second drive. In this respect, I suppose, hunting is even better than shooting, since tradition demands that you should have a drink before you start at all.

I have drunk sloe gin indoors on winter evenings and found it too cloying and sweet; the damson variety is sweeter still. They are both drinks to be swallowed under the open sky and, the sharper the air, the better they will taste. It was a perfect morning for sloe gin and the unctuous warming smoothness of it reconciled me to the prospect of a small bag and a disappointing day. I looked at my friends, as we sipped and talked, and I told myself that, even if they were lousy shots, they were honest men who worked for their living (apart from the two boys) and paid their taxes and did not deserve bitter thoughts from me. Shooting well is not a virtue; resenting those who shoot badly is most certainly a sin.

After comforts we went to the Strips, which were created seven or eight years ago when I fenced off an old hedge line by putting a new fence fifteen yards below the one that was already there. It is really one strip cut in two by a gateway half way along its length; each half is something like a hundred and fifty yards long and in each of them there is a pen. The cover is patchy but getting thicker every year. I have planted some spruces, some Scots pines, a few larches, a few mountain ashes and one or two oak-saplings. Birches, hazel and hawthorn were there to begin with as the surviving and mature or decrepit remnants of the hedge; there was blackthorn too and, with the sheep excluded, it is now beginning to run riot. The grass on the open ground between the trees is thick and full of rushy tussocks. Sometimes the Strips produce a good show of birds, although I have never found it possible to work out what sort of weather puts or keeps them there.

We have beaten them out on wild days of rain and wind, on cold and blustering days when you would have thought that every pheasant on my ground would have sought shelter in the gorse or beneath a thicker cover of trees – we have done the Strips on such days and pheasants have risen from them and flown like distressed angels. There have been days of serene sunshine when I have expected lots of birds up there and been disappointed by the few that have flushed, but I still think they usually show more birds on still and settled days; and so, as we trudged up through the gorse and the bright winter light, I was expecting more than enough pheasants for my friends to miss.

Usually I do the Strips as two separate manoeuvres, but today I lined my guns out along their whole length, about twenty yards below the bottom fence, and we did them as one. Austin and Phil started at the east end, while I acted on a sudden impulse and did something new. Perhaps it was because I wanted to get as far away as possible from the sight of birds untroubled by gunshot; perhaps it was because I wanted to swear loudly in the certainty that my language would be unheard.

Above the Strips, anyway, there spreads a ten-acre field called the Hag. It is a rough pasture full of thick beds of rushes which are sometimes full of birds. I went right to the western top of the Hag, where I looked down on five guns waiting below me on the sloping ground. I blew several long blasts on my whistle, a prearranged sign telling Austin and Phil to set their dogs to work; and then, while they advanced from the east, I came down from the west with Ross quartering ahead of me in the rushes, hoping that the pheasants he might flush would fly over the guns below me, hoping that my fellow beaters would provide sport for the guns on the far end of the line, and praying that, thus furnished with birds, my friends would manage to kill just a few of them.

And, glory be, it worked. Twice I saw what I love to see on a shooting day. Twice I saw a hen spring from beneath the nose of my spaniel – a cock would have done just as well – and climb steeply into the sky; I saw the sun in her wings as, rising still, she flew back towards Beck Bank; I saw a sudden convulsion in the sky and a headlong fall, with a few bright specks of feathers left fluttering and shining in the air. I saw these two pheasants, I shot another myself which flew away from the guns; I heard the sound of shots further down the line and began to hope that the bag would reach double figures after all.

The Strips produced five birds, with talk of one down somewhere in the wood. It would have to be left for the afternoon, and I decided that, if High Park ever again enjoyed the luxury of two beaters, then, for the Strips, one of them would turn into a picker-up and stand down by the beck to deal promptly with fallen or wounded birds. The land slopes away very steeply from the Strips and it is difficult for guns to mark where their birds come down.

Suddenly I felt in a better mood and the success of the experiment in the Hag encouraged my innovative spirit. Beyond the Hag there is a square field called the Stackhole; it has a spring in it and, by the way, if my fields have names I inherited them. I have already explained that I am not much good with names. The Stackhole, anyway, is the western extremity of my land. All over it there are clumps of rushes where pheasants often lurk, but beneath the spring, with its square fence, there is a very thick bed of them with outlying clumps and patches on either side. It is very rare to put dogs into these rushes without them putting a pheasant or two into the sky. Sometimes we have walked through it at the end of a main day; more often it has been kept for rough days towards the end of the season, when birds are getting scarce and I have abandoned attempts to drive them over standing guns.

I had been planning to do the Penside and then have lunch. But suddenly I invented a new drive. I stood two of my guns, spaced out in the field between the Strips and the top of the Rise; it has a name but I have forgotten it. One of the two boys stood by the gateway into the meadow; the other went down into the meadow itself, while I took Austin, Phil and Kyle Blue to the far end of the Stackhole, where we lined out and then brought it back. Kyle and I took the lower side, with guns over our shoulders, for I wanted armed beaters down in the rushes below the spring, ready to deal with birds that broke back. This was a good idea, because two birds leapt from the outlying rushes and went back over our heads. I shot one and Kyle killed the other.

The revelation came from the middle of the rushes, where four or five birds got onto the wing and went forward over the guns. I had been wondering how they would fly. With nothing to lift them except the line of a fence I had thought they might stay low and I was wrong: they rose quickly and they kept rising and they were fast; they were bright and high over the guns and two of them tumbled out of the sky. And then a bird crossed to my right and I swung through her and very soon Ross had brought her in, which meant that my impromptu drive had yielded five birds and been declared a regular feature of a High Park main day. It also meant that it was time for lunch.

I now felt ashamed of the dark thoughts, the brooding and critical thoughts that had festered within me during the first two drives, unless it was that I felt no shame at all but simply changed my mind, realising that my friends were not hopeless shots at all but had just taken time to get into their stride. There were twelve pheasants in the bag and, with all the best drives still to come – both sides of the wood and the Gully and the Gutter and the Whins – with all this still ahead of us we were, it seemed to me, almost bound to reach at least twenty, which would be more than enough for contentment at the end of the day.

I love lunch at High Park on a sunny shooting day. We sit by the hedge, on coats or on upended buckets, looking down the meadow with Beck Bank on one side and the Rise on the other. It is sheltered and beautiful and, even on a cold December day, cradled between steeply rising ground on three sides, it is warm down there beneath the midday sun; it is the heart of my shoot and I love to relax there for half an hour, deciding nothing, planning nothing, bossing nobody around, just chewing sandwiches and drinking whisky and talking to my friends.

Neil had brought whisky and so mine stayed in its flask. Coats came off. Each of the boys had a can of beer. The odd scrap was tossed to the dogs and we talked of nothing in particular, which is one of the things I like about my shooting lunches. There may be a bit of right-wing political stuff, but it will only be conventional and uncontroversial government-hatred inspired by hunting or shooting talk. On my shoot, at any rate, the state of the economy, the existence of god, the meaning of life and the problem of evil are topics seldom aired; conversation tends to be uncontroversial, anecdotal and there is no necessity to take part or even to listen. I have already forgotten most of what was said, which may be because I was not listening myself, although I do remember saying something about the weather and I did spend some minutes chatting to Phil, as we both suggested reasons why the little syndicate shoot of which we are both members was finding it so difficult to hold its birds.

After about twenty minutes, after a round of smoked salmon sandwiches and another of smoked bacon and tomatoes, after turning down a second dram and filling my mug with tea I began to think about the afternoon, about who should stand where for each little drive and where I should put myself. After about five minutes of this it was time to take command again and suggest that we returned to our sport. We would do the Penside first and then move onto my rented land.

The Penside is perhaps the best of my drives, but only when there are birds in it. It is very unpredictable. Facing it is North Bank, which always holds birds and does not show them quite as well; it always holds birds because they love the thick spread of gorse above the trees, whereas the cover in the Penside is less welcoming (and needs attention), but if

The Rise

birds are there and fly over the guns they are very good birds indeed.

The Penside takes time. First I must place the guns: one over the beck against the fence on Pheasant Hill, another at the bottom of the wood, one in an opening twenty yards into the trees, then another perhaps forty yards further up the wood, right down on the edge of the beck, which is where the best of the birds come: sudden, fast and high. After telling my guests that nothing will happen for at least a quarter of an hour, I go off in search of Austin, who will be trudging to the top of the wood in the pasture above North Bank.

Today, of course, Phil was with him as well and I caught up with them at the end of the fence. We stood for a moment and admired the view, then we went down the path through the trees, where the air was still sharp and cold, crossed the beck and climbed up the far side. Austin and Phil stayed in the wood, while I continued up onto the open ground above, a narrow stretch of almost flat land between the trees and my boundary fence, very thickly overgrown with rushes and brambles and briars.

Here I always pause for a minute to get my breath back; then I unsleeve and load my gun, shout to Austin and the beat begins. There were birds there this afternoon. They flushed from the wood and from the rough ground above the trees and nearly all of them went forward, shining as they rose into the clear air. There would be a shout from Austin or me or from Phil; there would be a pheasant in the sky and soon he would be lost to view before one or two shots rang out, and sometimes this was followed by one or two more as he went down the line and proved too good for at least some of my friends. For me the Penside is always the most exciting of my drives because, unless there is little or no shooting, I never have a clue how many birds have been shot – apart from any that I put in the bag – until the drive is over and we meet up at the bottom of Pheasant Hill.

Sometimes there have been a dozen or more shots but all I find is shaking heads and confessions of failure and perhaps a single bird. Today I came down from the old pen with a cock pheasant in my bag, the only bird that had flushed over the fence. He had risen high enough to persuade me that he was a respectable going-away bird and so I had pulled the trigger. I had not counted the other shots that had rung out. Some of them had obviously recorded a collective effort at the same bird but there had been enough to make me hope that four or five pheasants might have been brought down. There had certainly been some single shots, which is often a good sign, although birds from the Penside can be such fleeting chances that there is only time for one trigger.

Anyway there were six birds waiting for me at the bottom of Pheasant Hill and everyone was happy because everyone had managed to shoot one and clearly felt that in doing so he had done a difficult thing. There were now eighteen pheasants in the bag and there were still four drives to go. My view of my guns had changed, for it now seemed to me that if I could put birds over them they would shoot down a commendable percentage; they were a thoroughly workmanlike team of guns and I announced to them that there was every chance of a record bag. I thought it would inspire them to still higher achievements.

The High Park record for pheasants, when the possibility of beating it suddenly occurred to me, stood at twenty nine, shot on an early December day five years ago when snow threatened from the start and came at last in the afternoon. On that occasion it was the Gully that had made the difference and, on this occasion, it was to the Gully that we went next, climbing up Pheasant Hill, crossing the stile, which had been neither wired nor made firm, and then splitting into two teams. The Gully is the most complex of my manoeuvres. Today I sent Austin, Phil, Kyle and John up into the Rushy Pasture, to line out and bring it through, while I placed Neil, Tim and William as the three bottom guns on the north side of the Gully, and then I crossed to the south side, waiting there with Ross right at the top of the field where the wall, rising parallel with the line of the Gully, meets the fence that runs along the bottom of the Rushy Pasture.

The plan, as usual, was to beat out the Rushy Pasture, from which birds might provide sport for the walking guns or for those towards the bottom of the Gully or for me in the angle of fence and wall; then Kyle and John would take the two higher stands on the Gully while I left my position and, with Austin and Phil, worked our dogs down the Gully itself. The Gully forms a pleasing contrast with the Penside because, whereas I see little of what happens during the Penside, the Gully provides spectacle, with birds in full view as they curl over from the Rushy Pasture and rise over the guns, or clatter from the gorse and climb into the sky. Today there were no shots from the Rushy Pasture but a single cock came soaring over the Gully and crashed to the ground. Nineteen, I thought to myself, and waited for more.

There were a few more birds, but only two more were shot. There were fewer birds than I had been hoping and the Gully turned into something of a disappointment. I left it and toiled back up the hill with some sense of anti-climax, but I still thought that the record would fall, because North Bank is probably my most dependable drive. There was a problem with North Bank, however, because, when I had positioned the guns and reached the far end of the wood, when I was standing there above the trees, ready to work Ross through the gorse while Austin and Phil were busy in the trees below, I realised that we should be beating straight into the level light of the sun. It was very beautiful, with the edge of the sky stained and with spears of polished light striking through the branches and shining on the winter bark,

Shooting Beck Bank with Ross

with burnished clumps of rushes and long shadows behind them, with shadows everywhere between a radiance that seemed to be seeping out of things rather than laid upon them. It was very beautiful but I was not sure that pheasants would flush straight into the horizontal shine. You will often read that pheasants do not like to fly into the sun. I do not think it makes much difference when the sun is up in the sky, but when the sun is low on the horizon, pheasants usually fly away from it. And so it proved.

Three or four birds flew into the sunset, straight down the valley where the guns were waiting and two of them fell. At least a dozen birds came out at the sides: one I shot and one I missed and many I could barely see because my eyes were dazzled by the light. I heard the sound of wings and saw nothing but a blurred silhouette until it turned into a pheasant already out of range and skimming low over the field. I miscalculated with North Bank; if we had done it earlier in the day we should have shot more birds.

I should also have finished the day after North Bank, because by now the light was failing fast. I had thought at lunchtime that we had plenty of time for all my little drives; but both the Gully and the Penside take time and I had not taken this properly into account. We should have finished after North Bank, for the sun had gone, but the scent of a record had turned my head and I rushed through the last two drives, placing the guns down by the beck and then hurrying up to the top of the Gutter. Ross found a pricked bird on the way, which made twenty four. When birds flushed they were dark shapes. I rushed and poked and missed two, but William knocked down three chances in quick succession; they were fast and fleeting chances. And then it was the Whins and Tim shot a woodcock, and I missed a hen and shot another one that should have been left alone. It was the prospect of the record that corrupted my judgement and we did not beat the record; we did not even equal it. We ended with twenty eight and that single woodcock, and I cannot say that I cared very much.

We laid out the birds and I counted them solemnly. Then we braced them up and prepared to trudge down the fields beneath their weight. Kyle produced a bottle of sloe gin and we stood talking for a minute or two, in the sharp air and the deep shadows with a silver-rimmed sky all round us. Then it was back to the vehicles for more talk and a distribution of pheasants for those who wanted them, for farewells and best wishes for Christmas and then a drive home through the darkness with a dog sleeping in the back of the Land Rover and a front seat full of pheasants, two brace of which were dropped off with my friends at Tarn House.

I love the evenings of a High Park shoot. First the dogs are fed; then the birds are hung; then the gun is cleaned and then it time to clean myself in the bath after lighting the fire. Next, of course, comes sherry, two glasses of it as I write up my shooting diary and try to remember the main features of the day. Supper is almost always fillet steak, because it is easy to cook and very delicious as long as it comes from a good beast and has been well hung. With the steak there will be part of a half-bottle of good wine. There will be no washing up and the wine will be finished when the dogs have been out for a brief walk under the frosty stars.

I finished my wine very slowly this evening and each mouthful was a deep pleasure. Perhaps too much of this book finds me sitting by the fire with a glass of wine in my hand, or sitting somewhere with a drink and not doing very much. Books about sport should be full of vigorous activity. In this chapter, I suppose, there has been plenty of healthy exercise and, for me at any rate, the day to which it belonged had been a day of volatile emotions. I was tired at the end of it, ready for the soothing touch of sherry and of red wine; the end of it, justified by its earlier parts, also seemed almost the best of it, as I sat there in my chair, watching the dancing shadows of the fire, thinking how much I had enjoyed the day, thinking how well it had gone, looking forward to an easy day tomorrow with nothing more nerve-racking than filling the hoppers at High Park, deciding not to have a whisky when the last gurgle of wine was gone, then getting into bed before midnight and falling asleep almost as soon as I was there.

CHAPTER FIFTEEN

Shooting Invitations

High Park is the heart of my shooting life. I should be a happy shooting man if High Park were the whole of my shooting life but I am happier still because each season brings me a few days elsewhere: days when, if things go wrong, it is not my fault, days when my job is to stand in a line of guns, trying not to miss all the birds that fly my way and unbothered by nagging anxieties about why the last drive put so few pheasants into the sky or whether the next drive will put any there at all. It is good not to be in charge: merely to wait and see what the day brings without ever telling myself that it ought to be bringing more. And away from High Park it pleases me to see men missing pheasants; it means that I feel less embarrassed when I miss them myself.

At High Park the bag matters to me; doubtless it matters more than it should. Elsewhere I could care scarcely a fig about the number of dead pheasants on show at the end of the day. Ten or twenty pheasants may send me home in the best of good humours; a hundred or more of them has sometimes left me in a gloom, perhaps because very few of them were shot by me, sometimes because they were low and slow and unworthy birds, very occasionally because the company of my fellow guns was distasteful.

It seems to me that driven shooting, by the way, is essentially unenjoyable unless the birds are at least moderately challenging and unless you are capable of hitting a fair proportion of those that come over you. It is some years since I shot on a low-bird shoot. There are probably fewer of them around, but I remember a day nearly twenty years ago when I killed something like forty birds with fifty cartridges and drove away feeling miserable because I felt that I had just taken part in something unseemly. I suppose thoughts of this sort are bound to produce howls of rage from the enemies of shooting, who will protest that a pheasant killed high in the sky is just as dead as a pheasant killed ten yards from the ground and that both acts are equally repugnant. Shooters of driven birds see a world of difference between the two performances. Driven shooters – most of them at least – want high birds to test their skill; they think that a high pheasant falling from the sky has died a worthy death and they feel a sudden spasm of shame when – as most of them do from time to time – they forget themselves by shooting a pheasant that should have been left.

I probably get it wrong more than most shooters, not usually through greed or through a manic urge to kill, but because High Park is a hybrid sort of shoot where double standards operate. It is both a rough shoot and a bit of a driven shoot and, whereas rough-shooters take most of their chances, driven shooters take on the challenging bird. Sporting ethics, like most forms of ethics, are complicated: different situations demand different forms of behaviour and sometimes I get confused; sometimes, although I am standing in a line of guns, my rough-shooter's mentality takes over and I do what I ought not to do.

It happened only the other day on a shoot where most of the birds were fine and tall. It was the second drive and I had shot pretty well on the first; now I was on the end of a curving line of guns, with birds going forward and climbing steeply over the centre of the line. Those that came to me, out of the side of the drive, were not high birds; there were two or three that skimmed low and were left.

There was one that rose into the sky and was shot; then there was a hen that was somewhere in between, a crosser she seemed to me, the sort of bird to which a walking shot would certainly lift his gun if his spaniel flushed her from a bed of rushes. Almost instinctively I did lift my gun and pulled the trigger. I pulled the second trigger as well and the hen flew on, while a polite voice on my right said 'more air please.' The polite voice was, of course, quite right; I had shot at, and missed, the sort of pheasant that the driven shot should leave alone. I was covered with shame. At the end of the drive I sought out the polite voice, which belonged to my host, and grovelled. I was told to forget about it; I was told that everybody makes mistakes and that my peg was one that often produced exactly the sort of mistake that I had just made. But, knowing that the polite voice had been spot on, I could not forget about it and I shot very badly for the rest of the day. I have, by the way, been invited back.

Driven shooting, even for those swinging their guns, is partly a spectator sport. I take pleasure in watching my fellow guns tackling pheasants; I have already admitted that I enjoy seeing them miss, and this is not always because, by demonstrating that I am not completely surrounded by unerring dead-eyes, it takes the pressure off me. Watching pheasants fly is one of the pleasures of driven shooting. There is a noble defiance in the bird that goes down the line and, instead of falling to the sound of shot, rises each time and goes on his way in high contempt. There is pleasure too in watching an expert gun, watching the elegance and economy of his style and the way, almost always, his birds throw back their necks, falling steeply and stone dead.

You can also guess something of the personality of a gun in the way that he goes about the beginning of a drive. There are fidgety and restless shots who walk round their pegs as they wait for the action to begin. They move a foot this way or a foot that, before bending down to take an extra handful of cartridges from their bag to stuff into their pocket; they will probably break their guns at least twice to squint down the barrels and check that all is well, and quite probably the first bird will take them by surprise. I confess that I am something of this sort myself.

Other men stand almost like statues, like statues of tweeded squires put out in the countryside as memorials of a past age; these are often the good shots; sometimes they are also squires; they are the shots, anyway, who know that the pheasants soon to come over them are very likely to fall. Some men curse and grumble when they miss birds, which is a vice of which I am rarely guilty; others almost whoop when they bring down a tall one, which is something I never do, although I cannot deny that occasionally, on a bad day, I have greeted the sudden falling of a bird to my shot with a quiet 'thank God!' or a whispered 'at last!'.

I have watched men leave their pegs in the middle of a drive, moving whole yards forward or to one side because they think it will bring them more birds or make them easier to kill. These are greedy, disreputable and ill-mannered guns. I have watched men leave high birds to fly on their way in preference for birds half their height and many times easier to kill. I once watched a man, right at the beginning of a demanding driven day, miss seven birds in succession and then sleeve his gun before giving up the attempt to kill pheasants for the rest of the drive. It was a strange and temporary retirement. I seem to remember that he performed pretty well in subsequent drives and suspect that he was a skilled shot who could not cope with a rare and, for him, humiliating patch of incompetence. For my own part, I got used to it long ago, although consistent failure does still bring dissatisfaction and despondency.

We respond differently as shooters to success and failure. Most of us manage to keep our mouths shut when we shoot abnormally well and better than our fellows, though there is the sort who will tell you that he has shot nearly half the bag, or go through each drive and describe each bird that fell to his gun before announcing that his thirty for the day have cost him fewer than forty cartridges. Thank God shooting bores of this sort are few and far between; the golf course is their true home.

Most average shots take good days and bad days in their stride. They know that sometimes they shoot well and sometimes they shoot badly; they derive a modest pleasure from the good days and, in response to the bad ones, they acknowledge that they were off form or that the birds were too good for them. Most experts never mention how many birds they have killed on a drive or in the course of a day. I once stood next to such a man. On the first drive his peg saw a lot of action; all along the line the birds were high and I felt pleased with myself for killing five birds with something like a dozen cartridges; this had been Catlow at the top of his form. The birds over the expert had been more numerous and probably higher and I had watched a succession of them plummeting from the sky. I rather thought that the expert – I think he was a High Court judge – had killed every bird that came over him and, at the end of the drive, I asked him how many birds he had shot and whether he needed the help of a spaniel to find any of them. He replied that he had one or two down, that the pickers-up were on to most of them but that there was one on the edge of the river which Merlin might help by bringing in. Merlin promptly brought the bird in and the judge was loud in his praise. For the rest of the day, which continued to be one of my good days, Merlin was much busier with the judge's birds than with my own; and for the rest of the day the judge, who was otherwise an affable and talkative man, maintained a similar reticence about his performance with the gun.

I am not an expert; I am an average sort of driven shot who has never quite managed the average shooter's relaxed attitude to his sport. I become very miserable when I am shooting badly, whereas my good days still inspire an almost childish sense of elation, a feeling that the world is a wonderful place and that I fit into it rather neatly. It is absurd that killing pheasants should produce such a state of mind, although it is, of course, commendable to enjoy doing something well rather than badly. I have never quite understood what pleasure consistently bad shots get from their sport, unless it is the unquenchable hope that the next drive or the next day will be different.

Doing something incompetently is, it seems to me, intrinsically unsatisfying. At the same time average performers, whatever the activity, should be able to acknowledge their middling status and take it in their stride, which is something that I cannot do when I have just spent a day missing birds. I can tell myself that I do not do enough driven shooting to compete with the experts, many of whom are at it three and four days a week at the height of the season, whereas my own proper driven days rarely amount to half a dozen in the course of a whole winter. This is what I do tell myself, and there is some truth in it, but it never works.

Whatever I tell myself, bad days fill me with gloom. There is some sense of shame and wounded pride: a feeling that I am waving my gun to and fro and making an idiot of myself; there is the dark fear that a precious skill has deserted me and may never return; there is the sight of others doing with ease what I can no longer do; there is the knowledge that I have a role in the proceedings and that I am failing to perform it; there is the oppression of public failure and revealed incompetence.

I become downhearted when I am alone and shoot badly. It is much worse on a driven day when there are beaters and pickers-up and other guns to witness my cack-handedness. And it is, of course, pleasurable to knock down birds in the knowledge that others are watching and admiring your skill. Driven shooting is partly a spectator sport and, for me at least, this sharpens the edge of failure and success. Perhaps I am insecure and perhaps it is time that I stopped delving into my sporting mentality and took you for some driven shooting, for a day just after Christmas and a day at the beginning of the New Year.

I have a half-gun in a syndicate near Settle in North Yorkshire. It is an informal little shoot, which is the reason why I enjoy it so much. It provides driven shooting of a rough and ready sort rather than the more formal sort you find on grander shoots. It is not really the sort of driven shooting that I had in mind in the earlier pages of this chapter, but it is driven shooting after a fashion – a very enjoyable fashion – and, for a few pages, it will have to do.

On this rough and ready driven shoot thirty pheasants make a good bag. We beat for two of the day's six drives; the rest of the beating team is made up of friends with dogs, of wives and girl-friends with or without dogs. We have lunch in a barn and bring it with us. It is not a picturesque or cosy barn; it is not really a barn at all; it is a modern version of a stock-house, large and airy, a thing mainly of wooden slats and metal and concrete; sometimes it is very cold, and usually we share it with some of the stock for which it was constructed. We sit on plastic chairs round a couple of low tables placed end-to-end; the tables have some sort of plastic cover, on which we place our flasks of coffee or tea, our lunch-boxes with their sandwiches and pies; and we sit there, eating and talking and smoking in a good-humoured sort of way. There is nothing pretentious about the proceedings of the Wigglesworth syndicate.

Every member of the syndicate has his own view on how each drive should be managed and everyone expresses it; and somehow, although everybody's opinion is different and although the shoot captain has the final say and ignores every opinion that is expressed, we all manage to stay friends and enjoy ourselves. It is a shoot with no aspirations to be other than it is and I love going there. I was last there on the day after Boxing Day.

Usually I spend the days on either side of Christmas in London, which always brings a twinge of regret when I wake up on Boxing Day and realise that guns, spaniels and pheasants will form no part of the day's entertainment. I lie in bed drinking tea, congratulating myself for not having a hangover and at the same time remembering a few Boxing Days from the past; then I tell myself that I shall be back home in a day or two, that I shall perhaps go flighting on the first evening of my return and shall most certainly be out at High Park on New Year's Eve. It is thoughts such as these that reconcile me to Boxing Day in the suburbs of North London; even without the help of a dog and a shotgun I usually manage a pleasant day.

This year, for various reasons, I spent Christmas in Cumbria, and there was no regret at all that, having decided that my main ground needed more rest before we shot it again, I had organised no sport out at High Park on Boxing Day. I could have pottered round the outlands, in search of an odd bird and a rabbit or two. If the sun had been shining this is what I should have done; if it had been grey and cloudy I should have done the same; neither steady drizzle nor heavy showers would have kept me from the outlands; lying snow with flurries throughout the day would have made me very impatient to be there with a spaniel busy among the rushes and the gorse.

Come to think of it, a light cover of snow with sharp air and further flurries would probably have been best of all. But there was no snow; there was no sunshine; there was neither steady drizzle nor heavy showers of rain. I kept away from the outlands and, instead of going shooting, I sat by the fire feeling sorry for every sportsman who was out there suffering under the driving rain and the sodden sky. Most of them, I thought, would already have had enough before they started, and not many would keep going beyond lunch. It was a pig of a day: the sort of day when, simply by looking out of the window, you know that the rain is determined not to stop and will almost certainly decide to get heavier; and the wind was raging through the rain, sweeping it along in ragged grey sheets. I took the dogs for a brief run and got soaked in fewer than five minutes. Then I returned to the fireside, drank a glass or two and felt fresh waves of sympathy for anyone trying to enjoy himself outside. There were torrents of wetness, but, in spite of them, the weatherman's midday report was bright and breezy, insisting that these torrents would spend themselves sometime after midnight and that the morning would dawn bright and fresh. I think I refilled my glass in relief and celebration, and there may have been a hint of *schadenfreude* about it all; for next morning would come my turn to stand in a line of guns, enduring the sky's gifts to those stuck beneath it. I expected to cope pretty well with breezy sunshine and a few passing showers.

On the afternoon of Boxing Day I took Ross and Digby for some real exercise in the woods and got properly soaked. In its own way it was almost enjoyable; there is something exhilarating about wild weather, about the surge of streams in flood and the swaying uproar of the trees, but on this occasion the best thing about it was most certainly the thought that tomorrow was going to be different.

It is, of course, possible to enjoy being outside in wet weather. Fishing in soft and windless rain, for example, with indistinct horizons, with misty shapes, with subtle shadings of grey and green all round you, with running water sliding towards you in a cloudy gleam and with the sound of it muffled on the damp air, fishing on such days absorbs the fisher into a quiet world of benign and gentle wetness. Fishers, after all, depend on wetness for their sport; they would have none without it and to be fishing on a day of the sort described is most certainly a blessing.

There is nothing much wrong with the wilder sort of winter wetness as long as you can keep moving through it and find some sort of shelter from time to time. I have gritted my teeth and tramped squelching fields where rain was battering every standing pool, I have crouched beneath the inadequate canopy of a few bare hawthorns, trying to light

my pipe and deciding at the same time that I shall try another field and
the next in the hope of turning one pheasant into a brace. There can
be pleasure in this, although I suppose part of the pleasure is thinking
of the pleasure that will come when it is all over. There is, at any rate,
some satisfaction to be found in sport of the more vigorous type on wet
and windy days. But driven shooting in the same weather is almost pure
misery. It is difficult to stand in a line of guns while the rain pours down
from the sky and finds trickling access to those parts of your body from
which you thought it had been excluded, it is difficult to stand in a line
of guns beneath the rain, exposed and more or less motionless, confined
to your peg and committed to stay there for as long as half an hour, it
is very difficult to stand there beneath the relentless downpour, feeling
cold and wet and colder and wetter with each pelting drop, while at the
same time telling yourself that you are having a good time.

On the afternoon of Boxing Day I spent about an hour, unless it
was only forty minutes, out in the woods with my two spaniels; part
of the pleasure of it was relief that I was not part of a team of guns and
there was, of course, the prospect of better things the next day. There
were also closer pleasures with which to cheer myself as I tramped
through the loud and squelching woods; for in the evening there was
roast beef and claret, consumed while the rain rattled against the panes
and the wind sang wild songs in the chimney stack. The meat was
good, the wine was good and both were made better by those weather-
noises, because I knew that, some time after midnight, the wind would
soften to a breeze and the rain would turn into a few showers before
daylight brought back the sun. I drank a small dram and then took the
dogs out for the last time. It was still raining but it seemed lighter and
already the wind seemed less savage. The weather showed every sign of
doing what it had been told to do.

It was dry when I gazed out of the window at seven o'clock in
the morning. It was dry when I took the dogs out before putting them
in the back of the Land Rover, and the wind was no more than a stiff
breeze – a good shooting breeze. It was not dry when I pulled up in
the car park of *The Plough* at Wigglesworth, which is where we gather
on the morning of a shoot. During the journey, which takes rather less

than a hour, the sun had threatened to show itself once or twice, raising my trust in the weatherman still further. The wind, it is true, seemed to be strengthening, but I felt certain this was no more than a brief phase, a final gesture before it admitted defeat and obeyed orders. By the time I turned off the main road for the last two or three miles, the sun had abandoned any attempt to shine and the wind was indisputably wild. When I climbed out of the Land Rover into the car-park of *The Plough,* it was very cold and blowing a gale, there were sheets of wet snow sweeping over the fields, the sky was leaden, the snow seemed rather more than a passing shower and it was very plain, although no one said as much, that some of us were wondering whether we really wanted to be there; others had yet to desert the insides of their vehicles. I confess that I was doing a bit of wondering myself and my faith in the weatherman was beginning to fade.

The shoot captain, anyway, summoned us into a huddle to draw for our pegs. There were one or two defiantly hopeful comments; there were two or three downright gloomy ones. Then we all returned to our transport and set off for the first drive. Everyone cheered up marvellously when the shoot captain got his new four-by-four stuck in the mud as he turned a corner of the track which leads to the barn. He had got it stuck somewhere else on the season's first shoot and the repeat performance produced gales of laughter; I could almost hear them through my closed windows and the howling of the storm. I was laughing myself. Behind other windows handkerchiefs came out and they were being used to wipe eyes rather than to blow noses.

The shoot captain, with help from those closest to the incident, eventually extracted his vehicle from the mud. We all parked near the stock-house and set off shivering for the wood. The wind was roaring, from rim to rim the sky was dark, the blowing sleet was bitter cold, each step was a splash, a slither or a slide. There were troubled pools of water in every hollow of the land. It was just as bad as Boxing Day had been and the only comfort I could draw from it all was that I was beating the first drive.

At the top of the field I leapt over the wall that surrounds the covert we call Pipers; and there, in among the sheltering pines and spruces, I found some sort of refuge from the lash of the wind. It was damp and dripping, virtually every step brought down cascades of wet and spiky needles; but it was almost warm and it was a haven from the savage world beyond. It was heaven for Ross, for there were pheasants in Pipers; they rose and wobbled on the wind and swept away, rising still higher and curling over the guns. They were fine birds but the sight of them never made me wish that I was standing out on the bare slope beyond the wood, standing there with my face to the wind and the sleet and waiting to meet the challenge of those birds. Not many of them were shot and, at the end of the drive, a miserable band of sportsmen gathered on the lee-side of the covert, deciding without a single dissenting voice that, unless the passing shower got a move on and cleared away, lunchtime would definitely be enough. It was the only outbreak of unanimity that I have ever encountered on my little syndicate shoot.

Our main drives are from woods that cover the steep ground on either side of a small stream called Stinking Beck. It is called Stinking Beck because of sulphur springs that bubble up into it, and often it deserves the name. You could think, standing at one or two pegs, that you were shooting in the middle of St. Helens or of Middlesborough rather than in the clean air or rural north Yorkshire; at least you could think this as long as you closed your eyes, which would, I suppose, tend to impede the efficiency of your shooting.

On the day after Boxing Day, anyway, Stinking Beck was a brown and angry torrent and any influence of the sulphur springs was swept away by the wild rush of water. Down towards the beck there was some shelter from the wind and by now there was a rim of brightness on the weather-edge of the sky; the sleet was still sweeping over the fields and by now its shiver and its wetness had seeped into most of me. But that rim of hope seemed to be widening with its message of change. I shot two good birds, missed an even better one in between them and decided I was having a good time.

By the beginning of the next drive the bright rim had narrowed again and then disappeared. The snow was much heavier than before and it was beginning to lie; the land was turning grey and it looked as though before long it would start to turn white. I bungled the only bird that came over me and knew that I would rather be at home, perhaps tying a few flies with thoughts of soft spring days in mind, tying a few flies and looking forward to cold beef for lunch, with fried potatoes and a glass of wine. I was even more certain that my heart was at home, sitting smoking by the fire and tying half a dozen Orange Partridges, when I discovered that both my boxes of matches were now incapable of fire, so that the consolations of tobacco were impossible. I always used to carry a lighter with me, specifically to make smoking possible in the event of sodden matches; it is a practice that has lapsed, but it will almost certainly be revived as a result of the day after Boxing Day, when I found that I was cold and miserable and could not even smoke.

It was time for The Point, my favourite drive: a long, sharply tapering finger of conifers that usually puts challenging birds into the sky. The best of them flush from the very end of the covert, then turn back down the field over the line of guns, often swinging wide and rising all the time before they swing back into the main body of the wood. The Point is a fine drive. Over the years I have missed some wonderful birds there and killed a few as well. Whatever the weather, however cold the wind or heavy the snow, I look forward to The Point, even without anything in my pockets that is able to put a light to my pipe.

It was a pity that I got a bootful of water while fording Stinking Beck. My feet had previously been the warmest region of my body. It was also a pity that, on this occasion, few pheasants flushed from The Point. But a cock rose from almost the last yard of the trees and headed towards me at number five. I have seen much higher birds at The Point, but he was high enough and he was definitely long. When he stopped in the sky and then fell out of it, throwing up a shower of slush as he came down, there was, for at least a few seconds, no doubt in my mind that the morning had been composed of pure pleasure. And I was beating the last drive and would not have to stand shivering in the wind any longer.

The shoot captain who, God bless and preserve him, is a heavy smoker, now produced a lighter, so that I did the beating with a functioning pipe in my mouth. I had to take it out once or twice to shout 'over' and I banged it against one or two branches, but it was there smoking away for most of the drive. Ross put up a few birds and found the captain's runner from the second drive. Then we abandoned lunch in the barn and went to the pub. On entering the tap-room of *The Plough,* my first act was to buy four boxes of matches. After this I think I bought our captain a pint, and it was wonderful sitting there in the warmth and the smoke, drinking a pint of bitter beer and talking about sport in the comfortable knowledge that real sport was over for the day.

Driving home (only one pint) I decided that we shooters should accept a few cold and sodden days as part of the scheme of things. Shooting is, after all, largely a winter sport and cold, sodden days, along with days of a very different sort, belong to the pattern of winter. I also decided that the worst aspect of this particular sodden and very cold experience had been that I was expecting to spend the day in bracing sunshine. The sun was shining when I got home, which provoked a bitter thought or two but, all things considered, it had perhaps been better than spending another day inside. It gave me an appetite, at any rate, for half a pheasant and rather more than half a bottle of claret. At the end of the claret I was almost certain that the day had brought more pleasure than pain, but I am less certain now. Looking back, without a glass of wine at hand, it seems to me that my earlier pronounce-ment was correct and that driven shooting in sleet and wind and rain is chiefly misery.

CHAPTER SIXTEEN

Shooting at Scargill

Early in the New Year I was the guest of John Guthrie at his Scargill shoot near Barnard Castle. I was travelling there with a friend and, at the last moment, with snow forecast to fall throughout the day, we decided to take my old Land Rover rather than Neil's faster, sleeker and altogether more comfortable something-or-other. Scargill is a high shoot on the edge of a grouse moor and our way to it (past High Park, as it happens) was over exposed Pennine roads where, if the snow came heavily, a battered old Land Rover, even one with a broken heater, might turn into a blessing by managing to get us there and back again.

It was a blessing never needed; it was a cold and unnecessary blessing, although it did perform its function and get us to Scargill and then back again to Sedbergh, but it was never asked to demonstrate its special abilities. Not a single snow-flake floated down on our way to Scargill; there was not a single flake at any moment of the day which was dry and windy and cold and grey. Pheasants flew superbly and, to all of it, there was the special delight that comes from kind weather when you have been expecting it to be your enemy.

Shooting at Scargill is a very different experience from shooting at nearby High Park, which, as you have learned, once had two full-time beaters on the same day. Scargill is also very different from my little syndicate at Wigglesworth, where a day unfolds in genial chaos, where shooters are sometimes beaters and beaters are sometimes shooters, where the shoot captain is exposed to a barrage of contradictory advice and where not everyone is always entirely certain what is going on, or even what is meant to be going on. At Scargill shooters are shooters and beaters are beaters and there are pickers-up as well: they all meet each other, they enjoy each other's company but they eat apart and they move between drives in different vehicles. The beaters do not join the guns for comforts after the third drive. A day's shooting at Scargill is run along traditional lines; it is well-planned and managed by a full-time keeper called Michael. The grouse moor is his main concern, but he knows all about pheasants and he presents them with pride. You do not kill many birds at Scargill unless you are on form, and those pickers-up behind the line will see just how badly you are shooting when your form is letting you down.

I have shot very badly indeed at Scargill and I have shot moderately well. I have shot there perhaps a dozen times over the years and there is always some nervousness at the beginning of a Scargill day. Missing pheasants while the guns on either side of you bring them toppling from the sky is a demoralising experience. It makes me, at any rate, feel a fool; it makes me feel that I am wasting the keeper's and the beaters' time, that they are doing their job while I am failing to do mine.

At the beginning of a Scargill day I am conscious of the dark possibility that my spirits will fall with each drive and that, when at last all is over, I shall head back home over Stainmore feeling depressed. It is a possibility balanced by hope: the hope that I shall lift my gun and that pheasants will fall, high pheasants, and not just the occasional high pheasant but a succession of them throughout the day; which will mean that, at the end of the afternoon I shall climb behind the wheel of the Land Rover and set off into the night, filled with the childish sense of elation that I have already mentioned, filled with this elation that I should have outgrown and at the same time convinced that I know a thing or two about knocking down high driven pheasants. It has happened both ways.

Shooting well is much more enjoyable than shooting badly. It is much better standing in a line of guns when you are conscious that you are doing your bit. You can enjoy the good shooting of others without pangs of bemused jealousy; when the time for comforts comes round you can sip your sloe gin and masticate sausages without a secret sense of shame; between drives you can chat to the keeper without feeling that he despises you; you can tell the pickers-up that you have four down over the river; you can be beaten by an archangel and acknowledge cheerfully that he was just too high and too fast for you; you can look at your spaniel and tell yourself that sitting at a peg is not his idea of a proper shooting day, but that at least he is being given something to do at the end of each drive.

God definitely shaped Scargill with pheasant-shooting in mind, providing it with steep-sided woods and deep ghylls. There are pegs where you see birds coming and must wait for the right moment to raise your gun; there are other pegs, deep in the trees, where you have to be quick, very quick on a bird or it will be gone in a fleeting vision of wings. Scargill is made for pheasant-shooting and it is made even better by controlled and skilful beating: the slow and steady and quiet sort, with cunningly placed flagmen, that puts a regular trickle of birds into the sky rather than those wasteful flushes. Only six guns shoot and although, as always happens, each drive favours some pegs rather than others, I have never had a blank drive: I have finished a drive with no birds to collect but I have never stood through a drive without firing my gun.

I do not know how many birds are put down. I once asked Michael but I have forgotten his reply. Between twelve and fifteen hundred would be my guess. Birds cross the guns in the correct quantity; you do not have periods of continuous shooting; you have to wait between shots and I would estimate that, at the end of a typical Scargill day, you will have taken on something like forty pheasants. If you have hit more than half of them you will have shot well and the bag is usually roughly a hundred birds. Everything about this approximates to my vision of an ideal driven day. I do not really approve of a continual procession of birds and the enormous bags that are often its result.

On this particular Scargill day we gathered as usual in the yard of the keeper's house. Michael met us; I noticed that I was wearing odd stockings, but they were only slightly different shades of green and they did not look like a tastelessly exhibitionist sort of fashion statement, especially since only the tops of them were showing above my Wellingtons (eight pounds a pair from Eden Farm Supplies and very appropriately retailed as the Pennine Boot). We had been the first guns to arrive but John soon turned up and we had soon been introduced to all our fellow guns. We had soon drawn for pegs and before long we set off for the first drive. Keeper and beaters had disappeared ten minutes ago.

There was a brief journey along the road, then we took guns and cartridges and sticks and dogs, crossing the fields and climbing a stile before descending a steep path through the trees to our pegs along the side of the river Greta. I suppose the presence of the river is, in a practical sense, a blemish upon Scargill's perfection as a pheasant shoot, although the valley it has carved for itself provides the steep slopes that send pheasants high over the guns, while those deep ghylls are the work of small becks anxious to find their way to a larger watercourse as soon as possible.

Now that I think about it, the river Greta is clearly part of the divine plan, which denies us paradise on earth but allows a few close approximations. The Greta, anyway, like most other rivers, is beautiful: the sight and sound of it are welcome as you stand waiting at the beginning of a drive; the problem is that birds fall in the river and, if the water is up, not a few of them are lost to the bag. I once shot at Scargill with the Greta in big flood; it was a day when I shot well and most of the team shot even better.

At the end of the day Michael declared a bag of 129; it was a guess, based on his estimate that at least twenty five birds had fallen into the river and been swept away. At least five of mine had gone that way and the loss of so many birds left some sense of waste. The divine plan certainly intends shot pheasants to end up on plates.

On the morning in question there was no problem of this sort. The river behind me, as I stood on the end of the line at number one, was low and smooth, flowing between pale slabs of rock with the dark-polished shine of moving water on cloudy winter days. In front of me the land rose steeply in pale and faded colours beneath the grey sky; to my left, down the slope of the land, ran the dark shapes of the trees, slanting away from me along the side of one of those ghylls. Most of the birds, I knew, would follow this line of trees, but a few of them might show some independence of mind, might defy the flagman above me and insist on heading my way. Michael had already declared that the wind was wrong for my end of the line, but this did not stop me hoping for a chance or two. Waiting at my peg for the beginning of the first drive and the appearance of the first pheasant in the sky above me: this is the time when Scargill nerves touch me most sharply. Once my part in the shooting starts they turn into something else, into a grim acknowledgment of incompetence or an unspoken prayer for the challenge of the next bird. Just before the beginning of it all there is the tension of uncertainty.

It was not long before the first pheasant climbed into the sky, a typically high Scargill bird that was nowhere near me. I heard the bang but did not see whether she fell. More pheasants soon followed and a fair proportion threw back their necks and plummeted to earth or water. I was a spectator for most of the time. I had thought that, if birds came to me, this would happen early in the drive from the top of the wood before it cut away from me. I was wrong: my turn came late, with two birds that were quick crossers when they reached me; one of them was an indisputably high bird and, glory be, both of them fell to the first barrel. The drive ended almost with the fall of my second bird and very soon Ross had brought me a cock and a hen, both stone dead. It was a very good beginning to a Scargill day.

The end of a drive, when you are happy with your perform-ance, is a pleasant time. There is the sight of guns and pickers-up with long-tailed pheasants in their hands; there are dogs still hunting for birds, encouraged and controlled by the whistles and the voices of their handlers. There may be work for your own spaniel and there is the dissipation of the focused tension that should grip us all while we stand waiting and watching with a loaded gun. There is also the movement from the loneliness of your peg to the company of those who have made and shared the event that has just ended. For me there is always smoke, dissolving on the air all round me: a symbol of relaxation, a silent announcement that some sort of interval has arrived. And this time there was the pleasure of knowing that, although my shooting had only given two birds to the bag, it could not have given any more.

I handed my pheasants to Michael, who repeated that the wind had been wrong for my peg. I joined John and the other guns before we climbed up the steep path back to the fields, back into the wind and the grey light of a cloudy January morning. There was talk of one thing and another, easy talk, mainly sporting talk, a bit of school talk, since John is an old boy and a governor of my school and since the friend I had come over with – you have already met him – was Neil, the school's bursar.

Soon it was down through the woods, back to the river; soon it was back to the isolation of my peg. Michael showed me to it with something like a laugh, suggesting that, if birds flew over me, I would have to be very quick with them. It was the sort of peg designed to give the men who stand there stiff necks: it was a gap between the trees, tall firs or pines on level ground, with a steep, wooded bank rising in front, a continuation of that same, river-carved bank that had faced me during the first drive. The beat would not be straight towards the guns, but along the bank and past them, and it was clear that I should spend it staring up through the branches, waiting for the sudden shape of a pheasant in the patch of clear sky above.

I put a match to my pipe and inhaled a time or two, then I stuffed the pipe in my pocket and told myself that I must wait to light it again until Michael's horn proclaimed another interlude. I checked the barrels of my gun and put a cartridge in each of them. I spoke a word or two to Ross and I explored the view above me from different positions no more than a foot or so apart: none of them seemed to produce a broader view of the sky. The sudden sound of whistles told me that the drive had begun. I leaned to take a few more cartridges from my bag, put them in my pocket and waited for the pattern of the drive to unfold. As number three I could expect a fair share of the action; it seemed to me that it was likely to be of the demanding sort.

There was a shot or two back in the wood the way we had come; and then there was a pheasant above me, a dark shape on set wings. A swipe of the gun produced the sound of a bird crashing down behind. The swipe and the sound were both repeated a few seconds later and I began to think that I was no longer capable of missing pheasants, however high, however fast, however sudden their appearance over the trees. It was a thought soon exposed as a fantasy, but at the end of the drive Ross brought me six pheasants and, though forced to acknowledge that I was, after all, a fallible shot, I was feeling very pleased with myself.

The third drive at Scargill is similar to the first. There is a deep ghyll running back at a right angle to the river; the guns stand with their backs to the water and the ghyll is beaten down towards them. There is one peg on a rocky ledge above the river with the trees above rising from a sheer bank, with a rail to prevent the gun who stands there losing his balance and tumbling into the water. I have stood there twice and failed miserably with the pheasants that appeared so suddenly in the sky above me, missing them with the first barrel and rarely being quick enough to pull the second trigger.

This time I was on the far side of the ghyll on a less demanding peg. Birds came my way towards the end of the drive and I shot moderately well, shooting three of the six birds that flew over me. Then we moved woods, walking up through the ghyll, emerging from the sheltered and shadowed world of the trees down by the river into the grey windiness and sharp air of the Pennine fields. There was a short wait in a farmyard, until John and another of the guns had brought transport and taken us along and down the road, back down into woods that lined the slopes, not above the river Greta but on either side of a tributary stream. And there, in a clearing by the bridge, the ritual of comforts was performed.

There was a mug of soup; there were sausage rolls; there was a choice between sloe gin and damson gin and there was a slug of both for those eager to compare flavours (I was one of them). I cannot remember what we talked of, except that there was some grouse-talk and some talk with John about fives, an obscure game of which we are both inordinately fond. I thought the damson gin was marginally better than the sloe gin, but if the damson gin had not been on offer, I should have been perfectly happy with a refill of the sloe sort. I enjoyed comforts very much indeed, down in that little clearing by the side of the bridge, away from the wind, with a grey sky above and the sound of the beck on the quiet air; I enjoyed both sorts of gin; I enjoyed the soup and the sausage rolls (two of them); I enjoyed talking about grouse and fives and I enjoyed smoking; what I enjoyed most of all was feeling that I deserved to be there and thinking that, even if I made a hash of the two remaining drives, I had shot well enough on the three morning drives to avoid shame. We spent about twenty minutes comforting ourselves, and then Michael appeared and we prepared ourselves for the afternoon's sport.

I did not have far to walk. I was back to number one. Michael showed me to another and much smaller clearing on the other side of the bridge; he told me that there would be birds towards the end of the drive, which would be the longest of the day. I settled down to wait and decided that I liked my stand. The beat would be straight down the beck towards me. There was clear space in front of me but not too much; I should have time to see pheasants before they were on me but not enough time to start thinking about them. It seemed a good stand at which to kill birds, and I liked everything about my little clearing in the trees; it felt somehow comfortable, down there in the damp smell of the woods, and I was standing there after shooting effectively on three earlier drives. I liked the feel of the old Webley when I gave it a practice-swing and I liked being unable to see any of the other guns, which was not because I hated them (three of them were old friends) but because I prefer drives when I seem to be hidden away. It is probably because I feel that failure will be less public and may even go unnoticed, but it is also an aesthetic or atmospheric preference. I like the feeling of seclusion, as though I am standing and waiting for pheasants in a secret place among the trees.

It was not long, anyway, before the sound of shots told me that the far end of the line was engaged. I tend to think that double shots probably announce a missed bird (or a right-and-left), whereas the single shout of a gun proclaims the end of a pheasant, and I think it is true that most of us are more deadly with the first barrel than with the second. There is a point to this observation, which is that when, perhaps five minutes later, a pheasant appeared over me, it was the second barrel that brought him down, and this became for me a feature of the drive. They were good birds. They were not archangels, in fact they were probably rather less high than most of the morning's pheasants, but they were good fast birds and no one would have thought twice about lifting his gun to them. When I lifted mine, at least five times it took a second shot to produce the sudden dive of a dead bird. I killed only one with the first barrel; I missed a couple clean and either five or six fell to my second attempt. I am not too proud to be satisfied with second-barrel kills. Six or seven pheasants with fifteen cartridges is good enough for me.

At the end of the drive I disappointed Ross by refusing to send him for my birds, explaining to him that they had all fallen into the next and final drive and would have to be left for the beaters. Then I left my secluded clearing, apologised to Michael for being unsure whether I had six or seven birds down, pointed out to him where they had fallen and joined my fellow guns, wondering why I had just shot the only drive in my shooting life when I had consistently killed birds with the second barrel. It must, of course, have been the speed of my swing accelerating as I moved to the second trigger, but as someone who is more often than not a second-barrel bungler it still puzzled and almost delighted me.

The last drive of the day was a drive which I had never shot well before. It is difficult for me to explain this. The birds are no higher than the general run of Scargill birds. They are on you fairly quickly but not as quickly as at some stands and they certainly fly no faster than on other drives; they are probably slower, in fact, because they flush nearer the guns. There is no reason why a man who has killed his fair share of birds on the four earlier drives should not do the same on the last drive, and this is precisely what I told myself as I stood at my peg and sized up the situation.

I was number three. There was enough air above and in front of me to get a fair sight of approaching birds, which would come crossing from the left to begin with and I should be ready for them. It was not long before one came and I missed him with both barrels. Immediately after this the gun to my left shot a right-and-left and almost at once I missed another bird, which sneaked over me from an unexpected angle and only gave me time for a single shot.

There was a shot from the gun on my right and I heard the splash of what might have been my bird falling into the beck. Then I shot a hen, knowing as I lifted onto her and swung through that she would fall. It happens to all of us: there are times when we shoot a bird and are surprised by the kill, because somehow it all felt wrong, and there are other times when we pull the trigger and hope, merely waiting upon results; but there are occasions when everything is smooth, relaxed and easy and we know perfectly well that the pheasant above us is doomed. This hen was such a bird and she was not the first of many. I missed a very similar bird with two shots; I scratched down a cock with the second barrel, most certainly a runner.

I missed another hen and then the horn sounded for the end of the drive and the end of the day's sport. I went looking for my runner and found that one of the pickers-up had already marked and gathered him. I wondered why, on a day when I had shot pretty well, the same old drive had defeated me. Perhaps the problem was psychological. Whatever it was, I was not too bothered. Eighteen birds for something like forty cartridges is good for me and the bag for the day was one hundred and sixteen.

Unless I have shot dismally, I usually enjoy the end of a driven day. I enjoy realising that I no longer have to perform, that sudden shifts of mood are over for the day; I enjoy gathering wherever we gather to thank and tip the keeper and receive a brace of birds. At Scargill this happens in a barn next to Michael's cottage, before the guns drive to John's house for lunch.

There are those who like lunch in the middle of a shooting day and those who prefer it at the end. On the whole I am a middle-of-the-day man, but this is mainly when lunch is from a bag: a pie or a sandwich eaten in a barn or under the sky; an informal lunch of this sort is a pleasant break from sport and it does not take up too much time. You can also drink two glasses of wine, because you know that it will be at least three hours before you drive home.

But if lunch is a cooked meal, if it happens in your host's house, if it involves a drive to reach the house, a drive followed by taking off boots and putting on shoes and combing hair and washing your hands before you sit down to eat; in such circumstances, in spite of my middle-of-the day leanings, I acknowledge the compelling logic of shooting through. Midwinter days are short, too short to take an hour and a half out of them in the middle of a shooting day; beaters do not want to be kept waiting while the guns help themselves to another nibble of stilton and another inch of port. On true driven shoots, lunch after sport is a thoroughly sensible procedure.

Lunch after sport means that you will not sit down to it until four o'clock and it may be nearer five. This is something of a problem if you have been invited out to dinner, because at the end of a shooting day you will be very hungry and will want to eat a lot of food.

On the day in question nobody had asked me to eat and drink with them in the evening, and so, when the time for lunch came, I got stuck in. I should want my supper when I got home, but with home an hour away, and with dogs to feed and a gun to clean and the fire to light when I got there, not to mention a bath for my body and at least one glass of sherry to stimulate the appetite (my appetite almost always needs two); with so much to do before at last I sat down for supper, I thought it would be at least ten o'clock before I put the first pink lump of lamb chop into my mouth and, since ten o'clock was more than five hours away, since breakfast had been early and mainly coffee and since even comforts had faded into a distant memory of two sausage rolls, I accepted a second helping of John's beef stew – I am not sure that he had cooked it – and was particularly appreciative of the black pudding that was in there among the meat. I had only one slice of apple pie, without too much cream; I was moderate with the stilton and very properly restricted myself to a single glass of wine.

It was eight o'clock when I collected old Digby from the farm where he had spent the day. It was half past nine before I sat down for a glass of sherry by the fire; another glass followed and it was way past ten before I settled down to my three chops.

It was one o'clock when I went up the stairs after my claret, which was not because three glasses had led to three more. I had sipped my claret, very slowly and appreciatively, conscious that the fire was warm and that it was delightful sitting there at the end of a fine day, doing what I so often do at the end of such days, which is to take out my shooting diaries and wander back through the sport of earlier years. It is good to reawaken memories when you have just made a few more of them, and fireside shooting makes a warm and comfortable end to a day that has been full of the real thing.

Chapter Seventeen

Messing Around at High Park

The morning after my day at Scargill the alarm woke me at half past seven. I answered its call by staying put, by reaching for the flask that had come upstairs with me the night before, by lying there in bed and drinking tea and thinking how much I had enjoyed yesterday, thinking at the same time that I was glad it had been yesterday and that here I was, comfortably supine with no urgent need to do anything different for at least another hour. I did not have much idea what something different might turn out to be, for the activities of the day ahead had not been predetermined.

I could do with it whatever I chose; perhaps I would go to fill the hoppers at High Park, although this was a job that could easily wait another day or two if I decided to do something else. It occurred to me, about half way through the first mugful of tea, that my pond was perhaps ready for another flight and that, if I did go hopper-filling, I might stay on and see how many duck came in with the darkness; or I might leave the duck another week or another day and, if I finished feeding with time to spare, I might take Ross for an hour or so of rough sport, the sort of sport he really loves, the sort that does not sit him at a peg and ask him to do nothing for long periods, nothing but sit there and watch while the beaters' spaniels have all the fun.

Giving Ross the chance to do what spaniels like best seemed a good idea as I lay in bed drinking tea and half listening to radio four. It was not a good idea that turned into a firm decision: I might choose only to flight; I might go rough shooting in the afternoon and then wait for the duck; the weather might turn against me and I might do neither; I could, after all, stay at home and catch up with some work or spend the day splitting logs and building up the wood-store. I could do more or less what I wanted and that was what pleased me so much as I lay there wondering unhurriedly how much longer I wanted to remain on my back. I dozed for about twenty minutes; then I drank another mug of tea while resuming my consideration of the possibilities ahead. Eventually I got out of bed just before half past eight. A day earlier at this time I had been rumbling over the Pennines, waiting for the snow to begin, wondering whether the journey back would be difficult and would come at the end of one of those shooting days when, for most of it, I had felt embarrassed and ashamed to be in possession of a shotgun. Today there would be no tension at all; today, whatever it brought, would be an ambling sort of day and its first unstrenuous duty was taking out the dogs.

The weather had softened overnight; it was mild and cloudy with a moist breeze. Somewhere up in the treetops a mistle thrush was making loud and exhilarating noises, which pleased me with their message of stirring impulses without at the same time managing to stir within me any urge for immediate and vigorous activity. It was very enjoyable strolling along behind Ross and Digby. I felt almost certain that I should go to feed my birds, but I was not yet sure when I should set off. I could easily spend the morning doing other things and so the feeding might not happen until the afternoon.

Back in the flat I ate two boiled eggs with slices of delicious olive bread from the co-op in Kirkby Stephen. The eggs were delicious too and I declared boiled eggs with olive bread the best of all breakfasts; the eggs should, if at all possible, have been laid by your own hens and then kept for at least a week. When you decide to eat them they should be put in a pan of cold water and, when the water comes to the boil, the heat should be turned off immediately and the eggs left where they are for just four minutes (only three if the eggs are small). Do this and you will find the whites cooked through and the yolks yellow-gold, soft and unctuous. You will also agree with me that boiled eggs are the best of all breakfasts and, to use a fashionable phrase, the best of all comfort foods.

Now that I have just written it down I realise that I object to the implications of the term comfort food. On the face of it there is nothing much wrong in associating food with comfort. It is an association so obvious that you might think it barely worth making, but your modern foodie talks of comfort food with condescension; he seems to believe in the existence of superior sorts of food that provide something more profound than comfort and sustenance. Think for a moment about the idea of comfort food and you will begin to appreciate the revolting and fatuous snobbery that lies beneath it. What are these superior, and presumably uncomforting foods meant to do for us? Do they baffle us with their complexity? Are they some sort of metaphor? Do they challenge the intellect to wrestle with fundamental problems of flavour and smell? Can they shock us out of the dull complacency bred by foods that bring only comfort? Perhaps they feed the life of the spirit or lead us to the apprehension of ultimate truth? Do they possess something of the serenity and sadness of late Mozart? Do they reach beyond the realm of the senses to share the mysterious and sublime otherworldliness of Beethoven's last quartets? Food, whatever the French say, is not art; it does not explore and illuminate the human condition. It fills our bellies and, the better it is, the more comfort it provides in this imperfect old world. There are, of course, different sorts of comfort: it can come from a subtle harmony of different elements; it can be more or less exquisite; it can be rich and wholesome and uncomplicated, but none of this alters the fact that all food worth eating is comfort food.

The eggs, anyway, were delicious and they reminded me to take some leek-tops and potato-peelings to throw to the hens along with their three daily cupfuls of corn and three of layers' pellets, scattered round the pen together with my thanks to the hens for continuing to lay so consistently right through the darkest months of the winter.

It was time now to finish my coffee and look at *The Times* for twenty minutes, reading the leaders and the letters with mild interest in the great events of the world and their analysis by great minds. After *The Times* I did the washing up from the night before and, while sloshing water over plates and wiping knives in the slovenly way that means everything ought to be – but never is – washed again before it is fit for use, while washing up, anyway, with more thought for getting it all put away than for getting it all clean, I wondered what form of comfort food to eat for supper and what wine to drink with it. I remembered that there was a brace of birds that had been hanging for at least a week and realised that, if I plucked them, one of them would do for my supper and, since I had not drunk any Burgundy for at least a fortnight, a half-bottle of *Savigny-Les-Beaune* seemed a good idea. It would comfort me in a subtle and beguiling sort of way with all sorts of hints and nuances. Wine glasses left from the night before, by the way, receive an altogether different sort of attention than do plates and bowls and cutlery. They are washed, rinsed, dried and polished with exemplary thoroughness and also with good reason; a lump of steak on a dirty plate will, if it is good steak and has been properly cooked, taste wonderful; fine wine in a greasy or detergent-soiled glass may well be completely ruined.

The radio had been on during the washing-up. I had not really been listening to it, but I turned it off at once when I realised that the daily service had begun and that some female minister of religion was droning on to God about the needs of the world. I cannot cope with the daily service. The choir sing hymns in a horribly earnest sort of way, the prayers are prayed in a voice that positively oozes sincerity and, since any statement or opinion that might conceivably arouse contro-versy is avoided, the daily service, apart from being distasteful, is also a crashing bore. It is packaged religion and it puts me off Christianity. This is probably wrong of me; whatever it is, the daily service told me that it was time to switch off the radio and go down to the shed to deal with a brace of pheasants. I took a second cup of coffee with me.

The birds took about twenty minutes and I made rather a good job of them. The cock went into the deep freeze and the hen went on a plate in the kitchen. Then I made a sandwich (cherry tomatoes with bits of salad onion and coriander) and filled my flask with tea, still wondering whether I should try to kill a couple of pheasants as well as filling their hoppers, still uncertain whether I should stay on to flight Low Park Pond. Eventually I put the dogs and a gun in the Land Rover, got in myself and drove off towards Kirkby Stephen. By now it was half an hour before noon and the sun had come out; it was one of those winter

days of mild air and hazy shine and milky brightness; it was pleasant to
be sauntering through it in a Land Rover with flexible plans.

I forgot to mention that, as well as a dog and a gun and a box
of cartridges, I had a brace of unplucked pheasants with me. This was
because I had decided to call in at Tarn House and give them to my
friends Helen and Gerry. Only Helen was at home; Gerry was busy
somewhere on the fell feeding sheep. I drank the day's third cup of
coffee, sat talking for half an hour, left the pheasants, was given half
a Christmas cake and finally made it to Kirkby Stephen at about half
past twelve.

I stopped at the co-op to buy a bottle of sherry (co-op *fino* is
of high quality). I picked up half a dozen bags of grain from Eden
Farm Supplies, then, on the short journey from Winton to High Park, I
suddenly revised my plans, making the momentous decision that I was
not, after all, going to feed. I would carry bags of grain from the hut up
to the bins by the pens, but the hopper-filling would come tomorrow
(unless some of the hoppers were empty) and, as long as I had finished
with the grain-carrying by two o'clock, I should definitely allow myself
an hour or more looking for a few birds on the outlands south of the
road. There were one or two rough and overgrown corners where no
spaniel had disturbed the peace for at least twelve months. I should also
feed the pond and I should probably flight the next evening.

The sun was stronger by now and the fields were shining in
pale January light. Pigeons clapped away from the hoppers as I came
near to them. There was barely a crow or jackdaw to be seen, which
pleased me; there were, by my late-season standards, plenty of pheasants
running or flying from my approach, which pleased me even more. And
it is good for a man of fifty five to plod up slopes with a sack of grain
over his shoulder, panting somewhat but with no intimations of an
impending heart-attack; it persuades him that he is not yet as decrepit
as he sometimes feels; it convinces him that forty years' smoking has
not completely wrecked his health; it encourages him to believe that he
will make it beyond sixty and find that he is still capable of doing the
things that are inspiring these hopeful thoughts. They may, of course,
be a delusion but there is nothing much wrong with the delusions of

hope: they do at least promote cheerfulness.

It is also good, once you have plodded up your steep and muddy slope, to slip the sack from your shoulder, sit down on a convenient stile and take a little time to admire the strong contrasts of a winter landscape in sunshine, as the light explores a tangled and faded chaos of dead grass and rushes, with twining stalks of bramble that are defiantly clinging to green, with the brown skeletons of thistle stalks, some of them still tufted with matted clumps of seed. But above this jungle of decay there is the vital sharpness of winter branches against the sky, there is the purpling maze of the birch-tops above the white rise of their trunks, there is the grey shine of ash branches between those hanging clusters of brown keys, there are brown leaves on the oaks, there are dark crimson berries on the sharp and twisted hawthorns, there are still deep purple sloes lining the branches of the blackthorns. The hazels are hung with the tight shapes of unopened catkins waiting for the spring, holly shines out in polished green and bright red, while young spruces thrust neatly pointed shapes of silvered green up into the sky, and the dull green of the gorse is scattered here and there with loose patterns of little yellow flowers.

Sitting on my stile this afternoon I saw all this and I saw all over again how birds show themselves more brightly in winter. I saw redwings flying through the sky and knew at once why they were so called; I saw fieldfares among the sloes and admired the complementary glow of their purple. I watched a chaffinch sitting on a branch with the flush of palest pink on her breast; there was a robin outshining the holly-berries and there was the white flash beneath the wings of mistle thrushes. There was, of course, the metallic brilliance of cock pheasants running through the drab undergrowth, and over it all was spread the brightness of the winter sky.

I took three sacks up to the West Pen, two to the New Pen and three to the Old Pen. Then I decided that I had done enough carrying and ate my sandwiches down by the hut, watching a party of long-tailed tits move through the branches above me and wondering whether the old hut, which was a very cheap hut when I bought it ten years ago, would make it through the winter or be blown down by the next gale.

It was a very cheap hut and now it is a decrepit and very leaky hut. Many of the panels are loose and gaping, the rats have chewed holes in the floor, the grey squirrels have chewed a hole in the top of the door and the whole structure leans ominously towards the beck, probably in an attempt to warn me where I am likely to find most of it before long unless I help it to stay where it is. It will get no such help before the end of the shooting and, even if it survives the rest of this winter, it ought to be replaced. I suppose I could build a new hut myself. I also know that I never shall. Unless it falls down first I shall almost certainly try to bodge up the old hut and keep it in place for a season or two more. If I got a new hut, I ought to get myself a better hut and a better hut would cost two or three thousand pounds. I think I shall go for the bodge-up; if it lasts out this winter I shall spend some part of the spring encouraging my old hut to stay upright for a few years more.

My sandwiches, by the way, were delicious, and not only because they were made with olive bread from the co-op. Tomatoes are usually flavoured with basil or with chives: try salad onions and coriander and relish their subtle contrasts of taste and texture; they are delightful; perhaps the harmony they create is almost beautiful; but what all this does, when you get down to it, is bring pleasure and comfort. There was certainly nothing subtle about the strong dark tea in my flask. I rather wished that I had brought some sloe gin with me, for its sweetness would have gone well with my sandwiches. It was, by the way, no new striving for a more austere life that had left the sloe gin at home. I had simply forgotten to fill my hip-flask and shove it in my bag. After the essential comfort of tea and sandwiches, anyway, it was time to go looking for a pheasant or two. Ross and I were soon heading up the road for the outlands.

Almost as soon as he had started hunting through the spring pasture Ross pounced. I heard a brief flapping of wings in the gorse, accompanied by one or two snorts and a few scuffling sounds. These are the sort of noises that you want to hear when your dog is looking for a runner, not when he is supposed to be flushing pheasants for your gun. I assumed that a bird had been pegged and felt irritated, slightly irritated with Ross but more irritated with the pegged bird for not getting a move on and getting out of cover before it presented a spaniel with irresistible temptation.

There was, as it turned out, no need for any irritation at all because the bird that Ross brought to me was a winged cock from my last High Park main day, still fit and fat a whole week after the day of his wounding. For I told myself – and I was almost certainly right – that he must be the high cock that, rising from the top of the Gully, had flown over me, flinching to the second barrel before gliding out of sight through the misty afternoon. The day after the shoot I had looked for him and two or three other birds but had only found a pricked hen. His condition surprised me, for I put no feeders south of the road and I wondered what he had been eating to keep so much flesh on his bones. He was a lost bird found and, far from being a source of irritation, he was a pleasure. Immediately he made me hope that Ross would flush a hen for me to shoot and then hang with him in the shed at home. Almost immediately a hen jumped over the wall; she did it almost furtively and with no sense of sport, offering no chance of a shot.

We went next to the deep rushes right at the top of the forty-acre. There are not often pheasants there but a sunny day late in the season offers the best chance of a bird or two. I remember a bright afternoon just after the end of the season – I was there rabbiting with old Digby – when hen pheasants sprang out of those rushes all along the wall. There must have been seven or eight of them and, with the last two or three, I was tempted almost beyond resistance. If they had all been cocks, or even if just the last of them had been a cock, I know that my resistance would have failed. And I wonder if you have noticed how pheasants seem often to congregate in same-sex gatherings? You come across a little party of hens in one corner of a field; then in a gorse-choked ditch along the edge of the next field you disturb three or four cocks. It only struck me this season, but memories of earlier seasons support the view, and so do the later experiences of this afternoon.

It was, you may remember, an afternoon for neglected places and odd corners. From the top of the forty acre, where there were no pheasants, although a couple of snipe rose so far ahead of me that there was no question of asking myself whether I was in the rare mood to let off at them – from the top of the forty acre, anyway, I went down to the beck which, after flowing under the bridge where I often park the Land Rover, winds its way through flat fields that must once have been a bog: a place of squelching earth and muddy pools and rushes, an oozy paradise for fowl and snipe and shooting men. There is no longer much wetness, for the fields have been drained and they fatten sheep now, offering little to interest a man with a gun except along the edges of the beck, which is fenced off and flows two or three feet beneath the level of the surrounding land. The banks are steep and tangled and sometimes there are pheasants lurking along them; occasionally there is also a mallard down on the edges of the water. This afternoon Ross found nothing but interesting smells, until we came to the boundary of my shoot, where the beck approaches the road to Kaber at an angle that forms a small triangle of land between the water and the road, with a fence along its base, with rough cover below straggling willows everywhere else.

It is just the place for an old cock to shelter, brooding bitterly on the predatory urges that drive men to hunt him and all his kind. There was one there this afternoon until Ross put an end to his brooding by

Finn and Ross (right) in the back of the Landrover

putting him on to the wing. But he was a cunning old cock, flushing so low over the wall that I dared not shoot for fear of passing cars or walkers. Once he was settled into some other tangled corner, the brooding doubtless resumed in even deeper bitterness, though seasoned now with grim satisfaction that the old enemy had been thwarted once again. Meanwhile I was trudging back the way I had come, doing a spot of brooding myself because it seemed that it was turning into one of those rough-shooting afternoons when pheasants departed before ever bringing me the chance of pulling the trigger of my gun. Snipe were now most definitely on the hit-list.

It was back to the forty acre and along the bottom fence, where two hens rose high from the gorse, twenty yards in front of Ross and at least forty in front of me. They swung over the bank away from me with the sun in their feathers and there was, of course, no shot. A rabbit appeared and disappeared before the quickest shot in the kingdom could have had time even to mount his gun. I told myself that the gathering of a winged pheasant was more important than the killing of unwounded birds or rabbits; the afternoon had therefore been a success. Unconvinced by my own argument I crossed into the field below.

It is a steep field, rising up to the forty acre from the flat fields below, with a narrow plateau tapering to the north along its upper rim. It is also a bare field, except for a spread of blackthorn, perhaps seventy yards long and thirty deep, along the curve of the slope. From a field or two away it looks wonderful cover. It looks dark and dense and, perched on its slope, it looks just the place from which to drive wonderful birds. Unfortunately this is an impression that does not survive closer inspection, for it is, in fact, old and leggy blackthorn clinging to a cold and draughty bank; there are often rabbits in it. Only rarely have I disturbed a pheasant and always, on those rare occasions, if I have come at the thorns from below, the bird has run out far above me and flown away, whereas an approach from the topside has sent him out from the bottom, skimming low down the slope of the ground. I have never fired a shot at a pheasant flushing from those thorns.

And so I did not walk along the widening plateau towards them with much hope of sport, and in the bright sunshine I could see through

the spindly trunks to the open ground beyond, I could see how bare it
was beneath them and I saw all over again why pheasants were so rarely
to be found there; but suddenly there was a hen running from the far
corner towards the wall. I walked towards her, thinking she might
squat before she flew, but she flapped over the wall and was gone; and
now there were three or four hens running from the other corner and
leaping onto the wing at least sixty yards away from me. I have never
seen anything like it from the thorns and I have still to fire a shot at
birds coming out of them.

A wall runs down the north side of the forty acre, with patches
of gorse spreading along it; a ditch runs parallel with the wall, full of
rushes, especially right at the bottom of the field where the ditch is at
its deepest and wettest. Here at last a hen pheasant flushed within shot,
rose into the sunshine and fell over the fence somewhere in the field
of thorns. Ross was soon under the fence and I stood there waiting,
wondering whether he would return with my hen or whether I should
have to follow him over the fence and begin searching for a runner
while fearing that she would never be found. There are sights of which
we shooters never tire and one of them is most certainly the sight of
a muddy spaniel returning to his master with a pheasant between his
jaws. I have rarely enjoyed it more than in the bottom corner of the
forty acre towards the end of an afternoon when at last a bird had risen
into the sky and fallen to the ground; it would have been a deep disappointment if that bird had not been brought in.

The hen was dead; she went in the bag and I now sat smoking
in the rushes, admiring a tall holly that lifted itself from the sides of
the ditch, tapering to an almost regular spike lined with thick clusters
of blood-red berries. To the side of it rose a birch, with its flaking
trunk pale white; and the sun was bright on both the stiff holly and the
stirring birch. Even the rushes up the field had caught the light.

The long delayed and then successful shot, this and the brightness of the things all round me in the slanting glow of a late-afternoon,
this brightness of things and the sheltered seclusion of my corner down
there in the ditch below the wall; all this produced one of those inflows
of serene and deep contentment that come to me from time to time in

the course of shooting and fishing days. It is as though I breathe them in with the quiet air. I looked at my gun resting on my game-bag and tried to remember when first it had shot a pheasant for me. I looked at the pheasant that it had shot most recently and at the spaniel that had found her. I looked at the birch and the holly and wondered whether trees usually carried so much fruit into the New Year. I looked with admiration and gratitude at everything that I saw.

Soon it was time to put my pheasant in the game-bag, take up my gun, rouse my spaniel and plod up the ditch, working Ross through the rushes and the gorse. Every blade of grass was luminous. I was walking through a landscape transfigured by the late sun, until my contentment was disturbed by a twinge of disappointment when a woodcock flitted away from me and was missed by the one barrel I managed to let off at him. Then it was over the stile, back into the spring-pasture, where a hen rose from a tiny patch of gorse right against the wall; she rose for the last time and Ross had soon found her. She restored the contentment and she was the end of the afternoon's sport. I fed Low Park Pond with Digby and then drove home through a landscape sinking into shadows and dim shapes beneath a mother-of-pearl sky.

When I had fed the dogs and lit the fire and cleaned my gun and had a bath, when all this was done I poured myself a glass of *manzanilla;* then I poured another glass of *manzanilla* over the pheasant that was waiting to become my supper. I rubbed the bird with olive oil, shoved a slice of lemon into the cavity, larded the breasts with bacon and then roasted it for forty minutes with fennel and with thyme.

Modesty forbids me to proclaim it a triumph; honesty compels me to confess that it was very good indeed, very comforting. You must have pheasant stock (and white wine) to make the sauce, into which you put the bacon, cut into small strips, and all the bits of fennel. I ate my pheasant with leeks (fried briefly in olive oil) and spinach (simmered in oil and garlic) and with (almost) new potatoes, boiled without salt and then salted, sprinkled with rosemary and drizzled, I believe the term is, with olive oil. If I am in the mood I soak rather than drizzle, because I am very fond of olive oil; on this occasion I decided that there was already enough of it in everything else, and so on this occasion I contented myself with a generous drizzle.

There were twenty minutes or so full of contented chewing and gurgling. Then I left the washing up, took out the dogs, finished my burgundy and went to bed. Sleep soon came, but there was time for me to think, as I lay there drowsily, that the day just over had in a sense been more full of pheasants than the day before. At Scargill I had shot about twenty pheasants, but that is all I had done (apart from missing my share); on the High Park outlands I had picked one wounded bird and shot two others; but they belonged to a day on which I had also plucked pheasants, moved food for pheasants, cooked and eaten pheasant; it was a day that in its own fashion had been a complete pheasant day and it sent me to sleep in love with shooting and very happy that I had decided not to flight, so that, after tomorrow's feeding, I should be able to sit by Low Park Pond and listen to pheasants as they went up to roost while I waited there in the thickening light for the muttering sounds and the circling shapes of duck.

The view west, across Cumbria, from The Pens

Chapter Eighteen

In Search of Woodcock

It was towards the end of one of those January afternoons that I so enjoy: afternoons spent with a friend or two or just with a spaniel, afternoons spent hunting out a few late-season birds and perhaps a few rabbits. They are afternoons without any tension or strain, there is no plan to them, except to start somewhere and cover as much ground as possible and then finish with the failing light; and it does not really matter much if you end later than you should, when pheasants are already thinking of roost. It does not matter much because you are no longer trying to hold your birds for any grand occasions; on my shoot at any rate late January means that attempts at grand occasions are all in the past.

I like late-January shooting for many reasons. I like it, perhaps rather perversely, because the end of the season is now very close and, although I resent the ending of pheasant time, which comes at least a fortnight too soon, I find that approaching ends breathe off their own very distinctive atmosphere. It is true that the mood of late September fishing is sadder, more intense and more affecting than anything that hangs on the air of a January afternoon as the sun sinks low; for the end of the trout season comes with the deepening of autumn, with dying grass and falling leaves and early darkness.

In contrast, by the end of January, when the last pheasants are dropping from the sky, the days are already stretching themselves, mistle thrushes are already shouting from the treetops and winter, although it does not always seem so, is already in retreat. There are intimations of spring in late January; in spite of this, for the shooter, whatever the longer light and the first singing birds and the catkins on willow and hazel might be telling him, the sense of retrospect is always strong. Perhaps there will be a last flight in a few days; perhaps there will be another afternoon or two filled with the hope of a few more pheasants. But soon it will all be over; soon you will not shoot another duck or another pheasant until another spring and summer have turned into another autumn.

January shooting appeals to me for these reasons of mood. There is also a strong sporting argument for rating January pheasant-days very highly indeed, for January birds are without doubt the most exhilarating birds of the whole season. They are stronger on the wing than they were even a few weeks ago; they are much more cunning than they were before Christmas, more expert at using their legs to avoid the unwelcome attentions of a springer spaniel; there are many fewer of them too, which means that each one shot is worth more than it would have been a month or two ago. They are also, by the way, at their best for the table. Early in the season pheasant-flesh is often almost bland and covered with a layer of yellow fat which comes from lazy living and from rich pickings; but by January much of the fat has gone and the meat is full of the rich flavour, full of the earthy fragrance of game. Your January birds will, of course, need hanging. How long they need will depend entirely on the weather: no more than a week if it is mild, but up to a fortnight in cold and frosty air.

I hang my birds in an open shed, from a beam above the reach of prowling cats, and I rather enjoy the ritual, at the end of a shooting day, of slipping braced birds over the nails that I have driven into the beam and then, in the days that follow, inspecting them from time to time to make sure that corruption has not set in. I hate rotten pheasant; there is a world of difference between well-hung and putrid flesh. I do not, by the way, much enjoy the later ritual of plucking my birds when their hanging is over so I pay schoolboys to do it for me. They do a good job and spend the money I give them (a pound a bird) on food, or perhaps on beer and cigarettes; but sometimes they are on holiday and I have to do it myself. Over the years I have plucked and dressed enough pheasants to have become competent and fairly quick. It is not a skill that gives me much satisfaction and it is time to leave what happens to my pheasants when they are dead, turning instead to my efforts to kill a few living and flying ones.

I love January shooting: it does not matter much to me what the bag is at the end of the afternoon; two or three birds is fine; ten is rarely achieved but is indisputably better, especially since, as the season draws to its close, I begin to hoard dead pheasants in the deep freeze, so that the spring and summer can still, when the mood takes me, put a pheasant on my plate. On this particular January afternoon, anyway, it was just Ross and I out at High Park and things were going well. There were already four pheasants in my bag, although two of them, to be precise (which is something I can rarely bother to be), had spent some time in my game bag, but had then been taken out of it and were now hanging on short lengths of blue baling twine from nails on the outside of the hut.

And so, as it happens, there were only two pheasants in my bag as I stood on North Bank above a dense mass of gorse, listening to the sound of a hunting spaniel and waiting to see what he would put into the sky. I am not sure why there were still two pheasants in my bag. It seems odd that I had not hung all four of them from those nails when I had rested briefly by the hut before climbing up onto North Bank; but there most certainly were two birds in my game-bag, which – just in case you are interested in game-bags – was very cheap when I bought it second-hand something like twenty years ago. It is a green bag; both the strap and the bag itself are made of nylon, which is presumably why they have both proved indestructible. Anyway, I cannot remember why there were still two pheasants in my green nylon game-bag, but I do know that, if I regularly went into such detail about such trivial matters, this book would be four times as long and entirely indigestible. For some reason I have enjoyed telling you that there were not really four pheasants in my bag; I suppose writing a book gives you the opportunity to be a crashing bore.

It was a January afternoon of the soft sort, with short drifts of pale sunshine between longer periods of grey sky. There had been a hen from the Stackhole, from the rushes beneath the spring. She had flushed well in front but had turned back and flown straight over me on fast wings, a high bird for the rough-shooter, and her steep descent through the sunlight had pleased me. She embodied the strength and challenge of late season birds and, when Ross had brought her in, I sat down for a minute or two and sent smoke into the air. The cock that followed from the top of the hag was a going-away bird, but he was rising all the time until he fell and, as soon as he came down, he was going away again, but this time on his legs, which were not fast enough to save him from the gentle clamp of a spaniel's jaws. He made the brace and it was some time before the brace turned into three. We had searched the gorse along the top edge of the faraway, Ross had flushed a hen and I had missed her. Then we went down through the trees and crossed the beck, crossing it only after I had sat on a fallen trunk for a minute or two, sitting there beneath the trees and inhaling smoke together with the damp and distinctive flavour of a late January afternoon.

I do not bother with the wood when shooting alone, and so, once I had trudged up the steep and muddy slope on the other side of the beck, Ross got to work in the rough ground above it, but all his efforts put nothing on the wing. I said to myself, and probably to Ross as well, that pheasants were getting scarce and that we might have to be content with a brace, although I thought the Gully would probably produce the chance of a bird or two. It is not often that the Gully drives blank.

I left my brace at the fence, crossed the stile and put Ross into the pen-side gorse. There were a couple of pheasants here, but they flushed on the wrong side. Twice I heard the strong beat of wings and saw nothing until suddenly there was a pheasant rising over the trees and already way out of range. There was a bird or two in the Rushy Pasture as well, but they flushed half a field away from us and curled down the Gully. I watched them with admiration and regret, admiring the strength and speed of their flight and regretting that they had not flushed closer and that there were no friends waiting below to swing their guns and test their skill. My money would have been on the pheasants.

It was the same in the patches of gorse above the fence: again there were pheasants there but they flushed without the chance of a shot and all I could do was to watch their strong and high departure.

Solitary shooting often brings frustration of this sort, but I refused to let it trouble me and climbed over the fence that separates the top of the Gully from its long extension down the steep slope of the big pasture. And now I rested in the same spot where, back in November, I had sat down to smoke in the course of my boundary afternoon. The pipe came out again and you will know the sort of thoughts that came to me once it was lit. I thought how short pheasant-time is; how I had sat in the same place something like two months ago with a sense of prelude, whereas now I was sitting there with the end of the season almost upon me.

Acknowledging that there was so little time left made me very eager to harvest a few last birds and the Gully would surely provide a chance or two when I put my pipe away and got on my feet again. With its dense thickets of gorse and tangled clumps of brambles and briars the Gully always looks as though there must be pheasants sheltering there; there usually are and, even when you are unusually eager to add a few more birds to the bag, it is good to sit looking at the Gully in the expectation of imminent sport. I often guess from which bits of gorse my sport will emerge (I am usually wrong); then I light my pipe again and admire the view for just a little longer until finally I persuaded myself that winter afternoons do not last for ever and that it is time to be moving.

Ross had not been in the Gully for long before there came the sound of a pheasant that was suddenly finding the gorse less peaceful than he had been expecting. It is perhaps the best sound in rough-shooting: the sound of a bird making hasty preparations to emerge from cover; and there is always the uncertainty of precisely where and how he will flush. Already that afternoon I had heard the sound of wingbeats in the gorse at least half a dozen times, but only once had it brought me a shot. In the Gully it is very unlikely that a bird will flush without giving you a chance, which only happens if you let your dog work too far in front of you.

Anyway I heard the sound, and waited for the bird. Ross was above me and the pheasant he had disturbed, once it got launched, would fly straight down the Gully or out of one of the sides; it is very rare, though it has happened, for birds to fly up the line of the Gully. This one came straight down. He would doubtless have curled one way or the other but he fell before he could make any decision about curling. He was fast rather than high and he had spurs at least half an inch long. I fancy he was a survivor from some previous release.

The Gully rarely lets me down and, after this cock, there was a hen right from the bottom. She flew away from me, heading for the rough ground beyond the road, and she fell just over the wall. She made four and there were no more birds until I found myself standing on North Bank above that dense mass of gorse, with two pheasants in my bag, standing there above the gorse and waiting to see what Ross would put out of it.

I was perfectly happy with four pheasants, although I had no intention of turning down the opportunity for more; five would be better than four and six would be better than five. More pheasants would make me even happier than I already was, but I was, in fact, hoping for a change. I was hoping for woodcock and, quite apart from the fact that I love them on the wing and in the bag and on a plate, there was a particular reason behind this hope: I had been telling myself that the deep freeze was well-supplied with woodcock, but then a recent investigation had proved me wrong.

I must have eaten more than I thought, for I could find only three, which was only half as many as I needed. Usually I eat woodcock all by myself and two at once, feasting in solitary delight upon the richness of their flesh and at the same time gurgling my way through half a bottle of something rather better than average. A woodcock, in my opinion, provides the finest meat in the world and it is also my opinion that there is no point in wasting the world's best flesh on those who disagree with this verdict; the fact, moreover, that woodcock are roasted with their insides intact seems, for some reason that I have never been able to grasp, to put most of my friends off the idea of eating them, which makes my fondness for lonely woodcock feasts rather less selfish and self-indulgent.

I must admit that I no longer cook my birds with their heads on; these are now removed after plucking or before putting them in the roasting tray. Perhaps, under the corrupting influence of the modern age – which prefers not to be reminded that the meat it eats was once living flesh – perhaps I am becoming squeamish in my middle-age; at any rate I prefer not to contemplate the eyes and the long beak of a woodcock while I am chewing the dark flesh of its breast. Perhaps it is the beginning of a process: perhaps I shall turn against offal before long, deciding that rabbit livers are no longer the best part of a rabbit stew; perhaps I shall start feeding them to the dogs rather than slicing them with a knife, frying them for a second or two and then popping them into the casserole in the hope that most of them will end up on my plate.

Whether or not I am growing soft and semi-urbanised, I was still hoping that Ross would flush me a woodcock. The special reason for this – I am getting round to it at last – was that I was feeling generous and so, for once, I was planning a sociable woodcock feast as a change from the usual sort. This was because two friends, who more than once had listened to my eulogies of roasted woodcock, two friends with inquiring minds and inquisitive stomachs and no squeamish tendencies, were anxious to discover if my praise was justified. There would there-fore be three of us and we all had good appetites and the feast would be more like a hunger-lunch unless I could put two woodcock in front of each one of us. Even with six woodcock I was thinking that a mallard would be a necessary accompaniment, to fill us up just enough to leave plenty of room for the cheese and the port.

Up there in the gorse, anyway, Ross did what I was hoping that he would do. He made the gorse shake above him and very soon a woodcock, realising that it would be quieter elsewhere, sprang onto the wing. I was ready for it; I lifted the old Webley (very smoothly) and pulled the trigger (very confidently), and there was not a loud bang. Instead of a loud bang there was a feeble splutter of a sound; there was a feeble splutter and a soft hiss and that was all. In the confusion of my surprise I forgot all about the second trigger, bemused by the failure of the first to produce its usual result. Meanwhile the woodcock departed on erratic and graceful wings, while I, in compensation for the virtual silence of my defective cartridge, swore very loudly indeed. Ross knew none of all this. He was still questing in the gorse and so, in case another woodcock was about to decide that he had chosen the wrong spot for a quiet nap, I broke my gun and was on the point of reloading the first barrel when a warning voice, a voice whispering to me from some remote time in the infancy of my shooting life, suggested that it would be a good idea to look down the barrel before slipping another cartridge into the chamber.

It was a very wise voice, perhaps even a saving voice and I am very grateful to it, for when I looked where the voice had told me to look, I saw no gleam of light at the far end of my barrel; very clearly there was something still in there. By good fortune there was a cleaning rod in the hut no more than five minutes walk away. The obstruction was soon removed – it was, of course, the wadding – and I went on to shoot a woodcock, which brought my supply up to four. It was, incidentally, the last woodcock I shot before the end of the season and so the feast, when it came early in February, saw the woodcocks supplemented by two rather than by a single mallard. It was a good combination and my friends were full of praise for the richness of both sorts of flesh. Duck and woodcock were both toasted over the port.

But the feast is not what chiefly concerns me, which is rather what might have happened if the warning voice had never come or not been heeded? Would I have been a one-armed presence at my feast? Might it have been a memorial feast with just two gloomy revellers, sitting round a table to honour a dead colleague in the best fashion they could think of: with a solemn chewing of flesh, with a silent raising of glasses, with a torn and twisted shotgun lying between their plates as a sad reminder of their late friend?

This book has almost nothing useful to say: it rambles on about shooting and fishing and wanders where my fancy takes it. Just for once I am in a position to say something more than useful, something that is in fact very important indeed. Misfires are very rare events. I think they are probably much rarer than they used to be and, in the course of more than thirty years' shooting, I can remember only the one that I have just described. Perhaps my memory is letting me down; perhaps I have been unusually lucky with my cartridges, but none of this matters.

What does matter is that, since misfires are such uncommon occurrences, there is the danger of forgetting, as I so nearly forgot, the proper procedure to follow when one happens out of the blue. Wait a minute or two; point your barrels at the ground and, above all, make sure to look down them and see that they are both clear before you reload and then continue with your sport. Otherwise it is just possible that you are about to pull the trigger for the last time.

CHAPTER NINETEEN

A New Vice

The emergence of a new fault has made my performance with a shotgun even more unpredictable than it used to be. First appearing early in January as no more than an occasional impediment it was almost disregarded; on the recent day of the misfire it helped me to miss a hen pheasant, but that was the only sign of it. There have been no more misfires since that Saturday afternoon; there has been a final flight and there have been a few afternoons knocking round High Park in search of a few last pheasants.

I shall soon describe one of these afternoons and I shall also describe how this new fault seems suddenly to have become a settled, and very unwelcome, feature of what passes for my shooting technique.

As a sort of prelude to the main theme of this chapter you might like to hear about some of my old faults, some of the faults that I have lived with for years on end, somehow managing, in spite of them, to kill a few birds and to extract pleasure from the course of most shooting days. They will probably cheer you up, these old faults of mine; they will make you realise that your own faults, if you have any, are trivial in comparison with the long catalogue that you have just read with mingled pity and contempt.

You will probably wonder why I ever bother to get up early in the morning, put on a pair of breeches, and sometimes a tie, before eating two hurried boiled eggs, drinking a quick pint of coffee and then taking a gun from my cabinet and setting off through the dawn to parade my incompetence before yet another team of guns and another army of beaters.

The truth is that I have lived with my old faults for so long that, most of the time, I can put up with them. There are times when they get on top of me and ruin a whole day, but on the whole I manage to cope. Should it prove impossible to dislodge I shall have to cope with the newcomer as well; at the moment I am hoping that, however permanent it now seems, it will somehow disappear before the beginning of next season. I do have time to sort things out and I may decide to seek expert help.

Anyway, to begin my catalogue of old failings, the most obvious of them is a regrettable tendency to miss my target. This is, of course, a fundamental flaw and it happens for many reasons: because I poke at birds or misread their line or mount too early or too late. I do a dozen other things wrong: doubtless my feet are rarely where they should be; I dare say my balance is all over the place and I certainly miss really high pheasants because the sight of them excites and demoralises me at the same time, producing a mistimed swipe through the air which rarely puts pellets in the right spot. It is wonderful when a bird way up in the sky crumples and falls. It does happen from time to time and when it happens with something approaching regularity in the course of a single day, it is very wonderful indeed, convincing me that all my shortcomings as a shooter are finally in the past and that, from now on, high pheasants in my air-space are all doomed. It is a conviction that seldom survives much longer than the beginning of the next shooting day, which usually persuades me that the problem with my shooting is simply that I am an uncoordinated buffoon with no talent for any kind of sport.

Most shooters have problems with high pheasants. I wonder how many of you suffer from attacks of one-barrelitis, an affliction that takes two forms and has nothing to do with those fleeting chances that only allow time for the use of one trigger. A slow shooter, who pulls just his first trigger in a situation where a man with quicker reactions would pull both of his, is not suffering from one-barrelitis. He is just a slow shooter and I rather suspect that most of us get slower as the years roll by. One-barrelitis has no connection with the ravages of time, with failing eyesight or stiff limbs or slow muscles; one-barrelitis is pulling one trigger when, however slow or fast a shooter may be, there is ample time to pull the other one as well.

I suffer from both forms of the disease. The commoner strain is, I suspect, more widespread than is generally acknowledged; it makes a right-and-left almost impossible because it affects its victim in the following way. He hits a bird up there in the sky when, up there beside it, there is the chance of another, but he is so pleased with his success and so busy watching the stricken bird falling to earth that he forgets all about the possibilities of the second barrel. I think it is mainly a rough-shooter's complaint; it comes to those of us for whom two quick barrels at two different birds are a rare opportunity. We rough-shooters, moreover, are inclined to give our whole attention to a bird as soon as it has been hit, knowing that, if it comes to ground with its legs in working order, we need to get a spaniel onto it as soon as possible. Every pheasant matters to us. There are no pickers-up to hunt them down and we would much sooner pass up the chance of a right-and-left than lose a wounded bird.

The second and rarer form of the disease is the form to which I myself am more prone. There are times when I miss a bird – a straight-forwardly sporting sort of a bird – with my first shot and then just stand there, watching it fly on its way, flapping its wings or gliding through the air and doubtless feeling slightly bemused that no second charge of shot has come hurtling anywhere near it. Sometimes this is because I am shooting badly and have reached the stage when even the first barrel seems a waste of time. On such occasions one-barrelitis indicates a temporary bout of despair. More commonly it shows itself when I have lifted my gun onto an indisputably difficult bird of the sort that I nearly always bungle (long crossers spring to mind); I have not told myself that I will fire only once but, when the first shot predictably leaves the long crosser crossing no less freely than before, there is no resort to the second trigger. This is not the result of a conscious decision: it does not point to the sudden surfacing of nagging doubts about the morality of shooting living creatures; it is a puzzling sort of complaint and it is, I think, closely linked to another of my shooting disorders, namely obsessive-kills-to-cartridge-ratio-anxiety.

I have never understood my almost manic concern with whether I am taking five cartridges to kill each bird or ten or, on days of glory, two or perhaps even one and a half. I am not a famous shot, known throughout the country for my ability to knock pheasants from the sky with unerring elegance and efficiency. There are no tap-rooms or country houses where shooting men swap stories of my achievements in jealous and disbelieving wonder; there are no drives on famous shooting estates named after me; there is no peg on any shoot in the kingdom called Catlow's Corner in commemoration of the day when, standing there, I killed thirteen consecutive right-and-lefts at birds that were all forty yards high. I do not, in short, have a great reputation to preserve, and I know perfectly well that my friends could not care a jack straw whether I kill a bird with every second or every tenth cartridge; they would not bother much if I never hit a pheasant again but, in spite of knowing all this, I spend my shooting days doing sums in my head and feeling secretly miserable if they tell me worse than one for three.

One for two makes me happy; better than this finds me on the edge of disbelief, but for some reason it is one for three that matters. I am satisfied with it. I go home feeling that I have done my bit, that there is nothing to be ashamed of, that I can sit down in the evening in a mood of relaxed contentment. It is, of course, very foolish. We all prefer to shoot well rather than badly and it is natural to feel dissatisfied with complete incompetence; but nobody cares whether you take three or five cartridges to kill a bird and no shooter should be so concerned with his own performance that he cannot find pleasure in a day that finds him below his own standard of adequate form. It is, I suppose, a sort of pride.

There it is, anyway: there are the most obvious of my ingrained and almost certainly ineradicable faults as a man with a gun in his hand. And I have just remembered another one, one that only affects me at High Park and then only very rarely. Now that I think about it, this particular fault is arguably the worst of the lot, because it whispers insidiously in my ear, telling me to lift my gun at pheasants that should be left to fly. I have already described an attack of it in an earlier chapter; it is known as shoot-owner's-sudden-longing-for-record-bag-disorder and it is entirely discreditable, especially as it is a disorder that can be resisted. Its causes do not lie in our genes, it is a moral failing and I rather think that it is a sin. It is a disgraceful affliction, anyway, and I hope December's brief attack was my last.

Mention of it reminds me of a related, though much less blameworthy condition from which I also suffer and which you have already met: this is type-of-shoot-category-confusion, which persuades a man to treat driven birds as though they were the occasional chances that come his way on a afternoon's rough sport. It is embarrassing, you should try to avoid it, but it is not to be mentioned in the same breath as the most serious of all the many complaints that threaten those of us who shoot; for if we ever fall victim to the desperate-urge-to-kill-anything-that-flies-compulsion, then the time has come to sell our guns and join a golf club.

Now, at last, for the new problem, which is definitely not a sin and made its first appearance early in January while I was pottering round High Park with two friends. It was a soft, cloudy sort of day and here and there the spaniels flushed a pheasant which, more often than not, went into one of our bags. We had stopped for a sandwich and a dram by the meadow-gate. We had talked easy sportsman's talk and now we were up on my rented land, working our dogs through the gorse and the rushes, enjoying the wide view and the kind air and occasionally adding a further bird to the day's harvest. Mick had shot one from the gorse and Phil had shot another from the middle of the rushes. My chance came when a very dark hen sprang from beneath the wall-side and flew away, rising quickly on her strong January wings. I missed her with my first shot but, mercifully unaffected by one-barre-litis, I kept swinging and moved my finger towards the second trigger, strangely confident that my bird was about to fall.

Unfortunately the second trigger seemed to have disappeared; it took me a moment or two to realise that I had already pulled it in unconscious preference to the first, but by then the dark hen was crossing the road and heading into the next field. This was the beginning of second-trigger-syndrome. It had never happened to me before, but it happened with both the pheasants that came my way later in the afternoon, though both of them were killed. Then I more or less forgot about second-trigger syndrome, which had not then even been named. I went flighting and came home with four mallard (seven shots and so a fillet steak for supper oozing with rich satisfaction). I shot or missed a few more pheasants without even once pulling the second trigger before the trigger in front of it.

Then there came the afternoon when the implications of a duff cartridge were much more important than a hen pheasant greeted with the contents of only one barrel because my finger was groping for a second trigger that no longer seemed to exist. The naming day came a week later, on what was almost my last afternoon of the season. Phil was with me again; Mick could not be there but Austin made us three. It was a lovely afternoon for hunting out a few end-of-season birds. There were banks of white cloud between hazy and shimmering expanses of blue. The earth was soft, the air was almost warm. It was the sort of January afternoon that is impatient for spring, with cawing rooks and loud mistle thrushes and yellow catkins. The only sadness was that pheasant-time was so nearly over and that, every time I lifted my gun to a bird, my finger slipped onto the second trigger, leaving me clumsy and confused whenever one barrel was not enough.

We did the Gutter first, with me down by the beck as the only standing gun. I was thinking quiet thoughts, down there by the comforting gurgle of brown water, until from somewhere above the steep bank of gorse in front of me a cry of 'over' told me to think predatory thoughts instead. Suddenly there was the shape of a hen up there in the sky. I missed her with my first barrel and cursed when my finger could not find the second trigger. Perhaps a minute later the same cry, now rather nearer, told me to watch the sky and, within a few moments, exactly the same performance had been repeated with a somewhat higher hen. By now soft thoughts and predatory thoughts had been replaced by perplexed and disgruntled ones. Second-trigger-syndrome had been recognised as a problem and already I was wondering whether I should have to struggle with it for the rest of my life.

Things improved, but only because Austin and Phil killed some good birds and because I managed to kill four with the first barrel. The most puzzling thing was that, if I did a practice-swing at a thrush or blackbird, my trigger finger went where it was meant to go; but when practice turned into performance and I lifted the old Webley onto the shape of a pheasant, second-trigger-syndrome was again playing tricks with me. We finished with nine pheasants and a rabbit, which was a good bag for so late in the season and sent me home happy in spite of my new problem.

A few days later I went onto the outlands with Ross for an hour or two. Towards the end of the season going-away birds can be wonderful targets, especially if there is a wind blowing. From a deep bed of rushes, right under the long wall that runs along the top of the forty-acre, Ross flushed a cock that rose almost vertically into the sunshine, catching the wind and curling away from me. I missed him with my first shot, knew immediately that I had pulled the second trigger and then found the first in time to bring him tumbling from the sky in a shining glory of bright feathers. I felt this was something of an achievement, but I did not feel confident it was one that I should often manage to repeat.

I was out at High Park on the last day of the season. Instead of the old Webley I took my Williams and Powell, which is itself an old gun and was my preferred gun until the Webley came along. I wanted to discover if second-trigger-syndrome was specific to a gun or to a person. The Williams and Powell taught me that the fault was with me rather than with the Webley, although in teaching me this it also shot me a cock from the Gutter and a hen from the rushes of the Hag. It also missed a couple of birds, on an afternoon so mild and damp and splashy that the season finished with muddy breeches and a mired spaniel, a spaniel happily unaware that, apart from a few rabbits, it was all over for more than half a year, while his master stood beside him in his caked breeches, rather wishing that there was another week or two left for the sort of afternoon that had just ended.

Second-trigger-syndrome, at any rate, seemed suddenly less important than it had done a few hours ago. I told myself that it would surely disappear before I next lifted my gun onto a pheasant, which it did after plaguing me for one last time on a grouse moor near Barnard Castle.

I am now back with just my old failings. They are enough for one man to cope with and I have just remembered another condition which was with me for years, then faded very slowly and has now vanished except for a few lingering traces.

I never gave it a name but the first day of February was always the day when it struck, inspiring bitter resentment at the ending of pheasant-time and an almost savage impatience to be rid of spring and summer, to be standing beneath the autumn leaves and waiting for the first bird of the season to break over the trees.

In the years when this condition was strong upon me it made no difference telling myself that I was a fisher first and a shooter second, that once trouting started again I should be happy for my guns to rest in their cabinet for months on end, that only a sudden longing for rabbit pie would send me out to High Park with a mission to kill. In those years, in the early years of my association with High Park, the early-February prospect of at least eight pheasantless months seemed an impossible privation. It took me at least a week to come to terms with it as trout-longing slowly emerged from its winter sleep and began to tie a few flies.

I am no longer angry at the ending of pheasant time. I think it comes too early but I know this is unlikely to change. By the beginning of February I am within a few weeks of having done enough shooting for another season. I have seen the shape and challenge of almost enough pheasants flying through the sky; I have experienced the elation of a plummeting bird or the disappointment of the bird that flies on almost as often as I want to. By the beginning of February my mind is beginning to turn to a subtler, quieter and more binding sport; by the beginning of February, anyway, I am ready for a rest.

I rather like February. And it usually turns into less of a rest than I was expecting. There is usually some sort of project to occupy me out at High Park, which may involve digging, or slashing or hammering or possibly all three. February is sometimes a month of hard labour, but, in one sense, it is a restful month because it is rarely haunted by visions of failure and success. I never come home in February, sunk in gloom because I have missed a succession of pheasants, watching others shoot them rather than bringing them down myself. I never come home

feeling inordinately pleased with myself because I have swung my gun
and brought birds tumbling out of the sky; and February never brings
me to my fireside in the evening, wondering in bemused frustration
what on earth I might have done to catch just one or two of those
scores of trout that rose all day and refused to swallow any of the thirty
patterns I floated over them. February is an emotionally stable month;
it sends me forth in the morning quietly confident that I shall return for
my supper in a good mood.

And when the sun shines, February is filled with the excitement
of change, for there come days when spring seems a presence rather than
a prospect, when the air shines with a shimmering power to stir and
wake, when cock pheasants strut and shout and shake their wings, when
coltsfoot gleams yellow beneath yellow catkins of hazel and willow,
when rooks are noisily busy round their nests. This February I spent
some days of this sort out at High Park, planting a few trees, hacking
rides through the gorse, patching up a rickety fence and digging a hole
in the earth that might just turn into a flight pond. What I was doing
does not really concern me here, but rather the feeling that came over
me as I planted or hacked or hammered or drove my spade into the soft
earth; it was a feeling that egged me on in whatever I was doing until it
told me to sit down and light my pipe and drink in the shining vitality
of everything around me.

February is sometimes very exciting indeed. Towards the end of it
I start feeling impatient for March; ready once again for the uncertain-
ties of sport. I want to wake up in the morning, not knowing whether
the trout will rise at noon, not knowing whether my fly will deceive
any that do, whether the hook will hold, whether the nylon will stand
the pressure of the fight and draw a beaten trout over the net, whether
I shall open my door in the evening feeling full of the exhilaration of
early spring or still waiting for the spring of the year to take a proper
hold of me. It is March as I write these last sentences. The first daffodils
have opened and I am very eager for the chance of a trout; the despondency of failure is part of the contentment of success, but I should prefer
the contentment to come first. It is good to catch a brace on your first
day of the season and before long I shall be having a go.

Chapter Twenty

On Middle Age

What is it that a middle-aged fisher feels on the edge of another trout season or, to put it less representatively, what do I feel on the evening of the fourteenth of March, sitting here and fiddling round with a few words, sitting here aged fifty-four, drinking a glass of sherry and knowing that I shall have another one before my supper, drinking sherry and smoking and pleasantly aware that tomorrow the Eden opens for trout?

I have not the slightest intention of going to the Eden tomorrow. It has rained all day and the river will be in flood. It will be a warm flood and it will be good for the fish; if I did go to the river I might catch one or two trout with big flies worked along the edges of the water. I do not like fishing of that sort and I have to work anyway. I shall not go fishing tomorrow, but I like sitting here, pouring out my second glass and telling myself that the Eden opens at midnight. Just the thought of it – that trouting has started again – will make me feel cheerful in the morning and I may go to the river on Wednesday. Something important is about to start happening again.

When I was at university I used to get solemnly drunk on the evening of March the fourteenth (it was only the solemnity that set the evening apart). Tonight I shall go to bed sober. I shall drink a glass of wine with my supper, finish the half-bottle afterwards and that will be it; I am becoming almost moderate in my middle years and whisky is no longer allowed if there has been sherry to begin with (which there usually is). Even without whisky it will still be after twelve when I turn out the light then; as I lie waiting for sleep, I shall acknowledge to

myself that the move from one day to the next has just enriched my life
with the return of marvellous possibilities. I shall certainly think about
fishing as I lie in bed, but the thought of it is unlikely to keep me awake
for anything like as long as it would have done at the start of the season
twenty or thirty years ago.

I do not feel excited and restless this evening. It may be a whole
week before I get round to going fishing; it may not happen before
the end of term and by then the Wharfe will have opened as well.
But I know that, when at last I do go fishing, I shall be returning to
something that means just as much to me as it ever did. In fact I think
it means more to me than it used to and, being in the mood for a bit
of self-analysis (perhaps it is the sherry), I propose to examine where
the meaning lies, not in a whole book – I have tried that already – but

just in a few pages, exploring a few
strands of thought and seeing where
they take me.

It will, of course, be best to
start with obvious things and, to me
at least, it is obvious that a fisher of
fifty-four is relieved to find himself
at the beginning of another spring. It
is not that he didn't expect to make
it through the winter; it is rather that he acknowledged the uncertainty
and, in this respect at least, I think fishers of my age are well-placed,
because they have engaged with the grim fact of death, not just as a
remote idea but as an impending inevitability, which is something they
probably had not done as fishers of twenty or even of thirty-five; they
have acknowledged that they will not fish for ever, but they can still
reasonably hope for twenty or more years of living and fishing.

They can still lay down claret and hope to share it with their
friends. They can think that, when their old spaniel dies in a year
or two, there will probably be time for another spaniel and perhaps
another one as well. They can also begin to look forward to retirement
with the prospect of fishing just as often as they choose; but whatever
pleasure they take in the possibilities, they have come solidly to grips

with the fact that a man's purchase on life is precarious and that sooner or later it fails; and they are fortunate in this because they have at last confronted a truth and can hope to live with it for a decade or two more. This fisherman, anyway, finds daffodils and singing birds much more wonderful than he did thirty or even ten years ago. He has realised that, as far as he is concerned, they will not go on for ever.

I am not, by the way, consumed by morbid thoughts as I sit here on the eve of another trout season. I am very happy to be alive and fifty-four and looking forward to going fishing: to resuming something that has been an important part of my life for almost forty years; and knowing that something which has mattered for so long still matters is itself important and comforting. It is good to have bright threads running like rivers through your life. My love of fishing is undoubtedly such a thread.

I am glad to be alive and glad that I shall soon be fishing again; I am looking forward to all the delicate beauties of flyfishing and all the subtleties that belong to it. I am not a particularly accomplished caster. There are all sorts of things that I can't do at all and there are lots of things that I do very badly, but I still find great delight in casting a fly and feeling for half an hour and sometimes even for a whole morning that for once I am doing it rather well. I am looking forward to fishing a team of wet flies and seeing the little marks they make on the surface of the water before they go under. And I am looking forward to that little twitch on the end of the line, that little twitch or that faint slide against the current: that sign, whatever it is, that tells me to turn my wrist and hook a trout on the Waterhen or the Orange Partridge. I am very happy that before long it will have happened again. And before it happens the first spring olives will have floated down the river and fluttered through the air and just the sight of them will fill me with contentment.

I am also looking forward to my first trout on the dry fly, to seeing the rise and timing the strike and feeling the contact. I think, whether you are fishing wet or dry, that this is probably the central excitement of flyfishing: the way your rod and line, which have been moving in a quiet and easy rhythm that makes them seem almost insubstantial things, are suddenly charged with the solid and throbbing anger of a trout. Fishing has seemed, while you were just casting, a thing of airy delicacy and almost weightless grace, until suddenly it turns into strain and pull and pressure. It is always a surprise and there are times when you feel it like a shock, a shock that, even after many years, still brings a sudden surge of excitement.

At some stage of the season I shall probably catch a trout of two pounds or more, and I know now what will please me most in this: it will be the thought that he was caught on a rod weighing about three ounces, on a little hook attached to a length of almost invisible nylon of two or three pounds breaking strain. There is something so unlikely about all this that it makes catching a big trout on fly tackle wonderfully satisfying. The fact that the trout you catch – whether or not they weigh two pounds – are often beautiful beyond description, and also very beautiful to eat: all this beauty explains, I suppose, why it is no surprise that I am looking forward to going fishing again.

Catching trout does not become less important to me. Catching trout happens more often now than in earlier seasons and I suppose individual trout create less of a thrill than they once did. Thirty years ago a single fish could turn the whole day to glory; it needs more trout than that now and it usually needs something else as well: iron blues in April, a thick hatch of blue-wings on the Wharfe; these are the things that, as long as they come with a trout or two, are likely to fill my fisher's heart full of happy thoughts, unless it is some memory that comes wandering down the river and finds me receptive to its message, some memory or some quality of the light in the water or on the slopes of the fells. The beauty that surrounds me on the Wharfe and the Eden is perhaps more important to me than it was thirty years ago, but it always mattered and always moved me, and it still needs a trout or two to give it all meaning. I still go fishing to catch fish.

Perhaps I have become choosier in the methods that I employ to catch them, although I haven't exactly given anything up, or haven't, at any rate, announced to myself or to any one else that there are particular methods that I shall never use again. I haven't told the world that I shall never again fish for trout with the upstream worm. You will remember that I took some worms to the Wharfe late last summer, never got

round to using them and came home more or less convinced that my
worming days were over. I shall be very surprised if I ever again get as
near to fishing the worm as I did last August; I think I have done with
it for good, but I have not gone quite as far as formally renouncing it. It
is just possible that another savage summer drought will send me back
to the compost heap and then over to the Wharfe with a can of worms
in the back of the Land Rover; and it is just possible that, if the fly fails
utterly for two or three successive days, I shall end up impaling a worm
on a hook and seeing if it works as it used to in the old days. I might do
it just for old time's sake.

I used to fish big heavy flies from time to time, trundling them
through the pools and sometimes catching trout with them. Particularly in early spring I found that Wharfe trout were susceptible to the
crude charms of patterns that looked something like a cased caddis,
although I often used a huge Killer Bug instead and even flirted briefly
with goldheads. I think it is extremely unlikely that I shall tie an imitation cased caddis or a Killer Bug or a goldhead to my line at any stage
of the coming season, but, except for the goldheads, I have not actually
forsworn their use for ever. I can conceive that, at the end of a fishless
spring day, I might suddenly decide to try the caddis or the Killer Bug
for twenty minutes, just to see if they can pull a trout or two from the
deep places of the pools. There might be the odd caddis or Killer Bug
lurking somewhere in one of my fly-boxes and I just might, in my
eagerness to catch a trout, be tempted to fish them through the pools
towards the end of a spring afternoon; but, even if temptation comes, I
shall probably tell myself that I can't be bothered with the caddis or the
Killer Bug.

I have decided, more or less, that I like catching trout on or near
the surface of the river. I like fishing for rising trout best of all, but I
also like searching the water for willing fish. I like the dry fly and the
traditional upstream wet and I have no intention of experiencing the
Czech nymph. I have come to think that fishing for trout with deep
nymphs is ever so slightly disreputable; I have a feeling that bottom-
feeding trout are not the proper concern of the fly-fisher. It is not much
more than a feeling; it is very far from being a firm conviction. I may

just try that Killer Bug on a cold April afternoon and I do dress some of
my spring flies (the wet ones) on slightly bigger and heavier irons – to
get them down an inch or two more – and I fish fancy flies (particularly
a hackled Coachman and Simple Simon, which is merely a Coachman-
variant) whenever I think they are more likely to catch fish than more
refined patterns. But the refinement is very important and much more
than mere snobbishness; it is what flyfishing for trout is all about.

I am not meant to be holding forth about how I fish these days, I am
meant to be explaining how I feel about it, although it must be true that
the way you do something also reveals your feelings. I was wondering
how things have changed in my long and very happy association with
flyfishing. I know that they have changed, but it has been a subtle
development and I find it very difficult to put my finger on the important bits of it. The reason for this is perhaps that, over the years, what
matters has become blurred; things have run into each other like wet
colours on a piece of paper; they have merged and blended, making it
more difficult to see them apart and separately.

     Forty years ago there was no problem about seeing things clearly.
There was an aching desire for trout, and if it happened, if I caught a
trout or two, then even on a cloudy day the world shone and I exulted.
There was little concern with refinement. It is different now: I may
catch four or five trout and think how pleasant my day has been and
how, for all its drawbacks, the world is a pleasant enough place; or I
may catch just a brace, just two ordinarily good trout, and they might
bring me to the edge of tears; because it is September or because I have
just remembered something or just because I am in one of those moods
when things seem unusually affecting. My belief is that life, as it goes
on, tends towards complexity, which makes seeing things sharply more
and more difficult. Everything stays there and accumulates.

     It is the accumulation that blurs; it is this same accumulation that
is stirred to intensity by currents of thought and feeling. This, at any

rate, is what I think has happened to my fishing life. The trout are still there, right at the heart of it, but other things have moved nearer the centre, while many more things hover importantly round the edges. Catching a trout is a less savagely exciting business than it once was, although it still often thrills me and losing one still sometimes seems like a bereavement. Catching a trout does not always bring the wild joy that it once brought, but there are days when I drive home from the water, wishing that I could go fishing tomorrow and every other day until I die, and in possession of a happiness that seems more than an illusion or a passing mood and that has been produced by a river and a few trout.

It is a mystery and a blessing and, without becoming unbearably pretentious, I can say nothing else about it until I have been fishing. It will not be tomorrow and it will probably not be next Wednesday. Now that I am fifty-four I feel inclined to wait for my first fishing day until I can give myself over to it, knowing that all the blurred and impressionistic beauty of going fishing will seep into me more deeply, moving me in a quiet and intense sort of way, if it happens in the holidays, when I shall have time to do it slowly and then celebrate it later with sherry and with red wine.

Chapter Twenty-One

Upstream Wet

I was on the Eden and it was not my first day of the season which had happened a week earlier and left me without a trout. Then I had gone off to London for a few days. I like London, but on the whole I prefer the river Eden, especially in early April when spring olives are just beginning to hatch as I make my way along the banks, fishing the pools and other likely places and looking out for the day's first rise. The water was clear and full, the sky was cloudy, the willows were yellow with pollen and the air was still and sharp. It was just before one o'clock. I had seen my first olive about ten minutes earlier, just one of them floating down the river; then I had seen two in the air at the same time and now there were sometimes three or four together on the water, dark shapes where the river was white and grey beneath the light of the sky, but pale and yellow where the surface of the water, flowing smoothly beneath high banks or the cover of trees, shone with a dark shine.

The first rise that I saw, or thought that I had seen, was in a place where I wished it had not been: at the tail of a long pool where smooth water was gathering speed to spill over a shallow lip of rock into a long, lively run. These fast-sliding tails usually mean drag and frightened trout. I was not certain that it had been a rise; it might have been one of those strange tricks of running water that sometimes almost persuade us that rivers flow with free will. I half-hoped that it had been nothing to do with a trout, but stayed to make sure.

I sat down and lit my pipe, singeing my mittens with the match and then watching the river until I soon saw that it was most certainly a trout, feeding just beneath the surface and finding something to eat once or twice a minute between the odd minute of enforced abstinence. To put it precisely – or perhaps pompously – I was watching a trout eating nymphs just before eclosion in what was as yet a trickle hatch.

On the end of my cast was a Waterhen Bloa, with a fly of my own devising on the single dropper. I shall tell you how to tie it because it is a simple pattern and it catches fish. It catches them at any time of the season when trout are moving in coloured water; it catches best of all in the spring of the year when trout are chomping spring-olive nymphs. The thread is olive green; the herl wound over it is from the primaries of a Canada goose; the hackle is a well-speckled feather from the lesser coverts of a grouse. The hook is size twelve; at least it is what I think of as size twelve, although my interpretation of hook-size differs from that of many modern makers who now produce size twelve hooks that I should label as either fourteens or tens.

I could too easily become grumpily middle-aged about this; I could start moaning about the complexity of modern living and look back to a time when every fisher in England knew exactly what size twelve meant with reference to his hooks. But because I am in a good mood, I shall do nothing of the sort, merely saying that the hook for my fly should be on the big side for a pattern designed to imitate the spring olive. I call it the Grouse and Goose and I commend it to you. You will catch plenty of fish without ever using it; you will not necessarily catch fewer fish by tying it to your cast now and then.

I was in a wet-fly mood (I was, in fact, hoping for a wet-fly season) and, although I was unhappy with the place where my intended victim was rising, I was delighted that he was doing it just beneath the surface of the water. There was no temptation to replace the Waterhen with some sort of Klinkhamer. I thought the flies on my cast were the right ones, although I also thought that it was unlikely to matter much because, however appropriate my flies might be, and however cleverly I mended the line or wiggled my rod, their unnatural movement through the water would tell my trout that they were attached to nylon and best avoided, long before he opened his mouth to chomp one of them. Chomp, by the way, is a good verb, unaffectedly suggestive of the activity it represents, but it is not, now that I think about it, an appropriate verb for the behaviour of trout eating nymphs. You could probably hear him chomping a signal crayfish if you could join the two of them for a time beneath the water and listen to the performance; and perhaps trout chomp hawthorn-flies and bullheads and sticklebacks; but when they are eating ephemeropteran nymphs there is, I suppose, no chomping involved, no noisy munching, no loud mastication, just a suck and a swallow and another nymph added to the collection.

I thought of the trout I was watching, anyway, as a chomper and I thought that he was very unlikely to smack his lips before biting into one of my flies, since I was convinced that, whatever tricks I employed, they were bound to slide and drag through the water at least a few inches before they could float enticingly past his nose. The situation, when I got into the water, was in fact less demanding than I had assumed. It was immediately clear that, if I moved forward very slowly to the right spot, and as long as I held the rod tip high, I should be able to cover the rise and at the same time keep my line clear of the accelerating slide of water at the tail of the pool.

And so it proved. The trout rose once or twice as I was manoeuvring myself ever so carefully into position. The line fell lightly and the flies moved through his station with no obvious signs of drag. He rose again when my flies were past him and as I lifted my rod to make a second cast. I searched his lie at least half a dozen times and was thinking that I must have put him down when he turned and the line straightened and I found that I had hooked my first trout of the season.

As soon as I had hooked him I knew that he was big. He ran for his lair beneath the roots of the alders, swam down towards me and then ran again. The Loomis held him and he came across the river, floundering dangerously in shallow water. There is always a risk in trying to net a fish before he is beaten; sometimes, especially if there are snags in the river, or low and leaning branches waiting to catch your line, sometimes it is a risk worth taking and this time, though he was so far from beaten that he had barely begun, this time it worked and I waded ashore with, by my standards, a very large trout thrashing his tail in the mesh of my net.

Most experienced fishers can look at a trout and guess its weight fairly accurately. It is an ability that improves as the season advances and, by the end of September, most of us can glance at a fish – we gloat, of course, over the big ones – and get it right within an ounce nearly every time. We are not just as clever right at the start of the season and the first fish of another spring might just possibly mislead us by a whole half pound, although this is less likely to happen if he is only a half-pounder. My trout – at last I could call him mine – was definitely not a half-pounder; he was somewhere on either side of two pounds and my guess, as I knocked him on the head and got out the spring balance, was that he was somewhere on the right side, but it was not a confident guess. I always make a precise guess – although it is not so precise as to involve half ounces – before hanging my victim by the gills and seeing what the balance tells me. This time I went for two pounds two ounces, but I knew that I was out of practice and I would not have been surprised if my guess had proved an overestimate by as much as four or five ounces.

Not that it would have mattered much. I had caught my first trout of the season. He was fit and big and beautiful and I thought that I should make some mayonnaise before cooking him. I should not be much bothered if the spring balance told me that he was one pound fifteen ounces; then again it would be good to start the season with a two-pounder; it would be something that had never happened before; it would be something worth writing about, something just a bit special.

In the event my early-season estimate was six ounces wide of the mark. I saw that the spring balance was accurately set before I hung my trout and lifted my arm and studied the reading, which told me that the first fish of a new season weighed exactly two and a half pounds. And then I lit my pipe and laid my fish in the grass and loved his wild beauty and felt very happy, just a little happier, I confess, than if he had not quite made two pounds.

I looked at the water and the willows and the purple haze on the alders. I thought of the first big trout that I had ever caught, a trout just over the pound from the Wenning, caught on a cloudy and windy April day during an enormous hatch of spring olives; certainly it had been a bigger thrill than this trout more than twice its weight. I remembered that, almost as soon as it was in my bag, I had stopped fishing and gone home to find somebody to admire it and tell me that it was among the wonders of creation, which it certainly was; and so, of course, was my two-and-a-half-pounder, with his great tail and his long fins and his spotted flanks. But my response to the catching and to the contemplation of him was less impetuous than it would have been thirty-five years ago. I did not rush to the Land Rover and thunder back to Sedbergh; I did not burst into the headmaster's study, telling him to leave his report-writing and marvel at my trout. Instead of this I sat smoking on the riverbank in a mood of quiet festivity, thinking that before long I should try to catch a second trout and that, if this happened on a chilly day in April during a meagre hatch of olives, I should be very happy indeed. I felt happy enough already but I am, as you know, a fisher who likes a brace.

I found the second fish within ten minutes. He was easy to cover, for he was rising half-way down a deep and evenly-paced run, and I thought that I should catch him. I expected my first cast to bring him up but, just like the first fish, he ignored my flies until they had floated over him a few times; then he seized the Grouse and Goose and fought doggedly before surrendering to the net. My guess was much nearer this time. 'One pound thirteen' I said to myself; he weighed an ounce more. A very deep part of the pleasure of this brace, apart from the fact they were the first two trout of a new season and were both big and wild and beautiful, was that they had been caught on wet flies, on spiders cast upstream to float down over the rise.

I love the upstream wet. I began my fishing life with dry flies and learned the traditional method of the North very slowly and with great difficulty. It was a laborious conversion and, once it happened, it was for many seasons complete. I fished nothing but little wet flies cast against the water's flow. It is a beautiful style of fishing – and the old spider flies are beautiful themselves and often very effective; but there are times when the dry fly works better and at last I relearned this truth and fished very happily with flies that floated or flies that sank an inch or two. Then I learned something new – how to tie parachute flies – which brought the Klinkhamer into my life and almost persuaded me that nothing but variations upon the Klinkhamer theme was needed by a flyfisher, except perhaps during a fall of spinners.

By the time I discovered Klinkhamers I was old and wise enough to resist total surrender. I was not quite born again to their sole service; but, in spite of age and the beginnings of wisdom, it has often seemed to me that it would probably not matter much if I never used anything else. I do, of course, and I shall probably do it more this season than last. Things are settling down. With regard to Klinkhamers I suspect that, except with the really big ones, the parachute bit of them is more important than the specifically Klinkhamer bit of them. I am also beginning to think that there are times, not many times but just a few of them, when the conventional dry-fly hackle is more effective than the parachute version.

It was good, anyway, to catch my first two trout of the season on little wisps of silk and feather that sank a bit; it seemed like April as it used to be and it may have put a spring in my wadered steps as I went upstream in search of more trout. By now the sun had half come out and the early afternoon was almost warm; it was the sort of hazy light, grey and yellow at the same time, that gives a soft gleam to everything, to the pale grass, to the bare trunks and branches of the trees, to the moss on the bankside stones, to the brown backs of the sand martins, to everything but the river itself in those places where, especially in the spring, the perfect clarity of flowing water shines back into the light with startling purity and sharpness. And the air was still and sometimes the sound of the river – which we fishers very rarely hear because we are so used to it – reached my ears and sounded beautiful.

I ate my sandwiches – at about two thirty – sitting on a flat stone just upstream from the single limestone arch of Eastfield Bridge, chewing, rather than chomping, thick slabs of ham while drinking tea and watching a long willow-fringed glide where trout often rise to olives early in the season. I laid my fish in the grass and admired them, telling myself that such a brace had never come to me before as the first brace of the season. The sun shone on them very softly and they gleamed back and then I weighed them all over again to make sure that no mistake had been made. I thought the big one was perhaps nearer two nine than two eight. Meanwhile no fish had risen down the glide – the trickle of olives was very thin by now – and so I searched it with a few casts and moved upstream under the trees.

There were no rises here and I thought it was probably all over for the day. There were no rises on the edges of the fast water beneath the falls, which is another place where trout often show themselves early in the season. Beyond the falls, which consist of a single curving shelf of limestone perhaps two feet high, there is a place very dear to me. I call it Quiet Corner, because it is a peaceful place; the river runs over rock, shelving and smoothly grooved and ridged and channelled. In a full clear flow beneath bright light, with deep shadows in-between, you know, as you wade the pool, that you are treading on great art. The deep water is under the walled bank, which is on the right of an upstream fisher; there are tall trees on both banks, with high arching branches and lower-leaning or protruding ones which are much less welcome. Beyond the smooth folds of rock and the glide of the water there is a gravelly run along a slight turn of the bank, which might just be called a corner and gave the place its name. I planned to fish Quiet Corner, just for the pleasure of being there with a fishing rod, and then to finish. At the beginning of April a brace of big trout is enough.

The rise was unexpected. It was right under the walled bank towards the top of the glide, where the lowest branches were two or three feet above the water, although there were plenty of branches close behind my back. The fish rose several times while I stood there watching and wondering how to catch him. One floating olive disappeared but the other rises were just below the surface. Changing flies seemed unnecessary and so I pulled off line to cover the rise. My first cast was a sloppy sort of performance – something between a flick and a roll – but the flies fell without a splash and within a second the sloppiness had turned into a tight line and a bent rod. There were three or four short, strong runs when I feared for the nylon; there was a thrash on the surface and a savage flap from a broad tail. But it was soon over. Big fish do not, I think, fight long in cold spring water. I looked at my trout on the bank. He was in good condition and I killed him. I got out the spring balance, went for two pounds four ounces and got it wrong.

He was two pounds six ounces, which meant that my creel contained three trout weighing six pounds twelve ounces. It was a remarkable start to the season, quite unlike anything in my previous experience, and it was more than enough.

It was time to sit on the bank with my fishing over for the day, time to sit in the sunshine and drink the last mugful from my flask, looking at the river and watching my smoke dissolving into the hazy air. I did not stroke the Loomis thankfully as it rested on my creel though I might have done if it had been one of my old cane rods. But I did dry the two flies on my cast and tease out their matted hackles; and it was most certainly a grateful act. They were flies of the sort that had been fished on the Eden for centuries and the sense of tradition was very strong.

Two days later I fished the Eden again, although I began on Scandal Beck where nothing showed in spite of a thick hatch of olives. It is the way of things in early spring. I moved to the main river at about two o'clock, fished up half a mile of water and then caught four fish in ten minutes. They were newly stocked fish and it was the first time I had found them on the Eden. I learned a day or two later that they had been put in the day before I caught them and the whole thing made me very sad. I have fished the Eden for twenty years and it has, in fact, always been stocked, but this has been with six and seven and eight inch trout put into the river to help the spawning becks do their job; it has never before been done with fish of a pound and more, dumped into the water to provide fishers with easy sport, tipped into a great river in the false belief that the Eden will be improved by their presence.

I killed a brace of these stockies. I ate them the next day for breakfast and supper and I have to say they tasted delicious. With friends I had already eaten one of the great wild fish from the earlier day's sport and, in spite of the mayonnaise, it had not been quite as good. But it had left a better taste in my mouth, because the process that brought it to my palate had been a deep satisfaction to me. I do not think the Eden needs stocking with fish for catching. I shall spend the summer trying to prove it and I shall spend it on the higher stretches away from the stockies. I shall write to members of the committee and beg them not to repeat their mistake, begging them to let the Eden be what it has so long been: a river where big trout are wild or have gone wild and are beautiful and belong. I am not going to rant about polluting great trout streams with hideous monsters from stock ponds; I have done quite enough of it already, although it doesn't seem to have changed much. I am not going to rant; I am going to hope that, within a year or two, fish like those first three of the season will no longer be eating olives in the company of trout that do not deserve a serious fisher's attention. I don't promise not to return to the theme but I do promise to try my best.

CHAPTER TWENTY-TWO

Untold Treasure

There are days when I could go fishing and decide not to. There are, in fact, quite a few of them, but they do not often happen in May, not at least when my rivers have enough water in them for the hope of sport. Even in May, with rivers flowing full and inviting, even then sometimes I decide not to go fishing. The reason, I think (although this is the first time I have admitted it to myself) is that I do not want to risk the dissatisfaction that comes from ideal conditions and an empty creel.

Going for a walk in the hills does not bring with it a similar possibility of failure. You set off, you trudge up steep slopes and feel very happy when you reach the top of them; should heavy rain come down, you turn round and get wet and never once feel that it is your fault. As long as it stays dry you admire views and listen to the curlews and drink in beauty all round you; your dogs enjoy themselves enormously and, after a few or many hours, you come home feeling more or less tired and much more healthy and enormously grateful that, at the age of fifty four, in spite of the enthusiastic consumption of alcohol and tobacco, you are still able to take strenuous exercise and feel better at the end of it. Almost certainly you will reward yourself in the evening with an extra glass of claret or a slightly larger dram. And you will not feel guilty the next morning unless the extra glass turned into half a bottle or the generous dram was followed by two more.

Just sometimes in May I take to the hills when I could just as easily take myself off to the Eden or the Wharfe. It is, I have confessed, because the day seems too beautiful to end with me sitting under the blossom and the young leaves, sitting on the edge of water that shines differently in every particle of its flow, sitting there while a thousand birds celebrate the glory of their sexuality, sitting there surrounded by all this, and feeling angry or inadequate because I have failed to rise trout or failed to hook them or just lost what felt like a three-pounder. It comes to me occasionally, this unwillingness to give a beautiful day over to the uncertain emotions of going fishing. It did not come to me last Saturday. I was out of Sedbergh almost the minute my teaching was over and I was ready to start fishing just before one o'clock.

The Eden was full and clear, the sun was shining, the breeze was warm and lively and full of assorted black gnats, hawthorn flies and lots of other dark stuff. There seemed every prospect of catching a fish or two, and there was no need to think of returning to Sedbergh before six o'clock at the earliest. All in all, standing on the edge of Scandal Dub at ten to one, I felt very pleased to be wearing waders rather than walking boots.

So far this season, I have fished the Eden to the neglect of my other rivers. There has been just one day on the Wharfe, though there is a full week coming before long, and there have been three afternoons on the Ure. There have been at least a dozen excursions to the Eden and there is a reason for this, which is that I am trying to discover if I believe what has been said to me: I am trying to decide whether the Eden's store of trout has been as sadly diminished as one or two Eden fishers have insisted. I shall make up my own mind and it will take time, for April fishing is no guide to the stock of trout in a river. In years past I have seen huge hatches of spring olives bring scores of trout onto the rise in every pool; but only the next day, a hatch every bit as big has tempted only a few fish to make marks on the river's surface.

May tells a fisher more about the number of trout in his river, especially late May. Early May has not told me very much, except that, apart from witless stock-fish – thank God there are not enough of them to infest more than a few pools – there are trout of many sizes scattered through the Eden above the inflow of Scandal Beck. There are fish of three and four ounces; there are half-pounders and ten and twelve-ouncers and there are much bigger fish. Before today I had added a third two-pounder to the season's tally and a few fish well over the pound. But I had never seen a general rise; always it had been a fish or two rising here and a few fish somewhere else. There had never been many feeding, which was disappointing, but the trout had shown themselves in different places, suggesting that things might be better than they seemed; that there might come a day when all the trout in the river decided to put on weight at the same time, revealing themselves as numerous enough to need no help from stock ponds.

Last Saturday has not decided me, though it has left me hopeful rather than depressed. I was very hopeful when I started, which was not because I had suddenly come across evidence that the upper Eden was swarming with hordes of wild trout. It was rather that there come times of the year, and particular days within them, when hopefulness is the only possible response to what is going on all round you. Last Saturday was one of those days and it belonged to the year's best of all times, the time when spring has put on leaves and blossom but has yet to be engulfed by profusion, the time when all day long birds fill the air with male aggression and make marvellous beauty at the same time, the time when the smell of flowers drifts everywhere on the breeze.

Smells interest me, by the way, particularly the manner in which two smells can be almost the same and yet affect us almost oppositely. I loathe the smell of coconuts, but only the other day, wandering round my farm at Brough, I realised that my nostrils were full of their smell and that I liked it a lot; it was coming from gorse blossom and it was heavy on the air. I think what made the difference was just a hint of almonds, which meant that it was not a cloying smell; it was a structured and subtle smell and I thoroughly enjoyed it.

On Saturday, as I took the dogs out before morning school, it was the smell of may blossom that got up my nose: may blossom with petals still wrapped tight but beginning to reveal themselves from the green bud. The sight of them was lovely and restrained; the smell of them brought me a whiff of the urinal, an acrid sweetness that somehow, in spite of the association, managed to please me. Perhaps it is association that matters most of all: if it comes from piss it repels; if it wafts on the breeze from blossom along the hedges, then it charms the senses.

I like digressions but it is time to leave this one and return to fishing.

There were trout rising in the run immediately above Scandal Dub and I only caught one of them. I thought they were taking something very small; they were rising in a smooth glide of shallow water and they were very easy to put down. The one that I caught weighed twelve ounces; he was lovely and wild and went in the creel. He was also, together with the rising trout that I did not catch, a good sign to a fisher in search of some pointers to the health of his river. So was the trout I missed under the willows at the top of the run, and so was the second three-quarter-pounder that took my Badger Black about a hundred yards upstream. He too was a wild fish and was killed.

Perhaps it is wrong to kill trout when trying to assess the stock of a river; perhaps they should all go back until you decide that your river is full of trout and it is time for the killing to resume. I am afraid my policy is different: I will not fish in waters that insist on catch-and-release. On the Eden I shall continue to take a few fish here and there, but if at any time I decide that the stock is inadequate, then I shall fool

round with stock fish or stop fishing the Eden altogether. I do not, by
the way, really believe that there is much wrong with the Eden. It has
always – in my association with it until about a month ago – been an
almost wild river, and there have been times in the past when I thought
the stock of fish had been sadly depleted, only to find next season that
it was had not been.

Last April, and the April before, the river was full of trout, full
of big wild trout rising at spring olives and almost impossible to catch
in the low water. Last summer was a summer of savage drought and
in such conditions the upper Eden is barely worth fishing. The trout
disappear – doubtless they reappear at night – and you might think,
looking at long stretches of the river creeping on its way with no sign of
a trout, that they had gone for ever. It has never been so in the past and
I cannot see why it should have happened now. Blue-wings will reveal
the truth of it all. If, in June, the blue-wings come thickly through the
afternoon or the evenings and there are not trout feasting all over the
river – if this happens, or if the blue-wings never come, then I too will
begin to believe that a great trout stream has fallen on hard times.

After the brace I failed with a fish or too and sat down to smoke,
while listening to the birds and looking at elm blossom, for there was
a young elm leaning over the river, unravaged by disease. It was little
more than a bushy sapling, little more than seven or eight feet high, but
it reminded me how those lime-green and pale-yellow blossoms used
to hang in the sunshine ten and twenty yards up there in the sky, filling
whole valleys with the miracle of their beauty. As well as enjoying the
uncommon sight of elm-blossom – it was a regretful sort of enjoyment
– I decided that I was making a very rare mistake; I decided that the
black gnats were of the bigger spring sort – they come in all sorts of
sizes – and that my Badger Black was too small.

Tying on a larger fly, a black gnat dressed on a long-shank sixteen
with a body of floss silk and a swan-herl wing and a shiny starling
hackle, tying on this monster I went in search of rising trout, found one
and caught it and returned it because, although it weighed one pound
five ounces, it was a stock fish.

Had it been the first fish of the day, I should have killed it, but already there were two smaller and infinitely more beautiful trout in my creel and there was no thought of putting the stock fish to shame and disgrace by putting it there among two proper trout.

I came to the long run below Eastfield Bridge, spotted a little dimpling rise, covered it and realised almost immediately that I was connected to something much heavier than one pound five ounces. Now some big trout are dashing fighters; others are of the dogged sort. This one was somewhere in-between, although he was more dogged than dashing. Playing him turned into an arm-aching experience as he bored into the current, sulked in the nearest thing to deep water for a few seconds and then moved again sullenly and shook his tail.

I wonder if there are fishers who enjoy the fight? With a big trout every second of it is, for me, a sort of excited agony. There is that thrilling second of fulfilment when the hook takes hold; what comes next is a time of suffering tension which collapses into despair, or lifts itself into exaltation when the net receives its shining burden. The moment of the net is wonderful; everything that intervenes between it and the hooking is a form of pain.

As soon as the fight begins I want it over. I do not enjoy a second of it, and yet I recognise that it is one of the glories of fishing. In fly-fishing the moment of the take is perhaps the greatest moment of all, for it means that our deceit has worked; but our deceit cannot receive its reward unless the hook holds and the nylon stands the strain. Success in fishing comes in stages, which makes the whole thing more complex and much more satisfying when at last it does come. I do not enjoy the fight but I am glad that it is part of the fisher's experience.

This particular fight went my way, when my long-handled net received a large trout and I splashed to the bank with what seemed to me a huge shape still active in the bottom of the mesh. The shape I struck on the head with my priest and then prized the hook from its jaws, toying with the thought of kissing the fly that had just caught me a big trout that was certainly bigger than my normal experience of big fish. I felt certain that he was very big indeed, by which I meant that he was somewhere near three pounds.

There was no hurry in getting out the spring balance; I wanted

'As soon as the fight begins I want it over'

to glory in my treasure before learning just how much it weighed. The weight would be important, because I thought that I had almost certainly caught the biggest trout that had ever eaten one of my flies. The weight was most certainly important, but first I wanted to admire my treasure without knowing for certain just how many ounces of it there were. It was very beautiful in the way that wild trout are. It was in fine condition – except that it was dead – and every bit of it shone. Trout-treasure soon fades for the eye; there is still the glorious delicacy of the flesh waiting for the complement of chablis, but you should gloat over the beauty of a freshly-caught trout before you begin to think of it as food and before you make certain how much it weighs. Just for a minute or so you should concern yourself with beauty, for you have just pulled from beneath the water something as beautiful as the best of Raphael or Botticelli.

I drank in the beauty of my trout and I cannot deny that the bigness seemed an important part of it; there was something of grandeur about the head and the tail about the curve of the belly and the width of the back. Half and three-quarter pound trout are usually, in my correct opinion, more beautiful than the big ones: there is a delicacy to their tails and fins and markings, there is a subtlety of shine and colour that makes a more exquisite and refined beauty than you find in a two-pounder. But we fishers are aesthetically crude in that we most definitely regard big as beautiful. We do not tell our friends that we caught a half-pound trout so lovely that we wept tears over its still-moist and shining scales; we tell them that we caught a three-pounder and that it was magnificent. We prefer trout-beauty on the grand scale and we are wrong.

As big trout go, anyway, my big one was certainly beautiful, but it was not long before my mind had moved from the contemplation of a thing of beauty to the consideration of just how big it might be. The moment of the spring balance was drawing near but it was not quite yet. I had got it from my pocket – one of the many pockets of my fishing waistcoat – but I had yet to hook it under the gill cover of my trout, which was most certainly a two-pounder and might just, I thought, touch three. I had started the season with a two-and-a-half-pounder and I was convinced my present trout was heavier. I did not really believe that he was a whole half pound heavier, but there was the hope that the spring balance would prove me wrong. I went for two pounds twelve ounces, which would make him my heaviest ever trout by a whole two ounces, two ounces that would demand something special from the cellar in the evening.

There was now a further delay before Little Samson, which is what my spring balance calls itself, got down to its job; this was while I considered what bottle would do suitable honour to the occasion if, when its moment came, Little Samson told me that my trout weighed more than forty two ounces.

I will not bore you with all the wines that were considered and rejected, telling you merely that I decided *Langoa Barton '86* would do very nicely for a trout that weighed up to five ounces more than 2lb 10oz; if, on the other hand, I had underestimated the size of the fish in the grass at my side, if Little Samson insisted that he weighed three pounds and if my kitchen scales confirmed this, then it would have to be a bottle (my only bottle) of *Gruaud Larose '82*. There was now a third possibility that occurred to me: that the trout would turn out to weigh more than two and a half – I could not conceive that he weighed less – but not reach two ten. If this turned out to be the truth of it, should I go ahead with the *Langoa Barton* or content myself with *Chasse Spleen* from the same year?

There is, I suppose, nothing much more tedious than a wine-snob going on about the contents of his cellar, showing off his knowledge and expecting his audience or its readers to be enormously impressed by the store of bottles which his good taste and restraint have stashed away. I have finished now with this little display of wine-lore (I could not resist it, if only to annoy those who find such displays intensely irritating). Sitting there on the bank beneath the alders, I decided there was no more time to think of wine, because if I did not move to the moment of the spring balance, the trout that it was Little Samson's job to weigh might have lost at least an ounce through dehydration.

What Samson told me was a surprise and almost a disappointment. He told me that my trout was much bigger than two pounds but less than three. My trout was, in fact, exactly two pounds ten ounces, exactly as big as my previous biggest trout. It was a pity he had not fed more gluttonously in the week before his capture and put on just one more ounce of flesh, but there was no way – without plain cheating – that I could persuade the balance to change its mind. I think I should have preferred two nine to two ten; your biggest trout should stand alone until he is supplanted by a still bigger trout. Equal best sounds almost ordinary, but there it was and I decided to go ahead with the *Langoa Barton*. I relit my pipe and realised that two pounds ten ounces was very big and that, sitting there in the dappled sunshine, I felt very happy indeed, felt in one of those moods when I knew that being a fisherman was an incomparable privilege and the best blessing of my life.

I caught another trout before I finished, a ravishing pounder that went in the creel and made me happier still. He came from Quiet Corner, from the smooth ripple of white water beyond the shadows. After catching him it occurred to me that, although it was only five o'clock, it was time for me to be getting home; the *Langoa Barton* would need to stand for at least two hours before decanting and, being in the mood to celebrate, I thought that I should like to gather a couple friends to share wine and a leg of lamb. I gathered the friends and they knew what to expect, because they have turned up on similar occasions before. They knew that, at some time in the evening, I would start toasting rivers and trout and fishermen. I did not let them down, although there was not much of it. There was a toast to trout with the first course – an Eden fish from an earlier day – and there was a toast to all fishers with the lamb and the *Langoa Barton* (rich, complex and exhilarating). They got away with three toasts; I gave them the river Eden with the whisky and hoped to myself that the blue-wings would come in June and that I should come home one evening to feast alone and toast the river with every swallow, knowing that all was well.

CHAPTER TWENTY-THREE

On Form

I think that, for a fisher accustomed to rough northern rivers, the chief beauty of chalkstream fishing is the sight of trout below a sliding or rippling surface of clear water: trout lying over the weeds or the white chalk, resting or alert, or rising with calm deliberation to eat duns. You do sometimes fish for visible trout on rivers like the Eden and the Wharfe, but they are usually imperfect visions and much more often you fish to the mark of the rise or you fish the water. I like the mystery of fishing for unseen trout, not knowing whether I am casting over a six-incher or a two-pounder.

I know that experienced fishers are meant to interpret rises, deciding what a fish is taking and precisely where in the water he is taking it and whether he is worth fishing for. I am not very good at it and it is not very easy if your trout is feeding in rough water.

If a huge nose sticks itself out of the water, I am usually sharp enough to conclude that a large trout is eating surface fly; when the upper portion of a broad tail appears, swishing around above the surface of the water, I then tell myself complacently that a big fish is eating something – probably something very small – in or just below the surface film. That is about as far as forty years' fishing has got me with rise-forms and I get it wrong all the time, which makes for an exhilarating surprise when the fish you felt certain was a half-pounder turns into something three or four times as big. I think that, on the whole, I prefer invisible trout and the uncertainty of it all. But watching a feeding trout is a fascinating business and fishing for them, especially when you can see that they are big, calls for special skill with the strike.

I do not know what I do on my own rivers. There is no conscious decision when to strike a rise; I just do it and as often as not – perhaps a bit more often than not – I find that a trout is attached to my hook. With the revealed trout of a chalkstream you have to watch the fish move and you must do nothing to begin with – very difficult for an occasional chalkstream fisher – you must delay your strike for the moment when the mouth opens and the body turns. There are times when it is easier and times when it is more demanding. Sometimes even large chalk-stream trout get a move on, which means that you are much less likely to be too soon with them; at other times they drift with your fly and seem unable to make up their minds whether or not they want to eat it. In this case I am almost certain to pull the fly from their jaws just when they have at last decided that they could, after all, cope with one more blue-winged olive and open a lazy mouth to suck in my fly.

I was on form the other day at Driffield. It was a day of stifling heat. My beat was the Hunting Bridge; every step was a dripping labour and the beck was choked with weed. Fishing consisted of walking very slowly along the banks, looking for pockets of more or less open water and for trout in them. I had found one such pocket and extracted a fish from it; the strike, timed very nicely, had given me absurd satisfaction. Then I came across small portions of obviously flowing water with no trout lying there waiting patiently for the honed precision of my fishing technique to set a hook in their jaws. I wandered way up the beck, sweating all the way and beginning to wonder where my next fish would come from. There were no visible trout and there was almost no visible water; instead of water there was a damp matting of green leaves with a mass of long-stalked white flowers drooping over it. I had to remind myself that I was looking at a stream.

At last I found what I wanted, at least a full hour after the perfectly timed strike that had brought me my first trout. I found water again, at least ten yards of it with weed only along the edges of the bank; it was water flowing over chalk and, best of all, it was water with a trout in occupation. He was plainly a good trout and, as I stood there watching him, he moved at something under the surface. My fly was one designed to sink just a bit – I shall come back to it before long – and I thought that, if I managed to present it cleverly, it would probably do the trick.

One thing I have learned over the years is that, at Driffield, you should never cast from the bank if it is possible to get into the stream. It is not always possible and, even when it is, this is not always immediately obvious. There is often a layer of silt close to the bank and sinking into it, uncertain just when your feet will touch hard chalk, is a process that I find unsettling. There is likely to be weed as well as silt, tangled masses of it, which tends to make establishing the depth of the water a matter of mere guesswork.

I rarely return from my home rivers with wet feet unless my waders are leaking, which of course they usually are. This year I started with a new pair and they have been one of the minor delights of the season; it is good to know that, as long as your waders avoid close contact with barbed wire, you may well walk comfortably, without those gurgles and clammy squelches announcing every step you take, for the rest of the day. I have enjoyed putting on my waders this season, because I have done it in the knowledge that, unless I am careless or unlucky, there will be nothing much damper than sweat inside them when they are pulled off at the end of the day.

It is good to have waders that do their job. Mine rarely do and, at Driffield, it has rarely made much difference, for almost always water has flowed into them from the top-end. A good chalkstream trout is worth a bootful of water and you are much more likely to catch one if you are willing to get into the beck and risk some part of it getting where you would prefer it not to be. You can stand comfortably on the mown path along the bank, hoping that the border left by the keeper (a border tall and tangled with long grasses and meadowsweet and glowing willow herb) will conceal you from your fish while you lurk behind this lovely screen and cast for your trout and sometimes you will catch him, or at least bring him to the fly. Often you will put him down and it is always better to wade.

When I found my water and saw my trout I was, of course, on the bank, trying to blend in with the meadowsweet and the willow herb. It was a high bank, which made it all the more essential to leave it, stooping low and creeping back downstream until I found an almost convenient place to descend into the weed. I now slid down the bank and managed to stop myself just before I slid into the water. Prodding with the spike of my long-handled net, I thought that there was firm chalk no more than a couple of feet down and, after surrendering my feet to uncertainty, I found with considerable relief that the chalk was where my probings had suggested.

There was something of a struggle ahead. I had entered the beck at least ten yards below the patch of open water. I had lost sight of my trout and, to have any hope of hooking and playing him successfully, I should have to get much nearer. He was still there when I had pushed through a yard or two of uncooperative weed and came in sight of him. He moved to one side to take something. There were some blue-wings coming off; not many but it seemed likely that he was eating blue-winged olive nymphs. My fly fell very gently. It also fell an inch or two short and three or four inches to his right, but he turned and followed it and I managed not to lift my wrist until he turned again, this time to swallow it. He was well hooked; he was also a lively fighter and I was terrified that he would plunge into weed, for I have very rarely managed to extract a trout once it has buried itself in weed.

There was lots of it to go for and he kept trying, but I held him hard, even brutally, and he never got beyond the outer margins of the stuff. In the net he seemed silver all over. Struggling up the bank and then laying him in the grass I began the gloat, finding that he was indeed a silver trout, with two or three black spots on each flank. He weighed one pound fourteen ounces; he was fat and beautiful and he made me very happy. I tore off a spray of meadowsweet and of willow herb and put him on top of them, so that the silver would shine out in contrast with the rose and the cream. Then I sat there, smoking and sweating contentedly and telling myself that I had done well to cast a fly over two trout and catch them both.

The fly that had caught them was not a weighted nymph of the Sawyer sort, nor was it, as far as I know, created with the nymph of the blue-winged olive in mind. The genius responsible for its creation, if he separated the blue-winged olive from superficially similar duns, would most certainly have called it by a different name. The fly that caught my brace was a Partridge and Orange, one of the great spider flies and, in my admittedly limited experience, one of the greatest of all chalkstream flies.

My estimation of the Partridge and Orange as a fly for the chalk-streams is, as it happens, shared by others better qualified to judge. A friend of mine (perhaps I should withhold his name) swears by the Partridge and Orange (also the Snipe and Purple) on the Itchen and the Wylie. There is my anonymous friend and there is J.W. Hills, who has this to say on the subject, when arguing that nymphal patterns should offer no resistance to the mouth of a trout:

'One of the softest and most compressible patterns is the partridge hackle and, whether this be the reason or not, I consider it the best sunk fly on the Test. Its body, of silk, can be of many colours. I find the old Cumberland pattern, the Orange Partridge, the best.'

Yorkshiremen will probably disagree with Hills' opinion on the origin of the Orange Partridge, but since no one knows who first tied it, no one knows to which county it belongs. I think of the Orange Partridge as a Yorkshire fly (I am not a Yorkshireman) but I should not be massively disappointed to discover that its creator spent his whole life in Hove. What matters is that it is a great fly (almost certainly not from Hove) and that Hills has more to say about it:

'I have not decided whether the modern nymph type' (he means the patterns of Skues) 'beats the old fashioned copy, though I am inclined to believe that an ordinary hackle dressing is just as good as the more up-to-date article.'

Now these statements of Hills are very interesting. He is writing as a confessed beginner with the nymph on chalkstreams. I think that he was probably more experienced than he admits but, whether or not this was the case, he is suggesting that Skues (whom he admired) might have been wasting his time in developing his up-to-date articles. I suspect that Skues (whom I admire very greatly) *was* wasting his time and I also suspect that the old darling knew it perfectly well and was wasting his time for a very good reason.

Skues promoted his version of wet fly fishing on chalkstreams as a practice complementary to the use of the dry fly. It was not a universally popular programme and the idea that came to me, as I sat sweating and smoking on the edge of the Driffield Beck and looking at the two trout that the partridge hackle had caught me, was that Skues had indulged in a little bit of deceit. He may have deceived himself but I fancy that he was too sharp for that. My theory, anyway, was that Skues, knowing perfectly well that the old spider patterns of the North were wonderful imitations of nymphs, decided to devise his own range of patterns because he wanted to be in a position to argue that his nymph fishing was just as much a matter of 'exact imitation' as was the dry fly; he thought this would give the nymph a better chance of general acceptance on the chalkstreams.

In his first experiments with the sunk fly, Skues used, if I remember rightly, Greenwells dressed on doubles to get the fly down: a tactic devised specifically for tailing trout, for trout hunting in the weeds. His later patterns were designed for the ascending and emerging nymph and were famously successful; but I fancy that dear old Skues knew pretty well that a partridge hackle or a Waterhen or Poult Bloa or a Snipe and Purple would catch nymphing trout just as efficiently. He knew it well enough and he had his own reasons for pretending otherwise. I must delve into Skues – always a delight – and discover whether there are hints to support this theory of mine. I shall perhaps slip my conclusions into a later chapter, although, for reasons that I cannot bear to mention but will soon become plain, they may have to wait for a later book.

My Driffield thoughts, anyway, were not only about partridge hackles and G.E.M. Skues, for I also realised, as I lay sweating in the inadequate shade provided by the willow herb and the meadowsweet and the tall grass, that some fishers would be inclined to disapprove of spider patterns on chalk streams – not, in their opinion, proper nymphs – whereas they would regard huge weighted things – very improper nymphs, in my more refined opinion – as entirely unobjectionable. I wonder if anyone fishes goldheads on the Test; it is more likely than that anyone still dares, like Hills all those years ago, to use an Orange Partridge. Even if goldheads do not plop into the waters of the world's most famous trout stream, you can be sure that great big weighted things do, tempting trout in deep water where they would be better left

to doze or root through the weeds in greedy peace.

I have lost any interest in fishing heavy flies. I have decided that a flyfisher's art belongs in the upper layers of the water. I think it is good that a trout can sink beyond a fisher's attention and I think that the Piscatorials are quite right to allow only the unweighted nymph in the trout season (this is another thing to check, but I can't be bothered now). As I smoked by the side of the Driffield Beck what came chiefly to mind was that flyfishing should be graceful and delicate, and that once heaviness enters the act, much of the beauty is lost.

In flyfishing, ethics and aesthetics are the same thing and I think I have already written something very similar; but I cannot be sure because I make it a rule never to read anything that I have committed to print; it is rule that has arisen from finding that whatever I have written, once it has passed beyond the possibility of change, fills me with disgust, and so my earlier pronouncements on all this will be something which I shall most definitely not check. It sounds good, anyway, to announce that ethics and aesthetics coincide and, with regard to flyfishing, it is almost certainly true; it deserves repetition and it means that the fisher of goldheads is doing something less beautiful and less virtuous than the man who flicks an Orange Partridge over a feeding trout.

There is something about fishing a chalkstream that encourages me to sit down and think about the philosophy of flyfishing. Lord knows what will happen if I ever fish the Itchen or the Test; perhaps I shall become so sunk into reflection that I never get round to throwing out a line. The Driffield Anglers' Club has existed for more than a hundred and seventy years, but it has not, I think, been closely associated with famous developments in the evolution of the fisher's art. The Driffield anglers have just got on with it. They have not, as far as I am aware, much involved themselves in the controversies of our sport. They are, after all, mostly Yorkshiremen, which perhaps explains why, in their down-to-earth way, they have been more concerned with catching trout than with defining proper and improper methods of capture. There is no particular reason why fishing at Driffield should encourage ethical, literary or historical reflections. Perhaps it is just the chalk and the weed and my knowledge that, although the great Hampshire trout streams are bigger, they are essentially the same. When I fish at Driffield, anyway, I am always likely to sit down and look at the water – if any is visible – and then start thinking about Halford and Skues and Plunket Greene. None of them, to my knowledge, ever fished at Driffield (although Waller Hills loved the beck) but I still feel that, just for a day, I have wandered into their world, and the sense of communion and of tradition delights, making every day that I spend at Driffield special for the spirit of history that accompanies every cast. I drink the spirit deeper when I also manage to catch a trout or two.

The brace to the Orange Partridge was the day's only brace; there was not even half a brace for me in the afternoon. I went down to more open water where, in the stifling heat, the trout seemed fast asleep, except in just one spot where I found a rising fish and hooked him very briefly (not on the Orange Partridge) and that was it.

So it was back to the clubhouse to enter my catch in the register, surrounded by stuffed trout and maps of the beats, with windows looking down to the water over a sloping lawn and with an almost hallowed stillness hanging on the cooler air indoors. There is something of the mood of a temple about the clubhouse of the Driffield Anglers: not a dark and awesome temple where some dreadful presence broods, but a bright and airy one raised in honour of the kind spirits that look with special favour on fishers; the clubhouse of the Driffield Anglers is sacred to fish and to fishers and to their patron spirits; it is a beautiful place. Beginning and ending a day's fishing there, signing the guestbook and booking a beat at the start of it all, recording the statistics of your day before you leave: these are pleasant rituals performed in a room that has changed not at all in my twenty years' experience of it; the best thing about this room is that it is all about fishing and that is why I love being there, especially at the end of a hot and sweaty day when I have found three feeding trout and caught two of them on a fly that has been catching trout for centuries. It was a very good day.

CHAPTER TWENTY-FOUR

Fishing like a Fool

There are days, or parts of them, when I seem unable to stop myself fishing badly, and it happens even when I know perfectly well what it is that I am doing wrong. This time I told myself that it was because I had a headache. It was a headache, by the way, that had absolutely nothing to do with booze (making the point suggests, I suppose, that they usually do); it was partly the headache, anyway, and it was also because the beck had been so quiet, with the afternoon so still and soft and sleepy, that I had already decided no trout would move and that it would be a good idea to finish early and go home to do some packing.

Perhaps the packing was the real reason; perhaps it was also the reason for the headache, because the thought of it was preying on my mind. It was the sort of packing that had not yet started and would have to start very soon. It was not holiday-packing, which I can do in about ten minutes. It was the packing that precedes moving home. Before setting off for the Eden I had promised myself that it would start tomorrow (it didn't) and even the thought of it made me want to close my eyes and sink into a deep sleep. The thought of it was dreadful: the thought of putting twenty five years into cardboard boxes and then taking them somewhere else; it made no difference that somewhere else was less than a hundred yards away. The thought of it was appalling.

All the excuses in the world would still mean that I fished Scandal Beck very badly. It is true there had been few fish showing and that the water was low. But it was also a lovely afternoon for fishing, one of those quiet and cloudy July afternoons with warm air and no breath of wind: high summer without sunshine, with soft colours everywhere and sliding water and small sounds of birds. It was not an afternoon on which to expect the sport of a lifetime; it was an afternoon to delight in the gentle pleasure of casting a line, casting it with the hope that years of experience might just manage to unlock the secret of a brace from somewhere or other in the quiet splashings and slippings of the beck; it was most certainly an afternoon that deserved proper fishing. What it got instead of this, all it got was a fisherman with a headache, a fisher unwilling to do anything but to disregard whatever long experience had taught him, a fisher determined to fish in a way that was almost certain to send us home with an empty creel.

I did find some trout after an hour or so. I came round a corner and there was one rising under the branches of a sycamore. There were more, six or seven of them, feeding in the faster water above, and it was immediately clear to me that they were eating small black stuff. There was an odd blue-wing floating down the beck but it was only an odd one and these fish were busy. I did not think they were big fish, but they were rising trout and small trout are better than none, and there was probably a twelve-ouncer or two among them. Anyway, although I knew my fisher's duty, which was to take off the gold-tailed pale watery and replace it with something small and black, I sat there on the bank, smoking and drinking tea and wondering whether it was really necessary to change flies.

In the end I decided that it was not. I cast my little pale watery over those trout and, once they had seen it two or three times, every one of them went down. Perhaps a single trout nudged my fly playfully, or just to confirm his opinion that it was inedible. At the end of this mindless performance, which probably took about ten minutes, I sat down on the bank again, feeling depressed, lit my pipe and said to myself something like, 'I told you so!'

There was more than a headache and more than the thought of packing behind it all. Over the years I have, in general, got much better at changing flies once I have acknowledged that a change is needed; but, during more recent years, I have also spent much less time fishing little black things to trout eating live versions of them in or just below the surface film. There was a time when, for weeks on end, I did little else, and there were days when it caught me lots of trout.

The reason for this change is that I have discovered flies, neither small nor black, that sometimes work with smutting trout, discovering at the same time that these same flies, when they do work, give much easier fishing than do those little black things, which only bring trout consistently to net when the fisher in charge of them is on top of his form. I have had great days with them, but not for a year or two, which is largely because I have used them so infrequently; I have become frightened of their challenge and it is a mistaken sort of fear. By little black things, incidentally, I do not mean fairly small black things: the terrestrial gnats that wind and good fortune bring to the river's surface at various times of the year, most typically in May. These are monsters compared with the smuts and the midges and the other sorts of tiny insect life that I lump together very imprecisely as little black things, black things often so tiny that twenty or thirty of them could do a very lively line dance on the point of a very small needle.

The first fly that I tried as a relief from artificial little black things was a floater I call the Yellow Thing. I had already found it a great fly on the Eden for trout eating olive uprights. The Yellow Thing is neither more nor less than a Rough Olive. The first batch of them that I used was not of my own tying; it was given to me by a violinist who was also a retired fisherman and I called them Yellow Things because I was uncertain what they ought to be called, with their bodies of yellow-green wool and their olive-yellow hackles. They had no whisks, which I know only because I have kept one or two of the originals as models for my imitations. I have just looked at them and been struck by this feature for the first time. All my own Yellow Things, for something like twenty years, have been dressed with bodies of yellowish-green wool and with greenish-yellow hackles and five or six similar hackle fibres tied in at the bend. The tail has not ruined the look of them to the trouts' eyes.

I have had some great days fishing the Yellow Thing over smutting trout. I can remember the first time I tried it: I was on the Wharfe in July, the river was full and clear, the sun was shining and the trout were eating tiny black flies very greedily. I was fishing for them with an August Black and I was having problems, for the wind was in my face, a fresh and gusty wind, which meant that I never quite knew where the August Black was touching down. A trout would rise and I would be thinking that my fly was somewhere else before realising that I had just missed him; or I would strike a rise and find out that it had not been a rise to the fly on the end of my line. Knowing just where your fly is in the river is unquestionably a good thing, especially when you are fishing tiny wet flies. With the bigger sort, with those monsters tied on fourteens and perhaps even twelves, you can watch the end of your line and look for the draw; but with tiny flies you need to watch the rise and, for me at least, the wind often makes this a very awkward business.

The willows were shining in windy sunshine, the water was bright and lively and the trout were busy in it; it was the sort of July day that shows the underside of leaves, that shines on grass wet from overnight showers and brings back something of spring freshness to things. I thought that I should be enjoying myself and decided that this would be more likely to start happening if I could see my fly and mark the rise of any trout moved by a sudden urge to eat it. This should, of course, have led me to a little black floater with white wings or a white hackle. Instead of this, I tied a Yellow Thing to my cast and almost immediately I was enjoying myself enormously.

The unaccountability of it all bothered me not at all. There is, of course, a special pleasure in catching trout, especially choosy trout, with a pattern that you know is being taken for the fly that they are eating. It is good to see blue-wings coming down the river and to see trout sucking them in; better still is to tie on your own version of the dun and find that the trout take it for food. Somewhere in all this lies something of the essence of flyfishing and when it happens to me I feel very happy indeed; but, being a rather primitive sort of flyfisher, I am almost as happy to catch trout on a fly thirty times bigger than the insects the fish are swallowing. It certainly makes hooking them a much easier business.

On that fresh July morning when I first caught smutting trout on the Yellow Thing, I was soon almost as happy as a fisher can be. For I had found that, instead of fiddling round with almost invisible flies that only worked with precise and rather refined treatment, I could cast a bushy dry fly dressed on a fourteen, could watch it bobbing down the currents of the river and then turn my wrist when yet another trout forgot all about smut and came up very obviously to gulp the Yellow Thing down. And they were yellow-bellied trout with full and slender fins. And they seemed at my mercy, for very few of them refused my fly; they even took it from smooth glides as well as from more troubled water. I kept sitting down to smoke and relish my feeling of power over the river and its trout; it seemed that I could go on catching them for just as long as I chose and I wondered, as I sat there smoking in the sunshine, whether I might at last get bored with casting the Yellow Thing over a rise and catching another trout.

I cannot remember whether or not tedium finally set in, but the experience which did or did not end in satiety recurred in that and in other seasons. There was a wonderful day in late May above Kettlewell; there was an afternoon on the Eden round Wharton Hall; also an evening on the Eden just below Kirkby Stephen; there was a day on the Wenning above Clapham Station. There were these and there were perhaps half a dozen more fishing days when the Yellow Thing seemed irresistible to trout eating tiny black things. There were many other days when it put down two trout and rose the third, which is good going for trout occupied with the black stuff. There were days when it did not work at all and I rather think, looking back, that the Yellow Thing was most effective on sunny days with a high clear water. In its original form it has fallen out of favour with me; it has adopted the Klinkhamer look and this modish style of Yellow Thing has been very useful as a general pattern but it has only very occasionally killed trout eating little black things.

As a ploy for smutting trout, the true Yellow Thing fell out of favour. Klinkhamers are to blame, and the reason for this is that, once I had learned how to tie them and learned how deadly they were, I felt almost ashamed of knotting a traditionally constructed dry fly to the end of my cast. And Klinkhamers, big ones looking nothing like a black gnat or a midge or a smut, have sometimes been very successful on days when the trout have been busy with the little stuff, although they have never quite equalled the performance of the Yellow Thing on its best days. I must tie myself a new supply of Yellow Things with bright bushy hackles wound in the old-fashioned style. And a few long-hackled palmers would also be a good idea, because they were flies that often caught me a trout or two from fast water when I could not tempt – or could not hook –them with tiny flies. Even as I write I can feel a great affection for traditional flies stirring within me, but however much it stirs it will produce no action until the packing is done and the boxes are moved, until I have settled into my new house and drunk a few glasses of sherry and a few bottles of claret there. Meanwhile I should give myself some practice with little black things, especially the wet sort; re-establishing them as a central feature of my summer reper-toire is something that needs to be done.

On the Sunday afternoon, anyway, I put down those trout on the beck, acknowledged that I was an idiot and walked back downstream feeling uncertain what I should do when I got back to the main river. The headache had gone by now, but there was still the oppressive thought of packing and the dispiriting proximity of the hash I had just made of an opportunity to catch some trout. It might be better to call it a day and go fishing in the morning; it might be better to do an hour's packing and then go fishing for the whole of the next day as an essential form of recreation. I might find that an hour's packing and a night's sleep had turned me into a better fisherman.

It was the blue-wings that settled it. There had been a trickle all afternoon, but down on the Eden there was now rather more than a trickle and already a trout or two was rising to eat them. It was four o'clock. There was supper with friends waiting for me, but they were infinitely flexible friends who would not care a fig if I didn't turn up until nine; they were packing too (and had actually started), which meant that they would probably prefer a late appearance from their guest. They rarely ate much before ten anyway and, since Maz loved trout, it would be good to give her a brace. I could certainly stay on the river until eight and try to make amends for my performance on the beck; but first I would release the dogs from the Land Rover, give them a run and feed them, then I would sit and smoke and drink tea, putting recent events behind me and preparing to return to the river in a new spirit of enterprise and determination.

All this took about half an hour and the blue-wings were thicker when I started fishing again. It was not a great hatch; there was no strewn litter of fly on the water and the quiet air was not filled with the silent flutter of countless wings. There were little clusters of duns in all the eddies and they were coming down the currents two or three at a time. There was no wild profusion but there were plenty of olives to go at for any trout with a mind to swallow them. I tied on a parachute version of my BWO dun. Sometimes it works and sometimes it doesn't. I am very fond of it, partly because I invented it, but more because of an afternoon on the Eden when the blue-wings came in numberless thousands and it caught me four two-pounders in something like two hours. It was the greatest afternoon of my fishing life and the fly that produced it has been a favourite ever since.

With this fly on the end of my cast, I had soon put two three-quarter-pounders in the bag. I killed them with Maz in mind though, to be honest, I should probably have killed them anyway. The second of these trout came from the bottom of a long run. Once he was in the creel I spotted a second rise perhaps ten yards upstream on the edge of the fast water. As soon as I covered him, my fly disappeared and the little Sage was bent into a hoop by the wild rush of a very angry and very large trout. He ran downstream where there were willows on one bank and alders on the other; he obviously knew all about roots and when I held him from the willows, convinced that knots would slip or that the line would snap at any moment, he responded by rushing across to the alders.

He was very obviously another two-pounder and I can remember thinking – it was, I suppose, an attempt to prepare myself for his loss – that the Eden had already given me five of them since the beginning of April and that five two-pounders were more than enough for the whole season. I was, of course, quite right. Until this year my fishing diary has been conspicuously short of two-pounders. There was that glorious afternoon that brought four of them, but the chief wonder of it was that it was so untypical. I think those four fish were the only two-pounders of their season and most seasons have passed without any such trout, or perhaps with just one of them, shining at me from the pages of my diary in red ink and bold capitals, recorded and remembered as the crowning glory of a season's sport.

My diaries are full of fish that weighed almost two pounds, but, until this season and except for that afternoon in June when the blue-wings drove the trout wild with greed, the genuine article has been very thinly scattered through its pages. My friends have caught lots of them – and three-pounders too – but nearly all the trout that felt like two-pounders on the end of my line have hung from the scales and told me quite plainly that they fall just short of the weight that tells me to get out my red pen when I get home and then get out a special bottle for appropriate celebration.

As the latest two-pounder, anyway, careered from bank to bank and waved his tail in the air once or twice, just to make it plain that the unlikely event of his capture would most certainly demand the dignity of red ink, as yet another two-pounder threatened to break me with every second of the fight, the thought of five recent red-letter trout was no preparation at all for the virtual certainty of failure. The fact is, of course, that catching big trout does not make you less eager to catch more of them and does nothing to soothe the pain of losing one.

There is one exception to this great truth, which is a big fish lost at the end of a day that has already brought several similar trout to net; for a loss of this sort can be seen as a necessary reminder that trout snap nylon and throw hooks; a loss of this sort, nudging us back into the awareness that we inhabit an imperfect world, can be endured almost with equanimity. There is passing regret, there is the dark suspicion that he was the biggest fish of the day, but then we get out the fish already in our creel, laying them in the grass on the edge of the river, and almost immediately it seems that our longing for more of them was something close to greed.

That is the only sort of occasion when losing a big trout does not, for me at least, seem like a sort of bereavement. Big trout caught the day or the week before are no consolation at all; in fact I rather think they make things worse, for they are bright memories and they shine on the darkness of present failure, reminding a fisher of a time when he knew how to cope with the challenge of a big fish.

I have wandered away from the situation that produced this little stream of reflection and it is time to get back to it. The trout that had swallowed my fly on that early Sunday evening, a trout that I knew weighed at least two pounds and probably a lot more, made repeated attempts to find safety down among the roots. In my efforts to control him there was no judicious application of side-strain, no nice consideration of how much pressure my nylon (3lb test) would stand; I just held him very hard, hoping beyond reason that he would stay attached, and, by some temporary suspension of the laws of physics, it worked. Denied the roots he now set off downstream with a run of such ferocity that to my fevered brain he was no longer a two-pounder but a trout at least a pound heavier. He was a trout for the taxidermist, a trout for a bow-fronted glass case on the wall of my study. The memory of five two-pounders, how they had felt and fought on the line, only emphasised the difference between their puny struggles and the monstrous strength I was now failing to control.

I did not follow him, frightened that my rod or line would snag in the branches of the alders. He stopped and sulked and came swimming back towards me. There were two or three sickening moments of slackness as I hauled in yards and yards of line and still failed to keep in touch; each time there was the thrill of feeling the rod come to life again as the line tensed suddenly and contact returned. And that was more or less it. He hung in the current, he swung from side to side and walloped the surface of the water with his huge tail; then he surrendered to the net and I staggered to the bank, where I hit him with a stone and, leaving him for later contemplation, lay back in the grass and lit my pipe.

The swifts were screaming of the huge thing that had just been lifted from the water; the martins chattered and argued excitedly about his weight. Wagtails bobbed unsteadily in surprise. Sandpipers piped in amazement. Even the river was talking about it. Even the meadowsweet smelt of trout and the sun came out to take a look. It was one of the great moments of my fishing life and very soon I should be ready for the gloat and after that for the spring balance; but not just yet. Just for a little longer I wanted to smoke and enjoy nature's acclamation, acknowledging that I had hooked a great trout, had felt certain beyond doubt that I should lose him and had yet left the river with him beaten in the net. That shameful hour on the beck belonged to a different life; the thought of packing was an irrelevance. I was a fisher, lying on the bank with a great trout lying in the grass beside me; nothing else mattered, except that I decided to forget all about trivialities like packing and spend the next three days over on the Wharfe.

After about five minute's smoking it was time to take a closer look at the fish that might be a three-pounder. As yet I had barely glanced at him; I had seen that he was big and fit, and the relief that he was mine had been so great that I had wanted to do nothing but sprawl in the grass and inhale throatfuls of smoke. But now I took him from the net and admired him as the biggest trout I had ever caught, for of this I had no doubt. His tail was huge and concave; his head was massive; the body between was deep-bellied and wide-flanked. It seemed to me that some of his spots were almost as big as a small trout. I lit my pipe again and sat there looking at him as he gleamed in the pale sunshine, deliberately delaying the moment when I should learn whether or not he was a three-pounder.

I could not delay weighing him indefinitely, because I was keen to start fishing again and could see that the blue-wings were still fluttering from the river. Perhaps the second smoke lasted another five minutes; I spent part of it wondering whether red ink would be good enough for a three-pounder and contemplating a whole system of inks based on the size of the trout killed. There could be blue ink for fish under a pound, black for those between one and two pounds, red for the two-pounders and perhaps green – or even purple – for those of three and over. I thought there was a green biro somewhere in my store. I could, at least, be sure that it had not been packed.

At last I left my colour-coding and forced myself into action, reaching a hand into the inside pocket of my waistcoat where the spring balance lives. At least it usually lives there, but it was not there now (I had guessed the weight of the two earlier trout). It was not in the other inside pocket and it was nowhere at all in any of the numerous pockets of my fishing waistcoat. It was lost or, much less likely, lying somewhere at home and it was impossible to establish whether the trout in the grass was not only the biggest trout that I had ever caught but also my first trout over three pounds.

I was disappointed; I should have liked to know there and then rather than having to wait until I got back to Sedbergh. Denied immediate knowledge I admired the great trout once more, guessed him at three pounds three ounces, put him in the creel and fished on. There was a fourteen ouncer (correctly estimated as such), caught from a current that had turned white beneath the evening sky. His rising etched evanescent little black marks in the rapid slip of the white; his hooking and his brief fight filled the air with white spray. There were one or two other trout returned and then suddenly I had had enough. I suppose I wanted to find out the truth about my trout and there was also the thought that Maz might have found her packing so repulsive that she had given up on it and started supper untypically early.

It was half past eight when I presented myself with a bag of four trout. There were cardboard boxes all over the place. Maz was busy among them and food did not seem imminent. There was plenty of time to get out the kitchen scales, put a great gleaming trout in the brass pan and then solemnly place a black pound weight on the opposite plate. There was, of course, no movement and the second pound weight made not the slightest difference. The third weight was a half-pounder and the pan remained where it was. The next half-pound was what I had been waiting for. I added it gently to the little pile and very slowly the plate sank. I had not caught a three-pounder and there would be no need for any green ink. Fiddling round with smaller weights established that, although I had not caught a three-pounder, I had caught the biggest trout of my life, one of two pounds fourteen ounces.

I suppose it all ended in anti-climax, but it did not bother me much. I searched out a bottle of my best claret (I only live about a minute away from Ned and Maz, although very soon we shall be hundreds of miles apart); then Ned and I sat in the kitchen for half an hour, drinking sherry and insisting how much we hated packing. I,

of course, had yet to do any, but I knew that I should hate it every bit as much as Ned when I finally got down to it. I also knew that I was fishing until Thursday and that Friday was the first day when I should go looking for any cardboard boxes.

Supper happened shortly after ten; the chicken (not organic by the way, although how an un-organic chicken manages to exist until its neck is wrung mystifies me; I thought living creatures were all, by definition, organic) – the mysteriously unorganic chicken was delicious; the vegetables from the garden (doubtless at some time sprayed with noxious chemical compounds) were even better; the *Figeac '83* was a marvel of depth and refinement and slow change in the glass. The talk was easy and delightful though it was touched by sadness, and I kept reminding myself that I had just caught the biggest trout of my life. I also kept wondering how things would be in Sedbergh without my dearest friends. Just before leaving them I asked Ned and Maz what they thought of green ink; they were both scathing and I rather think that the three-pounder, if he ever comes my way, will have to make do with conventional red.

CHAPTER TWENTY-FIVE

On the Move

The pre-packing excursion to the Wharfe was a good idea; it was typical high-summer fishing, except that there was more water than there often is in July. I roamed the river, finding feeding fish here and there and catching a few of them. There was a windless afternoon of very fine drizzle, the sort of damp, soft afternoon that is best spent along the edges of a trout stream among quiet sounds of water. There was an early afternoon when the sun came out and it was suddenly hot; I ate my sandwich and drank some tea and then lay back on the bank and closed my eyes for half an hour, lying there with the warm air on my cheek, with the pealing of jackdaws and the murmur of the river in my ears, lying there lazily and drowsily and for brief periods unconsciously. There were four fishing days and there were no two pounders, but there were trout on every day and there was barely a thought of packing. It was ordinary fishing; it was absorbing and it was very enjoyable.

The packing was less satisfactory. There were good moments: there were the two silk lines found at the back of a cupboard; old Kingfisher lines, still smooth, supple and green beneath the dust; both of them last used at least thirty years ago. I thought they had been lost, or perhaps even thrown away in the enthusiasm of my conversion to plastic lines. It was a delight to find them, anyway, to wipe away the dust and then stroke the braided silk, admiring the subtle gleam of it, acknowledging that it was much more beautiful than the synthetic glare of any modern line and wondering whether I should give my silk lines another go. I think it was sensible to decide that I might try them one day – just out of curiosity – but that they would probably be better left to rest, like my cane rods, as venerable relics of the past.

They were a great pleasure, those two lines; they called for coffee and a break from packing while I sat smoking in the dismal chaos of my flat, trying to remember when I had last fished with either of those silk lines. I could not name the day but before long I remembered that it was, of course, the upstream wet that had forced them into retirement; for, as soon as I had begun to catch a few trout on sunk flies cast upstream, I had realised that a modern line, a white plastic line, would help me to detect and respond to the take of a trout. And then I remembered something else: I remembered the little green tins of mucilin with which the silk was greased and how half-way through the afternoon, especially on hot days, and however generously the mucilin had been applied, the line would refuse to stay afloat and would need stripping from the reel and then drying and greasing all over again. I decided that, all in all, I did not regret the passing of silk and more or less determined to leave those old lines honoured but unused. They were stowed, with something of reverence, in a cardboard box reserved for fishing oddments.

Another pleasure was half a case of claret that I did not know about, and there were one or two books unearthed after years and years in hiding; there were little broken bits of things that brought past enjoyment briefly to life again and there were other things, especially photographs, that stirred sadder but not unwelcome thoughts. Mainly it was a tedious and wretched business. Ned and Maz left in the middle of it, which made me feel lonely. They had been colleagues and friends for a quarter of a century and, although they were still my friends, they were now in Guernsey beyond immediate or easy intimacy.

The flat was bare and at the same time strewn with the discarded remnants of twenty five years' living. There were no pictures now on any of the walls, only squares and oblongs of unstained wallpaper where they had once hung. The flat was unsightly and unwelcoming. There was no longer the familiar jumble to make it seem the place where I belonged; there were windowsills with no piles of magazines or books; there were shelves with nothing on them but dust. It seemed a derelict place and I was anxious to get out of it as soon as possible.

After the packing came the move, which only took an afternoon. A friend and I carried the cardboard boxes sixty or seventy yards to the cottage that was to be my new home while the furniture and all the big stuff was moved by men who knew what they were doing. On the evening of the move I abandoned my jumble of boxes and chairs and tables. I left it all waiting for me the next morning and I went out and got drunk with other friends. The drunkenness was not planned; I did not say to myself, as I knocked on my friends' door, that I was determined to be carried out of it at the end of the evening. I intended to drink a glass of sherry and a few glasses of wine and then wander home quietly through the soft shadows of a summer evening. But, when the time to leave came, although I made it through the door, what followed was a stagger rather than a wander and I was already miserably conscious, in a fuddled sort of way, that the morning would be hell. I am not sure that my friends drank too heavily, but I certainly did; I guzzled, without meaning to. It must have been the strain of packing and the relief to find that I was sitting at a table rather than leaning over a cardboard box; it may also have been the thought that packing is necessarily followed by the slightly less dispiriting but still unpleasant process of unpacking.

Next morning, anyway, I felt ill and guilty and started to empty boxes. The only comfort I could extract from the whole ghastly business was by telling myself that, if I had been feeling vigorous and contented, then starting to unpack would certainly have plunged me into a black depression and might have driven me to drink; as it was I never noticed any descent of the spirit because I was already so profoundly demoralised, and there was no temptation to get out the whisky bottle at ten in the morning because even the thought of it made me feel sick.

Late in the afternoon I fled to Brough and wandered round my farm disconsolately, asking myself – without bothering to give proper answers – what needed to be done before the arrival of my pheasant poults at the beginning of August. The fresh air and exercise must have been good for me because at eight o' clock in the evening, with unpacking suspended until the next morning, I drank my first glass of sherry in the tiny cottage that was now my home. There would normally have been two glasses but the pricks of conscience – mere pricks now rather than tearing bolts of guilt – insisted that one was enough before half a bottle of claret. The drink, anyway, was important; it was the beginning of a process, the beginning of growing into my new home. By the next evening there were a few pictures hanging on the walls as I drank a glass of sherry with my feet on the coffee table; and my rods were already hanging at the top of the stairs next to an old print of a heron poised to strike.

An evening later at least half the cardboard boxes were empty. I wondered whether I should go fishing in the morning. I also decided that perhaps the best thing about my cottage was that it overlooked the chicken pen so that, while drinking sherry on a summer evening, I could look out of the window, watching the chickens scratching at the earth and listening to those strangely comforting sounds that chickens make. What I needed was an outdoor chair, where I could sit and drink outdoor sherry and enjoy closer proximity to my chickens and their sounds.

Thereafter, on three successive evenings, the evening sherry (I was back to two glasses by now) was taken under the open sky; on the third of them I decided that I was going to be very happy in my little cottage and also that there was no reason at all why I should not go to the Wharfe in the morning. It would be my first excursion to a river from my new home and very soon pheasant poults would appear at High Park and take over my life for most of August.

I did not go fishing the next day, because it rained bucketfuls overnight. Then there were things to get ready out at High Park and then my poults appeared. August was wet beyond belief; with wild thunderstorms and whole days of pelting rainfall. On two or three mornings the little beck that runs through my farm was so full and so angry that I had to make a long detour to cross it by a bridge and then tramp up streaming fields to feed the poults beneath a streaming sky. Even in the depths of winter the beck has never been impassable in wading boots; the wonder of it all was that my poults survived day after day of assault by rain. They stood there looking wet and miserable, but disease, though the pens stank of sodden pellets and it seemed inevitable, never broke out and no more than two or three of them died.

Sherry-drinking moved indoors again and, with rivers almost continually in flood, I abandoned any thoughts of serious fishing. There was an afternoon on the Eden (blank) and another afternoon on the Ure above Appersett (a brace). I never fish much in August, but the exquisitely subtle nuances of the evening sherry were sometimes turned almost to bitterness by the reflection that, last summer, drought had kept me for my rivers right through August, whereas this August torrents of rain had made them unfishable for almost the whole of the month.

It was not until the second day of September that I set off from my cottage for some proper fishing, for four whole days on the Wharfe. The evening before had been beautiful and warm. I had my two glasses of Manzanilla out-doors, and felt so happy sitting there that it was only stern insistence that stopped two glasses turning into three. I was happy because the sun was shining and the leaves of the birches behind the hen-hut were full of quivering brightness; I was happy because the hens looked happy as they pecked at the cabbage leaves I had thrown into the pen for them; and there were sparrows among them, searching for grains of corn, and they looked happy too.

Until I moved into the cottage, *al fresco* drinking was an irregular feature of my life, always associated with company, usually with large gatherings of which I was rarely sure that I was entirely happy to be a part. I warmly recommend the solitary sort, especially on a late summer evening when you can take a sip of sherry and then sit back in your green plastic chair to contemplate the scene.

You can follow the slow float of clouds, watching the glow fade out of them as they drift away from the West and turn innumerable soft shades of grey; you can look at the leaves on the trees and appreciate the complementary beauty of their difference: waving cascades of birch leaves, sharp spikes of ash like double rows of arrow-heads, sycamore leaves like the palms of imperfectly fingered hands, the thumb-like sturdiness of the leaves that hang from the old pear trees in the chicken pen and frame, often almost conceal, the rounded elegance of the hanging fruit. You can look at the swallows and decide that on the whole you prefer the erratic grace and freedom of their flight to the spectacular but drilled precision of the swifts' shrieking display; you

will only realise this in late August when the swifts have gone and your
eyes are no longer drawn to them alone. You can even enjoy the black
shapes of jackdaws ambling through the sky on shallow wing-beats,
and, as they move to roost and fill the air with playground noises, you
will feel the chill on the air which comes suddenly in September and is
so much better than the stifling heat of so many evenings in July.

Anyway, there were swallows in the sky as I drank my two glasses
of sherry the evening before my trip to the Wharfe; above the swallows
there was a slow drift of clouds and the leaves were stirring faintly and
shining in the light. A friend was in charge of my pheasants for the next
few days and the cottage was more or less as I wanted it for the time
being, with any still-unemptied cardboard boxes hidden away in places
where, as long as I did not need what was inside them, they could stay
unemptied for years to come.

The weather was set fair; I was going fishing for four whole days
and, although I did not want to dwell on the end of my fishing holiday
before it had begun, I knew that the cottage would seem more like the
cottage where I lived once I had returned to it from a few days' fishing;
it would have settled more comfortably into the important rhythms of
my life. All this I knew for certain as the jackdaws told me that it was too
late for a third sherry and high time to go inside and eat a fillet steak.

The first day of my fishing began very slowly. The Wharfe was
full and shining amber, the sun was warm, there was almost no wind but
what there was of it was drifting upstream. There was the sudden sense
of early autumn, coming from reddening berries and singing robins and
from dry and withered leaves; the heaviness of late summer was turning
into something else as the dark green of trees began to crinkle and fade;
there were just the beginnings of the autumn glow.

Calm and sunny weather in September is full of shining peace.
If trout rise and take your fly and, if one or two of them end up in
your creel, you will leave the river full of quiet and luminous thoughts.
September fishing is often wonderful and it is in this month that fishing
most often turns, indisputably and unpretentiously, into some sort of
spiritual experience.

The morning was very quiet and I was still blank at two' o clock.

I ate my sandwich just above Watersmeet, wondering if the blue wings would come in the afternoon. They did not, except for an occasional fly, but as soon as I started fishing again I realised that the mood of the trout had changed, that they were looking towards the surface of the river and looking there in search of food. I was fishing my gold-tailed pale watery and, from what I call the willow run, it brought up two trout that both weighed well over the pound. They were my first trout from the Wharfe since moving into my new home, which may seem a trivial observation, but to me it seemed important at the time.

There was a third trout from a long glide sixty or seventy yards upstream and then a fourth seized the hackle coachman on the dropper, gleaming through the water as he twisted and turned in the currents of the river. I sat down for the beauty and contentment of it all, then I fished my way without a take through a series of runs and pools that often give me good fish. I wondered what fly would be most likely to bring up a trout but in the end I did not make a change and from Mile House Dub I returned a stock-fish. In Spout Dub I stirred a big trout but failed to set the hook.

The Wharfe above Kettlewell

Above Spout Dub the river runs down a short and narrow gravelly run. Often I pass it by but, on this September afternoon, the level and the colour seemed both to be telling me that it was worth fishing and that it would be best fished with a big brown Klinkhamer to draw the attention of any trout lying along the edges of the rough water. It worked, bringing a trout of exactly a pound to the creel, one of those trout that, for some reason, bring to the fisher who has just caught them an inordinate satisfaction.

This one was a beautiful trout, unquestionably one of the river's own, but he was nothing exceptional in terms of size; he was, in fact, the smallest trout of the day. In spite of this he was undoubtedly the day's best. Perhaps it was because he came from a place where I had not caught a trout for a season or two and from a place where most fishers never bother to cast a fly; perhaps it was because, when I caught him, I knew that it would not matter if the day brought no more. Partly, I suppose, it was because he seemed the reward of my fisher's instinct, which had told me that, on this particular day, this particular spot would be worth fishing with this particular fly. These thoughts had something to do with it, but there was certainly more at work; I believe there are trout that, through some strange alchemy of time and circumstance, embody all the beauty of fishing and all that it means to us as fishermen.

It may be the mood we have brought with us to the river; it may be the light in the sky and the sound in the water; it may be the time of day or the place of capture; it could be the season and the drift of thistledown on a soft movement of air. Whatever it is there is some power, some mystery that transforms ordinary trout into trout of special blessing. This pounder was such a trout.

It was as I sat there on the edge of the river, looking at him, that the evening slant came over the valley. I realised that the breeze had sunk into perfect stillness and across the water the high fields and the fell-edge above them were all shining in golden light, but the shadow had already crept over me and over the river. Soon it would be time to finish, but I would fish on for half an hour. It was the first evening of my autumn fishing and it was too beautiful to leave.

A couple of half pounders would have been good. There would have been no thought of not returning them, but there was no sign of a fish until I came in sight of the Stepping Stones. It seemed that the evening chill had put them all down. But then, under the walled bank on the far side of the river, I spotted a rise. My fisher's instinct took charge again and tied a Dry Simon to the end of my line. It fell on shadowed water but I could see the bright hackle and I watched it down the run until suddenly it disappeared.

He was a much bigger trout than any of the five that had come earlier in the day. The fight was savage and brief and, in the net, I could see that my trout was dark and fat. He weighed exactly two pounds, with copper-coloured flanks and a black back. I have not learned the trick of returning two-pounders to the river and so he went in the creel and I went off to *The Falcon*.

There were three more full fishing days. The trout were choosy but on each day I managed a leash or a brace. They were not special days in the bags they brought but, in among them, there was a half-hour which was remarkable in itself and also in its similarity to a wonderful half-hour last season. There had been a day in late May spent above Kettlewell, a day of frustration and defeat that was suddenly turned to glory in the space of about ten minutes. On that day the fish had been eating small black fly, and I was still fishless at three o' clock in the afternoon, and then I came round a corner and very soon there was a brace of big trout in my creel.

On the recent September day I came round the same corner some time after three o'clock in the afternoon. I was not quite fishless, for I had killed a trout just over the pound, but the fish – lots of them – had been busy with tiny black stuff and, apart from this one trout, they had gone down almost as soon as I had cast over them. In spite of the golden sunshine and the still air I was despondent, resigned to a day of one dead trout and innumerable others too cunning to be fooled by my crude deceits.

Feeling that I was not quite ready to call it a day, I declared that it was time for shock tactics. I had tried my little black things and now it was time for something else.

I shall just remind you of the spot: a straight run of streamy water with dappled light falling onto the river through the overhanging leaves, a straight run between two sharp corners about a mile upstream from Kettlewell. Rather more than half way along this run there was a fish rising persistently right on the edge of the gravel on the far bank. It did not seem the place for a big trout but I put the Greenwell Klinkhamer over it. Two or three times it floated over the spot unmolested, and then it was taken. There was a long surge downstream, there was a plunge for the willow roots, there were less savage demonstrations of discontent and before long there was a large trout in my net. 'One pound fourteen ounces,' I said to myself, but the spring balance told me that he was two pounds, not an ounce more but most definitely not an ounce less. He was the second two pounder of my holiday and the eighth of the season.

There was another rising trout above the willows. The Klinkhamer was taken as soon as it fell and this trout weighed one pound and a half; he made me very happy and he turned my mind to the earlier time when the same place had produced a very similar brace and a very similar mood of surprised and sunny contentment.

Altogether it was a good holiday, in which experiment and persistence were rewarded with a scattering of good trout. For part of the first afternoon fish had come easily; at other times they had come only at intervals and each one of them had been both a relief and a delight. When I got home I collected the dogs and made a phone call to check that disease and predators had spared my pheasants. Then I sat outside for my sherry, watching the chickens and the sparrows and the swallows and the clouds and the light in the leaves, feeling that life was back to normal again, that there was nothing in urgent need of packing or unpacking and that very soon it would be time for a day on the Eden.

Chapter Twenty-Six

Innocence and Experience

It was almost the end of September and my Monday afternoon was free; the day was cloudy and still and so, as soon as morning lessons were over, I drove off for the Eden. The preparations for that evening had been made before breakfast: I had cleaned out the fire and laid it, which is something that usually happens just before it is lit in the evening; I had taken a bacon chop from the freezer and made sure that I had some white wine and an onion and some olives and capers and tomatoes and grain mustard, these being the necessary ingredients for baking your bacon chop; I had taken out a bottle of powerful Italian red, knowing from experience that it would stand up to the capers and the olives and the mustard; I had checked that there was sherry in the fridge and put all my tackle in the Land Rover; I had filled a flask with tea and filled four slices of brown bread with slabs of ham.

The reason for all this was that, although it was not the last day of the season, I thought that it would probably be my own last fishing day. I wanted to get away as soon as possible and, when I returned to the cottage, I did not want to mess round for an hour getting the evening ready; I wanted to have a bath, prepare my chop and stick it in the oven, and then settle down to a glass or two of sherry and three or four hours full of fishing thoughts. The day that is probably the last fishing day of another season deserves a touch of recognition. There is also the pleasant possibility that it might turn out not to have been your last day, in which case you can do it all again.

The fishing, on what was probably my last day of the season, was unremarkable. The Eden did not present me with any more two-pounders to help me through the winter, although I passed each of the six places from which they had come and one other place, beneath a yellow-leaved willow, where I knew there was (or had been) a trout that was certainly two pounds and more likely three. He had stuck his nose out at my fly one August afternoon and I had been so shocked by its colossal proportions that I had promptly whisked my fly out of harm's way. Now, at the end of September, I searched for him in the water beneath the yellow leaves with a big dry fly, but there was no re-emergence of a frighteningly huge snout.

There were no two-pounders and the afternoon was more restless than the morning calm had led me to expect. There was a gusty wind blowing dead leaves through the air and onto the water; it was a downstream wind, which made fishing a dry fly an awkward business. I caught a fish just two ounces under the pound and just inches from the spot where the two-and-three-quarter-pounder had taken my fly among the blue-wings on that early evening in July. I thought this fourteen ouncer would make an appropriate breakfast on the morning after my last fishing day of the season and so he went in the bag. I can usually find compelling reasons for killing fourteen ouncers, although perhaps the best of them is that they are certainly the perfect size for breakfast, on the day after the end of the season or, for that matter, on any other day.

There were a few blue-wings, there were a few pale wateries of one sort or another, there was some black stuff, but there were very few rising trout. There was the one I caught, there were one or two that I put down, blaming the wind. It was turning into a rather dissatisfying last day, threatening to be unworthy of the preordained honour it was to receive in the evening. It was drab and bleak and dispiriting and I was beginning to think that, however difficult and unprofessional it might be, I should have to make time to go fishing on Thursday after-noon; but then, late in the day, the wind died and the autumn calm descended. The mood was helped by the quiet singing of robins and the dipper's water-song, by the whisper of my line, the slow fluttering of leaves and the much slower fading of the light.

Suddenly it was autumn fishing as it ought to be, with a fisher

casting his flies onto the quiet murmur of sliding water and himself
moving very quietly between the banks where yellow and brown
and pock-marked leaves hung motionless from the trees. A trout rose
towards the bottom of the run below Eastfield Bridge. I covered the
rise with a little brown Klinkhamer, hoping that the maker of the rise
was a good fish but not a two-pounder, for the evening was too calm
to be invaded by the excitement of fishing a great trout. I covered him
and the fish was on, pulling the line through the indistinct ripples of
the water and splashing in the shadows. The fight was felt and heard as
much as seen. He weighed a pound and the gentle gleam of him from
the grass was beautiful beyond belief. By now it was deep evening and
time to finish, but the spell was on me.

I waded under the arches of the bridge, listening to the resonant
echo of my splashing steps, and then cast over the run along the edge
of the willows. I could barely see the fall of my fly and I saw no rise.
Passing under the trees, where the river flows smooth, I thought I saw
rings spreading and fading on the water ahead of me, then I thought I
glimpsed a movement to my fly and immediately the rod told me that
he was hooked. There was a pulling and shaking on the line, there
was a bending of the rod. I knew at once, and with relief, that it was
not a huge trout; there would be no drama in the soft evening air, no
savage struggle, no exultation or emptiness. Instead of this there was
brief resistance, with the dim suggestion of a splash or two and perhaps
another tug and another short run when I thought that he was beaten;
and then there was the soft shine of a trout drawn over the net in the
sudden knowledge that, beyond any doubt, he was the last trout of the
year.

He was two ounces over the pound and he was infinite contentment. The blurred shape of him, lying on the grass with my two earlier
trout on either side of him, told me why I was a fisherman and also told
me that I would not fish again until next spring, for the three of them,
lying there with the brown stillness of an autumn evening deepening
round their dim silver – the three of them lying there composed a
perfect and wordless epitaph for the end of another season. After them
there could only be disappointment if I fished on. So I went home,

knowing that it was all over until some morning late in March when something in the feel of the air or something in me, or perhaps just the opportunity, would tell me that it was time to go looking for the first trout of spring.

I had my bath and then drank two glasses of sherry while the bacon chop baked and waited for me to eat it. The evening was warm and, although it was dark, I sat outside for the first glass, sitting in the light from my window and thinking of nothing in particular, except that it was only two months since I had sat there for the first time and that already it seemed a good place to be. For the second glass I went inside and lit the fire, more for the lively patterns of its brightness than through any need of heat; partly in recognition that, with fishing over, my summer too was past and the time for winter things was approaching. While drinking this second glass, I went through my diary totting up how many fish I had caught in the course of the season and how many I had killed. I made a list of the flies I had used and worked out how many trout each of them had brought to the net.

Then I ate the bacon chop with a glass of splendidly rich *Primitivo di Salento*, thinking how delicious the chop and the wine were and also thinking what a privilege it was to be a fisher. I wondered whether I should flight duck next evening or whether I should leave it a day or two. I did not come to a firm conclusion, although I decided that, whether or not I went flighting, I would nip out to Brough after school to check that all was well with my pheasants.

Shooting thoughts mingled themselves with fishing thoughts. I told myself, with more than a hint of self-congratulation, that I had chosen the perfect wine for the bacon chop, with its sauce of tomatoes and capers and olives and grain mustard, but I still left the rest of the half bottle and did the washing up, which took about five minutes. I made a cup of coffee and smoked, thinking of the six two-pounders the Eden had given me, trying to remember in some detail the capture of each of them. The last, I decided, although the biggest, had not been the best. Perhaps the first of them had been the best, for he had been the first fish of the season (and there is something wonderful about those early fishing days of sharp air and bare branches in late March and April); perhaps he had been the best, unless it had been the fourth of the two-pounders, the one that had come to a little black floater on a Saturday afternoon early in May. He had, I thought, been the most beautiful, and the delight of him had filled the rest of that Saturday and then woken up with me the next morning.

I took the dogs out and told them we should be going shooting very soon. Then I ate a lump of bread to clean my palate and settled down to finish the wine. I tried to decide what I really thought about the health of the Eden. Six two-pounders were, of course, too many for the headwaters of a northern trout stream. In William Nelson's time they had not caught two-pounders on the Eden, but a score or more of six and seven ouncers in a single day. In Nelson's day a two-pounder would have set the whole valley talking for weeks on end, for, in Nelson's day, the river had been so full of trout that there was no room for two-pounders, except for a few old cannibals down in the darkness of the deepest pools. I seemed to remember that Pritt, in about 1870, fifty years before Nelson published *Fishing in Eden,* had killed more than three hundred trout on the river in just three days. Nowadays even the thought of three hundred dead trout, all slaughtered in less than half

a week, seems – even to me – an abomination; nowadays it also seems an impossibility.

There was, of course, no doubt in my mind that there were fewer trout in the Eden than there had been eighty and more years ago. What puzzled me was why things had changed in the last half dozen years or so, for it did seem to me that I had seen fewer trout rising this season than I expected to see when the blue-wings were coming down; there were pools where I had not seen a feeding fish all season; there were places where ten years ago I had counted a dozen fish or more rising, but where, this season, I had been lucky to see two of them eating flies in the middle of a big hatch. There were small trout in the Eden, three and four ouncers, there were half- and three-quarter-pounders and true pounders and fish all the way between pounders and the true red-letter-trout of two pounds and more; there was therefore no missing generation, no evidence of one or two bad spawning seasons, but rather the suggestion that each successive year was producing too few trout. Had that wonderful afternoon of four two-pounders, which certainly deserves one more mention before this book ends, been a final demon-stration of the river's richness, a last revelation of the Eden's glory before the beginning of decline.

I was not in the mood to pursue these gloomy thoughts and, anyway, not being a scientist, it did not seem likely that they would reach any worthwhile conclusion. The wine was rich and comforting; perhaps it was its influence that prompted me to hope that whatever was wrong with the Eden would soon mend itself and fill its pools with trout again. There were, at any rate, still enough trout for me to take two or three now and then without feeling guilty about it; I should be eating one of them for breakfast in the morning.

Fishing thoughts were now interrupted by the last swallow of wine and by a brief struggle with temptation. I make it a rule never to drink whisky if I have drunk sherry before supper. I did not always make this a rule; in fact it is a rule I only introduced this year and it is a very good rule indeed. Sherry – two glasses, proper glasses rather than a bare thimbleful in one of those ridiculous midget-sized glasses sometimes falsely called sherry glasses – sherry, anyway, followed by half a bottle of red wine and then by a half an inch of whisky in a tumbler (there is no point in less than half an inch): all this means a bit too much and a headache the next morning, a headache, moreover, accompanied by the nagging guilt that always gnaws away at me when I feel that I have been overdoing the booze. There are ways of lessening the guilt. You can, for example, say 'Ernest Hemingway' three times very slowly; if you do this you will usually find that you feel in control of your drinking again, but the best course is undoubtedly to avoid the headache in the first place.

My new rule is a very good rule and I had never broken it, scarcely even thought of breaking it until, with my wine finished, and with trout fishing also finished until next spring, it suddenly seemed to me that the occasion demanded a dram. I had not reckoned with the last day of the trout season when I invented my new rule. I had toasted the end of the season with a measure or two of Glenmorangie for as long as I could remember, so that the thought of missing out this final act of the ritual suddenly seemed a gross impiety.

I did toast the season with malt whisky and then I modified my new rule, declaring that whisky is not allowed after sherry, *except on my last fishing day of the season when it is allowed (one half-inch measure in a tumbler) as long as* (in future) *the sherry has only consisted of a single glass.* I think the modified rule is now even better that it was in its original form and I shall have to decide whether the last day of the pheasants will be another exception. I already know that it will be, and it will be very important from now on to be absolutely certain which is the last day of each shooting and fishing season. I must not allow myself to cheat and I have already decided that if I catch myself, after fishing my last day and commemorating the occasion appropriately, finding to my surprise that I can after all go fishing two days later on the official last day – I have already decided that, if ever this happens, my new rule will be restored to the inflexible austerity of its original form.

The Glenmorangie was wonderful. I sniffed, sipped and swallowed and thought what a splendid innovation *the exception* was. I got out some of my older fishing diaries and flicked through them, trying to recapture past days from the bare statistics my diaries so often set before me.

Sometimes I could do it; sometimes a few lines of scribble, telling me that I had been at Yockenthwaite on such and such a day in September and had caught five trout weighing whatever they weighed, sometimes this was enough to bring back a day and some of the feelings that had belonged to it. The record of other days roused no memories at all. But they had all been fishing days, much better days than just ordinary ones.

It felt a great privilege to be a fisherman, drinking whisky and roaming through fishing memories; there stirred within me a deep sense of the beauty of flyfishing – perhaps it was the Glenmorangie at work – and perhaps it was also the Glenmorangie that inspired a conviction that often comes to fishermen, usually when they are by a river and have just caught a memorable trout, perhaps for no more than a minute or two, perhaps for only a few seconds, when they know that the world is an infinitely beautiful place and that inhabiting it is a wonderful blessing. Normally it happens on the edge of running water. This time I was sitting by the fire with a glass of whisky in my hand, but I knew that what I felt was true and I did not wake with a headache the next morning.

There will be no whisky tonight, which is just an ordinary night, but it is already eight o'clock, I have not gone flighting and it is most certainly time for the first glass of sherry. I shall be drinking it indoors and I don't suppose I shall drink sherry under the sky again until the next trout season comes along. I wonder whether the first as well as the last day of the season should be made an exception to the Great Rule.

The Wharfe

To Arncliffe

Skirfare

Tennant Arms

Kilnsey Crag

Amerdale Dub

Throstle Nest Dub

Wharfe

Watersmeet

Coniston